Autobiographical Comics

AUTOBIOGRAPHICAL
COMICS

Life Writing in Pictures

Elisabeth El Refaie

University Press of Mississippi / Jackson

www.upress.state.ms.us

The University Press of Mississippi is a member
of the Association of American University Presses.

Copyright © 2012 by University Press of Mississippi
All rights reserved
Manufactured in the United States of America

First printing 2012

∞

Library of Congress Cataloging-in-Publication Data
El Refaie, Elisabeth.
  Autobiographical comics : life writing in pictures /
Elisabeth El Refaie.
     pages cm
  Includes bibliographical references and index.
  ISBN 978-1-61703-613-2 (cloth : alk. paper)—
ISBN 978-1-61703-614-9 (ebook) 1. Autobiographical
comic books, strips, etc.—History and criticism.
  2. Narrative art—Themes, motives. I. Title.
  PN6714.E4 2012
  741.5'35—dc23   2012005656

British Library Cataloging-in-Publication Data available

Contents

Acknowledgments

It is not possible to mention everyone who has contributed, either directly or indirectly, to the creation of this book, but a few people deserve special thanks. My colleagues at Cardiff University have been unfailingly encouraging. I am especially grateful to Alison Wray and Adam Jaworski for all their support and advice, as well as to Nik Coupland for suggesting several useful readings on the theme of authenticity. The original idea for this book was conceived during my research leave in the spring of 2009, part of which I spent as a visiting scholar at the University of Technology Sydney, supported by Theo van Leeuwen and funded by a Cardiff University International Collaboration Award.

I would also like to express my thanks to the friendly community of European comics scholars, especially Martin Barker, Roger Sabin, Paul Gravett, and Charles Forceville, whose work greatly inspired me. I am indebted to Thierry Groensteen for his generous assistance and helpful feedback on one of the chapters.

The staff at University Press of Mississippi were exceptionally efficient and supportive at all stages in the development of the book. I would also like to pay tribute to the three anonymous reviewers for UPM, from whose expert opinions I benefitted greatly.

This book would not have been possible without the support of family and friends, particularly Tanja Nause, Susan Wood, and Thomas Spielhofer, who read parts of the manuscript and offered many invaluable comments, and Sheila Spielhofer, who is the most patient and perceptive reader anyone could hope for. Finally, I must thank Amr, who kept me going with his encouragement and thousands of cups of tea.

Autobiographical Comics

Introduction

The autobiographical comics genre provides fascinating new opportunities and challenges for both comics artists and autobiographers. On one hand, the creators of autobiographical comics, who come from a wide range of backgrounds, often disregard established norms and conventions and invent new narrative techniques. For this reason, the examination of autobiographical comics allows us to rethink preconceived notions about the nature of the medium and to explore the many resources for creating meaning available to comics artists. On the other hand, autobiography has been greatly enriched by drawing on the sociocultural traditions and formal features of comics, which offer new possibilities for autobiographical storytelling.

The roots of autobiographical comics began in the underground comix movement in the U.S. of the early 1970s, when comics artists first produced subversive and often sexually explicit stories for adults, which were often based on their own experiences. This development opened up the field of life writing to a new group of people, thereby changing the constraints of traditional assumptions about "who gets a life and who doesn't: whose stories get told, why, by whom, and how" (Couser 1997: 4). Due partly to the critical and commercial success of works such as Harvey Pekar's *American Splendor*, Art Spiegelman's *Maus*, and more recently, Marjane Satrapi's *Persepolis*, the graphic memoir has surged in popularity on both sides of the Atlantic and led to a greatly increased acceptance of comics by the political, cultural, and educational establishment.

The medium's long history of skirting the margins of "polite" society, however, continues to influence how comics artists tell their life stories, with taboo-breaking subject matter, subversive humor, and irony still playing a central role in many such works. Autobiographers working in the comics medium are also constrained (and empowered) by its unique characteristics, particularly its heavy reliance on images. For example, the requirement to produce multiple drawn versions of one's self necessarily involves an intense engagement with embodied aspects of identity, as well as with the sociocultural models underpinning body image. The formal tensions that exist in the comics medium—between words and images, and between sequence and layout, for instance—offer memoirists many new ways of representing their experience of temporality, their memories of past events, and their hopes and dreams for the future. Furthermore, autobiographical comics creators can draw on the close association in contemporary Western culture between seeing and believing in order to persuade readers of the truthful, sincere nature of their stories.

My aim in this book is thus to identify the key conventions, formal and stylistic properties and narrative patterns of the autobiographical comics genre. In the choice of my title (*Autobiographical Comics: Life Writing in Pictures*), I was inspired by Will Eisner's (2007) collection of autobiographical stories, *Life, in Pictures: Autobiographical Stories*, and by Jessica Abel and Matt Madden's (2008) course book on creating comics, *Drawing Words & Writing Pictures*. I was also influenced by Adams's (2000: 225) discussion of the etymology of the word *autobiography*, and by his claim that the ancient Greek word "graphe" is more accurately translated by *marking* rather than by *writing*. An autobiography is often defined as the story *of* a life, whereas a memoir is used to designate a story *from* life (Barrington 2002: 20). "Life writing" typically refers to the broadest range of personal narratives, including, for instance, journals, letters, travel writing, and oral history (Adams 2000). In this book, however, I use the terms autobiography, memoir, and life writing more or less interchangeably.

Serious book-length comics for adults are often discussed and marketed under the label of "graphic novels,"[1] but, like many other comics scholars, I object to the way this term is used by some as an "all-purpose tag" (Hatfield 2005: 5) for a vague new class of cultural artifacts, particularly when applied to works that have little to do with "novels" in the conventional sense. Instead, I will strive to rehabilitate the term "comics" and rid it of its close association, in the minds of some, with childish humor and trivial fantasy. Other scholarly terms with a similar semantic scope as "autobiographical comics" are "graphic memoirs," "graphic life writing" (Herman 2011), and "autographics" (Whitlock 2006; Whitlock and Poletti 2008).[2]

My work builds on and extends existing comics scholarship, which is flourishing as never before. Several scholarly books include chapters on individual examples or particular aspects of autobiographical comics (Beaty 2007; Hatfield 2005; Miller 2007; Versaci 2007; Witek 1989; Wolk 2007). More recently, two complete volumes about the genre have appeared: Hillary Chute (2010) draws on literary and cultural theories to offer perceptive critical readings of the work of five female graphic memoirists, and Chaney's (2011) edited volume brings together a lively collection of essays on autobiographical comics, written mainly by U.S.-based scholars. Several international journals, including *Belphégor* (4 [1], 2004), *Biography* (31 [1], 2008), and *Studies in Comics* (1 [2], 2010), have dedicated special issues to the genre.

Like Hatfield (2008: 130), I believe comics are "a protean, expansive, fundamentally challenging object of study, one inevitably located at the interstices of existing disciplines." In order to analyze some of the changes brought about by the fusion of autobiography and comics, I have found it necessary to look beyond the disciplinary boundaries within which much of the current research—particularly in North America—is taking place, namely English literature. Thus, one aspect of my book that distinguishes it from the majority of previous scholarly work on the genre is that it applies concepts from several disciplinary fields to the study of comics, drawing not only on literary and cultural theory, but also on (social) semiotics, linguistics, narratology, art history, philosophy, psychology, psychoanalysis, sociology, and media studies. This brings my work closer to the tradition of European comics scholarship, which often spans the Arts and Humanities and the Social Sciences.

While the vast majority of the existing scholarship on the graphic memoir focuses on just one or two specific books or artists, the aim of this book is to analyze a large number of works in order to discern general patterns and trends. The drawback of my approach is that I cannot consider individual books in any detail; so, for the benefit of readers who would like to study more on the subject, I have included references or footnotes to more comprehensive discussions of particular works, where these exist.

My choice of eighty-five books was based on a desire to demonstrate the broad spectrum of autobiographical comics currently found in North America and Western Europe.[3] Although other regions of the world, most notably Japan, also have a thriving comics culture, the graphic memoir genre is not yet as established there as it is in the West, and such works as do exist have typically not yet been translated into English or into any European language I can read. Moreover, as different cultures develop their own specific forms and contents, a consideration of comics from too many different countries would exceed the limits of a single research monograph. For similar reasons I have also restricted my discussion to work that has been published in book format, thus excluding the ever-increasing number of autobiographical comics published only on the Web.

Many of the works I consider are by established comics artists, while other creators come from a background of fine arts, graphic design, or book illustration. Some authors of graphic memoirs have no formal training in any of these fields. Consequently, the style and quality of the artwork and the relative weighting of verbal and visual meaning varies greatly across the body of works I discuss. There are also significant variations with regard to the period of time covered in these comics, with some creators recounting the story of their whole life so far, and others focusing on a specific issue that affected them for only a few weeks or months. Finally, comics creators make stronger or weaker claims about the veracity of their tales; while several works might legitimately be classified as travel writing or reportage, others constitute prime examples of "autofiction" (Masschelein 2008).

Despite this huge variety, I argue that the books I consider nevertheless share a number of key properties as a result of the communicative functions they have in common: all autobiographers must find appropriate ways to represent their sense of self, convey their memories of past events and dreams for the future, create a sense of authenticity, and engage their readers. These key communicative goals provide a structure for the present book.

Chapter 1, "Life Writing from the Colorful Margins," offers a general introduction to the graphic memoir genre. I begin by summarizing the ways literary scholars have tried to pin down autobiography, starting with Lejeune's (1989) notion of a "referential pact" between author and reader. More recently the focus has shifted away from the finished product and toward the process of life writing. Identity is now generally seen to be constructed in and through the stories we tell, which are shaped in turn by those genres and media of storytelling our culture makes available to us. Because of its distinct formal resources and sociocultural associations, the comics medium offers new ways of telling life stories and of representing the self. The discussion then turns to the context in which autobiographical comics creators have operated over the last four decades. I argue that the comics medium's long history of "powerful marginality" (Versaci 2007: 27), together with the more recent promise of greater legitimization, has given a new impulse to life writing in pictures throughout North America and Western Europe.

Chapter 2, "Picturing Embodied Selves," examines the nature of the autobiographical self and its relationship with body awareness and body image. Current theories stress the dynamic nature of identity and the important role played by the experience of our own bodies in sustaining a sense of a continuous self in the face of this unsettling flux. This notion of embodiment is very relevant to the graphic memoir genre, since producing multiple drawn versions of the self entails an explicit engagement with physicality. In works that deal with adolescence, illness, and/or disability, the bodily aspect of the self is particularly evident. Moreover, comics artists cannot ignore the sociocultural assumptions and values that render bodies meaningful, for instance, those related to gender, class, ethnicity, age, health/sickness, and beauty/ugliness. I introduce the term "pictorial embodiment" in order to capture the different ways in which graphic memoirists' sense of self is linked with the act of visually representing their bodily identities.

Chapter 3, "Commemorating the Past, Anticipating the Future," begins by exploring the human understanding of time and its unique contribution to our sense of identity. In both everyday discourses and conventional structuralist narrative theory, time is commonly conceptualized as something regular, linear, and measurable, but our actual experience of temporality is much more complex than that. For instance, time seems to speed up or slow down depending on our experiences at any particular moment. Time acquires a further dimension in our memories, since our minds often replay some events swiftly, whereas others are remembered in minute detail or merged in startling ways. Human beings also possess the unique ability to abstract from the here and now, and to imagine alternative future situations. When graphic memoirists decide to share their experiences with readers, I suggest, they engage in a process of "commemoration" in the sense that private memories are shaped into a narrative for public consumption. Indeed, sometimes the author deliberately stages events because of their potential for making a good story. Due to its unique spatial properties and its inherent "gappiness," the comics medium is well suited to the task of conveying these different human experiences of time, with their irregularities, fissures, and obsessions.

As I argue in Chapter 4, "Performing Authenticity," most readers now accept the idea that truth is always subjective and relative, but they are nevertheless likely to expect autobiographies to be in some way "authentic." The concept of authenticity is notoriously difficult to grasp, as the meaning varies according to the specific areas of life to which it is applied. According to Goffman (1969 [1959]), the authentic self is best understood in terms of an individual's ability to choose the most appropriate roles for the different types of social interaction in which he or she engages, and to perform these roles skillfully and convincingly. Seen from this perspective, authenticity in autobiographical comics inevitably involves an element of performance and is produced jointly by the artist and the audience in a process of constant renegotiation. Since autobiographical comics tell *and* show events from a person's life, the notion of authenticity in this genre applies not only to the verbal narration but also to both the content and the style of the visual representations. Many autobiographical comics creators draw on the mythical sense of indexical referentiality associated with photography, while others use a deliberately "artless," spontaneous style to suggest their fundamental honesty and integrity. I also discuss examples of mock and fake graphic memoirs, which openly challenge or subvert the very possibility of autobiographical authenticity.

In the fifth and final chapter, "Drawing in the Reader," I maintain that all graphic memoirists aim to appeal to their readers and to produce some kind of emotional or intellectual response in them, be it compassion, understanding, admiration, or simply entertainment. As several scholars and artists have noted, comics typically achieve a high level of involvement on the part of their readers by inviting them to contribute to the process of creating meaning. Drawing on the theories of discourse analyst Deborah Tannen (1989), I take this argument one step further, suggesting that in the case of graphic memoirs it is not only the oft-mentioned gaps between panels and between words and images but also common rhetorical devices such as verbo-visual metaphor, humor and intertextuality that invite readers' active participation. These narrative strategies often fulfill another function as well, namely to invite what I refer to as "affiliation," the reader's emotional engagement with the protagonist. The frequent depiction of protagonists in close-up and the visual alignment of the reader with their point of view may also encourage various patterns of affective engagement.

In the conclusion, I return to my central argument and provide a brief summary of the unique verbo-visual narrative strategies autobiographers draw on in the comics medium. I also risk some cautious predictions about ways in which the graphic memoir genre is likely to evolve, before ending in the traditional way by suggesting possible areas of future research.

Chapter 1

LIFE WRITING FROM
THE COLORFUL MARGINS

Lynda Barry's *One! Hundred! Demons!* (2002) is a first-person account of a young girl growing up in Seattle in a lively household that includes her eccentric Filipina grandmother. Two panels from the introduction (see Fig. 1.1) show a thoughtful-looking woman, who, as a label on the previous page has informed us, should be taken to be the "author." Floating above her head, in soft handwritten loops, are the questions the "author" is considering: "Is it autobiography if parts of it are not true?" and "Is it fiction if parts of it are?"

Literary scholars have struggled for decades to pin down auto-biography, trying to answer questions that are in essence not dissimilar to the ones raised by Lynda Barry's alter ego. As I show in the first section of this chapter, since the genre was first subjected to scholarly debate in the late eighteenth century, there has been a shift in the perceptions of who may legitimately be regarded as an "autobiographer" and of what forms autobiographical writing can and should take. For a long time, theoretical writing about autobi-ography was dominated by essentialist notions of a universal, rational, masculine self, a situation Sidonie Smith (1993: 3, 4) describes as "the tyranny of the arid 'I,' which obscures through a gray and shapeless mist everything colorful that lies within its vision." More recently, however, definitions of the genre have expanded to include a broad range of narrative forms that document the lives of men

FIG. 1.1 Lynda Barry (2002) *One! Hundred! Demons!*, p. 7 (original in color). Copyright © 2002 Lynda Barry.

and women from all kinds of colorful and often marginalized backgrounds.

Many commentators conclude it is impossible to draw strict boundaries between factual and fictional accounts of someone's life, since memory is always incomplete and the act of telling one's life story necessarily involves selection and artful construction. This realization is reflected in the terms now commonly used to refer to the genre, with many scholars preferring to talk about *life writing* (Adams 2000), *autofiction* (Masschelein 2008), or *periautography*, which translates as "writing about or around the self" (Olney 1998: xv). The name Lynda Barry gives her own creation, *autobifictionalography*, is a wonderful tongue-in-cheek comment on the inflation of terms coined in an attempt to wriggle out of the fact-fiction conundrum.[1]

Roger Sabin's definition of a comic (1993: 5) as "a narrative in the form of a sequence of pictures—usually, but not always, with text" seems to describe Barry's work very well. In two panels from the book (see Fig. 1.1) the author sits at her desk with her hand poised above a single sheet of blank paper; in the second she contemplates a half-finished version of the very page the reader is currently reading.[2]

Some people, however, are likely to be surprised by the designation of this work as a comic, since, particularly in the English-speaking world, this art form is still more readily associated with childish tales of superheroes, swashbuckling adventurers, or funny animals. Indeed, the term itself implies a humorous intent that to some people may seem incompatible with the art of life writing. Moreover, Lynda Barry's work does not look at all like a traditional comic—it is a book with more than two hundred full-color pages, most of which are made up of just two square panels with vivid, childlike drawings and text boxes containing the narrative commentary handwritten in large capital letters.

Each of the eighteen stories is introduced with a double-page collage made up of scraps of printed or handwritten texts, drawings, photographs, pieces of fabric, buttons, and other objects relating to the topics discussed in the following pages. The page discussed above is also unusual in that it is painted on lined yellow legal paper and the margins are not just neutral background—instead they constitute an important narrative space populated with demons inspired by a Zen painting exercise that gave the book its title (see Fig. 1.1). Given that this work seems to contradict everything people expect from a comic, is it still valid to use this term to describe the medium in which Barry works?

This question is addressed in the second section of the chapter, which discusses both formalist and sociological/historical approaches to defining the comics medium. Scott McCloud (1994: 6), who has used the comics form to write a semi-scientific treatise about the inner workings of comics, starts his book by insisting on a clear separation of form from content: "The artform—the *medium*—known as comics is a *vessel* which can hold any *number* of *ideas* and *images*." While this sounds deceptively uncontroversial, a closer look reveals that the distinction between form and content is in fact not that simple. Over the years the term "comics" has described an entire range of different cultural objects, including nineteenth-century illustrated stories, strips, cartoons, American-style comic books, and Franco-Belgian *bandes dessinées*. Most attempts to define comics by formal or aesthetic criteria have tended to privilege one of these forms and to ignore the process of evolution and reinvention the medium is constantly undergoing. Therefore, it is necessary to consider the historical development of comics and the varying sociocultural and economic contexts in which they have, over time, been created, distributed, and consumed.

Since the origins of the medium in the nineteenth century, some have considered comics to be trashy, subversive, and, because of their visual quality, detrimental to literacy in the traditional sense. Both sides of the Atlantic have witnessed repeated attempts to censor or even ban comics, particularly during the 1950s and then again in the early 1970s when the underground comix movement attempted to break every existing social taboo. Since then, an ever-increasing number of writers have utilized comics to tell all kinds of fictional and non-fictional stories not traditionally associated with the medium, including such (relatively) prestigious genres as history, reportage, biography, and, notably, autobiography.

The final section of this chapter traces the origins of autobiographical comics back to the underground comix movement and follows their development over the past forty years. I argue that the genre can only be understood properly in the context of the restrictions and opportunities for creativity and subversion offered by the medium's long history of marginality, as well as by the more recent promise of greater prestige and legitimization. Creators of autobiographical comics are able to exploit the subversive connotations of a medium long associated with humor, satire, irreverence, and counterculture, and simultaneously claim to be considered as authors of serious literature. It is this creative tension that offers such a fertile ground for comics artists to come up with new ways of understanding their own lives and the concept of the self more generally.

Autobiography: A genre in the borderland between fact and fiction

Autobiography was first recognized as a distinct literary genre in the late eighteenth century (Anderson 2001). Initially scholarly debates about autobiography concentrated on texts by "great men" like Saint Augustine, Rousseau, and Wordsworth. In their discussions of such texts, scholars tended to draw on essentialist notions of a unique, autonomous, rational, purposeful, and coherent self. Because this self was regarded as "separated off from the contingencies of that most personal entity, the body and its irrational desires, and from the vagaries of tradition" (Smith 1993: 8), it could, paradoxically, also be considered universal in the sense that a shared core identity would allow one individual to understand and identify with another.[3] Many of these ideas persisted well into the twentieth century.

However, the profound social and cultural changes of the late 1960s and early '70s challenged comfortable assumptions not only about who could legitimately produce autobiography but also what form autobiography can and should take. An enormous shift in values affected the status of men and women, the relationship between social classes and ethnic groups, and the contract between the generations. Anyone's life story could now lay claim to being equally worthy and intrinsically interesting. Autobiography thus gradually became an important tool by which marginalized individuals of all descriptions could make their voices heard and claim validity for their unique experiences of the world.[4] The concept of autobiography has also expanded to include all kinds of personal narratives, including diaries, confessions, letters, travel writing, as well as collaborative forms of autobiography in which, for instance, a ghost writer or an oral historian recounts someone else's life story. The term is even used to refer to discourse practices not "literary" at all in the traditional sense, such as genealogy, autoethnography, and self-narratives on television talk shows (Adams 2000).

Paradoxically, at the same time as autobiography was starting to colonize larger and larger areas of discourse, literary theorists were busy dismantling its very foundations as a separate genre. These scholars were inspired by poststructuralist thinking, most particularly its radical questioning of the concept of a single, straightforward Truth and its view of the self as fractured, dynamic, and plural. The realization that all texts consist of a blending together of a variety of writings, none of them original, prompted Roland Barthes (1977a) to declare the author to be "dead," because a text's meaning can no longer be guaranteed by reference to the one "Author-God" alone.

These ideas are reflected in *Roland Barthes by Roland Barthes* (1977b), a book that claims to be an autobiography, while challenging from within all the major assumptions about the genre. For instance, the traditional chronological sequence is replaced in Barthes's work by memory fragments in a completely random order, described from a range of different perspectives. De Man (1979), too, attacked traditional assumptions, claiming that it is impossible to distinguish between fiction and autobiography and that the latter is not a separate genre at all but rather a manner of reading or understanding that can operate across a range of different texts. As a writer is necessarily implicated in his or her work, it is possible to read any text as at least partly autobiographical.

The reliability of memory as the basis of the autobiographical process has also come under scrutiny. In everyday discourses, the act of remembering is sometimes conceptualized by means of the analogy of an archaeological dig, which would imply that the experiences of the past are there for us to uncover. However, both cognitive and literary scholars now tend to reject this analogy in favor of a view of memory as a continuous process of reinterpreting, or re-remembering, the events of a life in the light of current interests and concerns (Wägenbaur 1998). Kerby (1991) points out that our recollections of the past "cannot escape the historicity of our gaze and our interests" (p. 31), and that, consequently, "truth" in autobiographical narratives becomes "more a question of a certain adequacy to an implicit meaning of the past than of a historically correct representation or verisimilitude" (p. 7). Indeed, imagination may sometimes provide a more adequate expression of subjective truths than can be achieved by sticking to the literal facts, if they are even accessible. This applies particularly to traumatic memories, which often enter into our conscious life story in oblique ways, through allusions, symbols, or metaphors (see Chapter 3).

For all these reasons, it has now become virtually impossible to establish with any certainty whether or not someone's autobiographical account is "true," as there are multiple selves to be described and several different truths to be told.[5] Autobiography has become a particularly unruly genre, which is seen to exist somewhere on the "borderland between fiction and nonfiction" (Adams 2000: 20). Indeed, the very concept of genre has now shifted. Genres are no longer seen as sets of static formal features but rather as networks of conventions and patterns of expectations that circulate among text producers and audiences, and that are constantly developing in response to changing orthodoxies (Bateman 2008). Nevertheless, publishers and writers continue to refer to autobiography/memoir as a separate genre, partly perhaps in order to cash in on its popularity. As the healthy sales figures for celebrity memoirs, in particular, clearly show, the public's appetite for "true" stories of "real" lives has apparently not abated at all; if anything, it seems to have increased over the last few decades.

Some scholars dealing with autobiographical texts have rediscovered Philippe Lejeune's (1989) concept of the "autobiographical pact," a sort of tacit understanding between author and reader by which the former commits him- or herself not to some unattainable historical exactitude but to the sincere effort to be as truthful as possible. This, of course, raises the difficult issue of how a reader can possibly judge the intentions of a finally unknowable authorial consciousness. In response to this problem, Lejeune identifies a textual criterion by which to distinguish autobiography from fiction: In the case of autobiography there has to be identity between the author, the narrator, and the protagonist, an identity which can be established by checking the proper name given on the title page. He argues that once the reader has grasped this central self-referential gesture, he or she will approach the text in a particular way. Autobiography should thus be seen as a mode of reading rather than simply as a way of writing.

These arguments have since been subjected to intense debate and developed further. Genette's (1997) concept of the "paratext," for instance, has made it possible to look beyond the title page for a set of guiding directions as to how to read a text. Paratext refers to all the supporting texts that frame the contents and offer readers relevant clues. It includes physical elements of the book such as the cover, title page, titles, and any dedications, inscriptions, prefaces, or notes (the "peritext"), and the various public and private communications about the book, such as interviews, press releases, reviews, letters, and diaries (the "epitext"). An author may, for instance, choose to refer to his or her work, in the title or subtitle, as a memoir or autobiography, and the identity of author, narrator, and protagonist can be emphasized on the dust jacket, in publicity materials, and in media interviews. According to this view, any book can thus be considered autobiographical if it is designated as such in the text itself or in the paratext.

A more interesting and productive response to the dismantling of the concept of a singular truth is a shift of focus away from the finished product and onto the process of life writing itself. Despite—or perhaps because of—the unavoidable fluidity of our self-identity, there still seems to be a deep-seated human desire for something more stable and coherent, which means that we "instinctively gravitate to identity-supporting structures: the notion of identity as continuous over time, and the use of autobiographical discourse to record its history" (Eakin 1999: 20). Many scholars now stress the way in which identity is constructed in and through the stories we tell ourselves and others. These, in turn, are strongly influenced by the forms of storytelling our culture makes available to us. Autobiography thus has an essentially intertextual character: the way we understand our experiences and how we convey them to others is always at least partly influenced by our own and other people's accounts of events in our lives, as well as by other life stories we encounter. Literature, in particular, provides us with "a rich vocabulary for articulating, and thus interpreting, experience in ways previously unsuspected" (Kerby 1991: 103; see also Bruner 1993).

In contrast to traditional autobiography, which was "rather prone to monologism" (Egan 1999: 23), contemporary life writing is often explicitly "dialogic" (Bakhtin 1981), in that it incorporates the voices and perspectives of several different people. It also draws on a host of different genres, which may support, subvert, or destabilize one another. This dialogism, in which each voice and each perspective exists in relation to others equally valid, creates a sense of ironic ambivalence, where "truth" can never be established once and for all, since it is always being simultaneously avowed and dismantled. Another characteristic feature of postmodern autobiography is "metadiscourse" (Hyland 2005), which incorporates all the ways writers refer to themselves, their readers, or the text itself, and which can include writing that openly displays its own condition of artifice.

Seen from this perspective, autobiographical comics offer potential new ways of conceptualizing the self. Creators are able to draw on models not only from literature but also from art and photography and their long tradition of (self) portraiture, for instance. They can also exploit the particular formal properties and sociocultural affordances of the comics medium itself, which has had a long history of marginalization but which is currently enjoying something of a cultural renaissance.

Comics: A distinctly unruly medium

Comics are not prose. Comics are not movies. They are not a text-driven medium with added pictures; they're not the visual equivalent of prose narrative or a static version of a film. They are their own thing: a medium with its own devices, its own innovators, its own clichés, its own genres and traps and liberties. (Wolk 2007: 14)

As this quote suggests, it may be easier to define what comics are *not*, than to try and pinpoint what actually makes them distinctive. What most commentators do seem to agree on, however, is that comics should be considered and discussed as a separate medium and not as a genre (Bell and Sinclair 2005; Chute 2008; Fingeroth 2007). Ryan (2004) believes that the property of "mediality" or "mediumhood" is relational rather than absolute and will depend on the purpose of investigation. Speaking from the point of view of a narratologist, she suggests that what counts as a medium "is a category that truly makes a difference about what stories can be evoked or told, how they are presented, why they are communicated, and how they are experienced" (p. 18). Comics certainly offer unique ways of presenting and evoking stories, which, according to this definition, means that they can legitimately be called a medium (see also Ewert 2004; Herman 2011; Walsh 2006).

While some scholars still try to define the comics medium by the formal devices it typically employs, others have concluded that it makes more sense to look at the many products that have historically been called comics and how they have evolved. In my view, the specificity of the comics medium can only be understood properly by drawing on formalist *and* sociocultural perspectives, since the storytelling opportunities in a medium are always shaped both by its specific material properties and the way it is used by particular sociocultural groups at certain points in history. In the following, I will discuss these two different perspectives in turn. Then I will draw on both perspectives in order to introduce the graphic memoir as a unique means of articulating and understanding the self.

Formalist perspectives

Much of the critical work on the distinctive formal characteristics of comics coalesces around two distinct claims: that comics engage the reader's imaginative involvement by putting single images into a sequential relationship, and that comics constitute an art form that combines words and images in a particular way. In order to explore the strengths and drawbacks of these formalist approaches, I would like to introduce an example from *Pyongyang: A Journey in North Korea*, Guy Delisle's (2006a) account of being sent by a French animation studio to oversee production in its Pyongyang

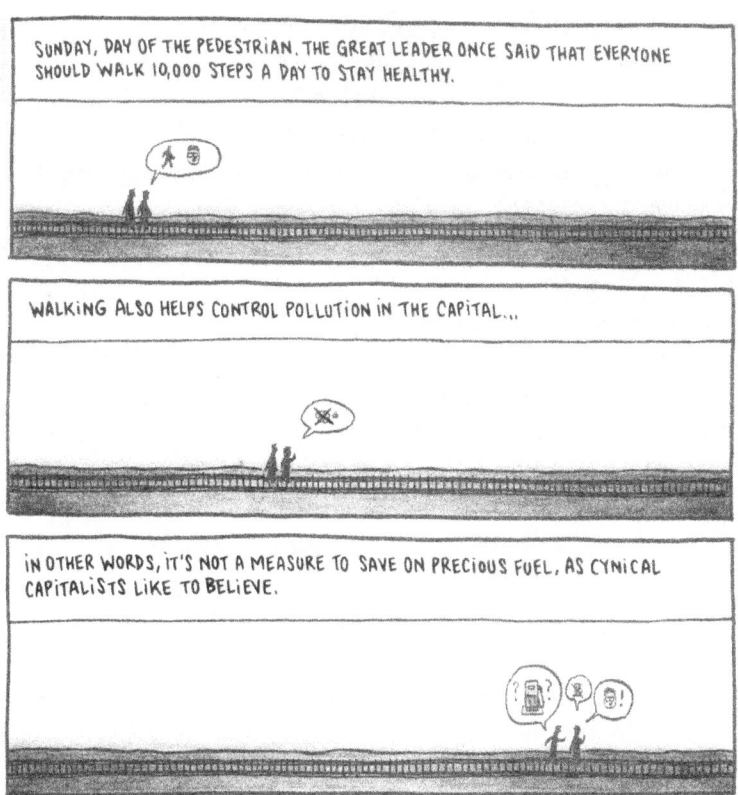

FIG. 1.2 Guy Delisle (2006a) *Pyongyang: A Journey in North Korea*, p. 119 (extract). Entire contents copyright © 2003, 2005 Guy Delisle and L'Association; translation copyright © 2005, 2006 Helge Dascher.

office. He describes his sense of boredom and alienation in this strange new environment, where he is not allowed to go anywhere without his "guide."

In a scene where he recounts his reluctant participation in a visit to a battleship, three equally sized panels show two small figures on a railway line leading through an empty, utterly desolate landscape (see Fig. 1.2). Any reader familiar with the conventions of comics will understand that the three panels are to be understood as logically linked, representing different moments in time as the two figures move from left to right along the track. The text in the captions informs us the scene takes place on a Sunday, "day of the pedestrian," and goes on to explain the "Great Leader's" official justification for not allowing any traffic on this day. The caption in the third panel introduces an alternative viewpoint, but then pretends to accept its explicit rejection by the guide. The ideograms in the speech balloons provide a humorous gloss on the conversation as it is recounted in the captions.

For some commentators, the essential feature that allows us to call this excerpt a comic is the fact that readers are encouraged to perceive the individual images as forming a coherent sequence. The concept of "sequentiality" was given particular prominence in the work of American comics artists and theorist Will Eisner (1985). His central claim was that comics work by cutting up the continuous flow of experience into segments separated by gaps, which the reader is then invited to fill. Scott McCloud (1994: 9) later took up this idea, offering a provisional definition of comics as "[j]uxtaposed pictorial and other images in deliberate sequence, intended to convey information and/or produce an aesthetic response in the viewer."

In contrast to film, where the transitions between shots tend to be smooth, all the gaps and transitions in the comics medium are obvious and laid out before us, allowing us to examine them freely. One leading European comics scholar, Thierry Groensteen (2007: 18), stresses the principle of "iconic solidarity" in comics, which describes the way in which multiple images in a series can be connected through patterns of plastic or semantic correspondences across the page, the double page, or even the whole book. Many American comics scholars similarly believe that the combination of sequence and layout is a vital feature of the medium (Versaci 2007; Witek 1989). This is clearly exemplified (see Fig. 1.2) where the progression of two figures along a railway track is represented through three identically shaped panels that stretch across the width of the whole page and are arranged precisely one on top of the other, with regular spaces in-between. This layout creates additional temporal meaning, powerfully evoking a sense of monotony and tedium.

The second major approach to defining the comics medium by formal means stresses the way in which it seamlessly combines words and images. Robert C. Harvey (2001: 75, 76) claims that the inclusion of words is absolutely integral to comics and that "in the best examples of the art form, words and images blend to achieve a meaning that neither conveys alone without the other." Comics can use words in the form of verbal narration in text boxes, as part of the landscape of the storyworld, to indicate diegetic sounds, and, perhaps most distinctively, in speech and thought balloons.[6]

Over the years, much effort has gone into cataloguing the relations between words and images in comics. More than three decades ago, Roland Barthes (1977a) coined the terms *anchorage* to describe the way that language is often needed in order to fix the meaning of images, and *relay* to refer to a situation where "text (most often a snatch of dialogue) and image stand in a complementary relationship" (p. 41). The latter, he suggested, is characteristic of sequential forms of communication, such as comics and film. Since then, scholars have come up with a whole range of different relationships that exist between the verbal and the visual mode in comics. McCloud (1994: 153ff; 2006: 130ff) lists seven different ways in which the two modes can combine, ranging from *word specific* or *image specific*, where one mode carries the meaning and the other merely adds non-essential detail, to *interdependent*, where both modes together produce meanings that neither could convey alone. In *parallel* word-image relationships there is no logical intersection between words and images at all. A similar concept is that of *ironic juxtaposition*, where pictures belie words (Varnum and Gibbons 2001: xiv). Cioffi (2001: 98) has added *disjunctive* to the list of possible word-image relations, describing it as a situation "where the word and image seem to follow a similar course yet in fact express opposing alternatives."[7]

On the face of it, the distinction between words and images is perfectly straightforward, with each possessing specific semiotic properties. In Peirce's (1960) semiotic theory, words are *symbols*, based on an arbitrary and utterly conventional connection between signs and their meaning. Images, by contrast, are *icons*, which are founded on a close physical resemblance between signs and the objects to which they refer. However, it is becoming increasingly clear that the boundaries between the two modes are in fact quite fuzzy. As Mitchell's (1994; 2009) concept of *imagetext* suggests, much visual art includes writing in some form, and, by the same token, all texts "incorporate visuality quite literally the moment they are written or printed in visible form (2009: 118)." The size, weight, expansion, and regularity of type often convey a vast amount of connotative meanings. Written words can also assume more explicit pictorial qualities, when either individual letterforms and words, or the shapes of text lines or blocks on the page, are made to resemble specific objects (Stöckl 2005; van Leeuwen 2006).

The visual potential of words is exploited to the max by comic book artists, with story titles, for instance, sometimes doubling up as pictures.[8] When onomatopoeic words are used to create the illusion of sound, these also tend to be represented in a way that integrates them visually into the pictorial context. Another good example of the hybridity inherent in the art of comics is the speech or thought balloon, which, while acting as a "container" for written language, simultaneously forms an important part of the visual design. The shape, size, and placement of the balloon itself and of the typically hand-lettered words it contains combine to convey emotions and/or important paralinguistic information, suggesting a particular volume, pitch, or intonation (Forceville, Veale and Feyaerts 2010). The reader of comic books is encouraged to actually "hear" the dialogue that is presented visually: "There is an interaction between the pictureness and the verbalness of the speechballoon, to produce the meaning of sound. We 'hear with our eyes'" (Barker 1989: 11; see also Khordoc 2001).

Conversely, the drawings in comics are often characterized by a high level of abstraction, which means that their meanings become less purely iconic and more reliant on convention. At the most abstract end of cartooning, pictures can be used to stand in for something other than what they depict, thus operating as word surrogates (Beronä 2001). An example of this is the drawing of a light bulb above a person's head to signify he or she is having an idea. When such pictograms or ideograms are placed in word balloons (see Fig. 1.2), they become "verbalized."

Charles Hatfield has developed a particularly cogent account of the formal properties of the comics medium, which offers a productive synthesis of the two major approaches outlined above. Hatfield (2005: 37) agrees that words and images in comics are often so completely intertwined as to be virtually inseparable, but he believes that learned assumptions about these different codes mean that they are nevertheless likely to be recognized and interpreted as different types of signs. He considers word-image relations to be only one of several tensions that characterize the comics medium. Two further tensions he identifies—namely the one between the single image and image-in-series, and between sequence and layout—have already been touched upon in the discussion above. The former relates to the mysterious way in which a series of individual images is able to evoke in the mind of the reader a coherent sequence of events, while the latter describes the constant tug-of-war between the functions of the single image "as both momentum-sequence and design element" (Hatfield 2009: 139).

The fourth tension of the art of comics, according to Hatfield (2005; 2009), is that between text as narrative and text as material object. As readers, we are often completely absorbed by the storyworld being presented to us, yet we are also more or less aware of the materiality of the comic book we are reading. This includes such factors as the shape, weight, printing, and binding of the book; the quality and thickness of the paper; and the design of the page, including, for instance, the layout, monochrome or color, the quality of the line, and the surface of the page. These characteristics carry symbolic value, while also acting as indices of the mode of production, "bearing traces of hand, gesture, mechanical and photographic means, or digital techniques" (Drucker 2008: 50).[9]

The materiality of the comic book can also be seen to relate to the creative process. In an interview with *The Comics Reporter* (Spurgeon 2008), Lynda Barry describes the making of her second autobiographical work, *What It Is* (2009), as an intensely physical act, which involved creating collages from whatever was "blowing by on the floor while I worked": "[I]t seemed that the actual physical act of cutting things out and gluing them down, or of using my paintbrush—that actual physical act was the thing that generated the content."[10]

Comics artists thus have a vast array of different formal features at their disposal, and the comics scholar is often subject to conflicting impulses: "on the one hand, the nigh-on irresistible urge to codify the workings of the form; on the other, a continual delight in the form's ability to frustrate any airtight analytical scheme" (Hatfield 2005: xiv). One possible response to this dilemma is to stop trying to pin down the medium through formalist descriptions and to look instead at what sort of cultural artifacts have over time been referred to as comics.

Historical and sociological perspectives

Scholars searching for the antecedents of the comics medium have come up with several different answers, depending on what formal properties they regard as essential and on how widely they cast their nets both historically and culturally. McCloud's (1994) definition of comics by their sequential nature, for instance, allows him to trace a line all the way back to ancient Egyptian tomb painting, the Bayeux Tapestry, and Pre-Columbian Mexican picture manuscripts. A more credible case is put forward by Roger Sabin (1996), who insists that comics are essentially a medium of mass circulation, and that the invention of the printing press should thus provide the starting point for historians of the art form. The earliest precursors of comics he identifies are fifteenth-century broadsheets, anonymously produced woodcuts on a single sheet of paper, typically on religious subjects or current affairs. The discovery of copperplate engraving techniques in the eighteenth century allowed artists to produce much more detailed satirical illustrations, exemplified in Britain by the work of James Gillray, George Cruickshank, and William Hogarth, whose moralizing stories in sequential pictures are also often cited as important forerunners of the comics medium (Bartual 2010). However, most scholars now agree that the prototype of the modern comic was invented in the 1830s by the Swiss schoolmaster Rodolphe Töpffer, who used sequential images with handwritten captions to tell lengthy picaresque adventure stories for adults (Kunzle 2009). While Töpffer's work was certainly pivotal in the creation of the medium, many formal conventions that have since become familiar in modern comics were introduced quite gradually. In the 1840s and 1850s French artists such as Cham (born Amédée de Noé) and Gustave Doré played a major role in further developing the art form, which subsequently spread to other Western European and American countries (Mainardi 2007). German nineteenth-century forerunners of the comic included Wilhelm Busch's illustrated tale of two naughty children, *Max und Moritz* (published from 1865), and Heinrich Hoffmann's *Struwwelpeter*, which told moralizing stories in verse about what happens to children who misbehave.

In Britain, modern comics developed out of the tradition of satirical monthlies such as *Punch* (from 1841), which focused on political caricature and was aimed at an educated middle-class readership. It was followed by several much cheaper titles for working-class readers that used less text and emphasized slapstick. The first of these to introduce a central character was Gilbert Dalziel's *Ally Sloper's Half Holiday* (from 1884), a tabloid weekly that drew on music hall traditions and mixed cartoons, comic strips, and prose stories (Sabin 1996). The eponymous character, Alexander Sloper, is a working-class drunk who enjoys all the leisure activities available to Victorian society, while constantly getting into trouble with the law and making a fool of himself when trying to mix with his social superiors. The huge financial success of this weekly led to the creation of a flood of copycat titles.

The main precursors to comics in the U.S. were not satirical magazines but newspaper comic strips, which, from the end of the nineteenth century were used to boost the sales of papers, especially to the immigrant populations in the big cities (many of whom struggled to read English). These strips grew into full-color Sunday supplements (the "Sunday Funnies"), and many of the most popular strips were syndicated and sold to a large number of newspapers across the nation. The most famous of these strips was Richard Outcault's *Hogan's Alley*, which ran in the *New York World* from 1895 onwards and featured the Yellow Kid, an obnoxious yet strangely endearing child resident of a fictional urban slum tenement, and offered a satire on the life of the immigrant poor (Hajdu 2008). Many of the newspaper strips were humorous, often using funny animals and domestic comedy. Around the turn of the century they started to be reprinted as books.

In both Britain and the U.S. of the early twentieth century, the newly emerging comics attracted the adverse attention of conservative society, which saw them as emblematic of declining moral and cultural standards and a threat to literacy (Lent 1999). In the States, this class prejudice had added religious and racial overtones, as the strips were published on Sundays for often non-Christian immigrant populations. These attacks set the tone for a whole series of anti-comics campaigns over the course of the last century.

The early twentieth century saw the main target audience of the English-language comics industry shift from adults to younger people, to the extent that the medium gradually became associated almost exclusively with juvenile entertainment. In the UK, humorous magazines such as *The Dandy* (from 1937) and *The Beano* (from 1938) reached millions of children, and there was also a glut of deliberately naïve and innocuous comics targeted specifically at either boys or girls. Although some critical voices were again raised, there was generally a more tolerant attitude towards these titles: "They may have had their faults, the thinking went, but, after all, they were a part of a particular, and special, time in life: a time symbolic of a state of innocence" (Sabin 1996: 42, 43).

Belgium and France had also developed a strong comics tradition. *Tintin* by the Belgian Georges Remi (Hergé), which appeared from 1929 as a children's supplement and then in the European album format, was phenomenally successful. It introduced the "clear-line" technique that was to dominate much of European comics art in the following decades. From 1959 onwards, *Tintin* was joined by *Asterix*, written and illustrated by Frenchmen René Goscinny and Albert Uderzo. Bolstered by the enormous success of these and other children's comics and by limits imposed on the number of U.S. comics that could be imported, the Franco-Belgian industry developed largely along its own path, appealing to both juvenile and adult audiences and enjoying a much higher level of prestige than anywhere else in the Western Capitalist world.[11]

Meanwhile, in the States, the magazine format we now associate with the emblematic American comic book gradually came to dominate the market. In terms of content, the 1930s saw the emergence of the superhero genre, which, as Fingeroth (2007: 17) points out, was mainly created by Jews, and had its origins in their specific, historically situated experience: "The creation of a legion of special beings, self-appointed to protect the weak, innocent, and victimized at a time when fascism was dominating the European continent from which the creators of the heroes hailed, seems like a task that Jews were uniquely positioned to take on." Although originally aimed at a younger audience, World War II provided the perfect conditions for the expansion of superhero comics, as young soldiers used the mildly engaging diversion they provided to survive the tedium of military routine. With the arrival on the scene of the funny animal genre and the expansion of the Disney empire, the comic book had, by the 1940s, become the most popular form of entertainment in the U.S., selling between 80 and 100 million copies weekly (Hajdu 2008: 5). Publishers reaped huge profits from the legions of writers and artists employed in factory-style comic art shops, where they were paid by the page to churn out as much work as possible. This trend led to countless run-of-the-mill stories and bland house-styles, although individuals such as Jack Kirby created some highly innovative work, partly by adopting film techniques such as rapid shifts in scale and perspective.

The popularity of superheroes faded somewhat in the late 1940s, and the 1950s saw the emergence of a whole range of new genres, including Western, war, romance, science fiction, crime, and horror stories. Many of these comics contained graphic depictions of violence, sex, and criminal behavior and often told extremely lurid stories that displayed an open disdain for any form of authority. They appealed to a large number of young people but were anathema to parents and the cultural and political establishment, which was in the grip of anti-communist paranoia and regarded anything hinting of rebellion with intense suspicion. Moreover, the same period saw a startling rise in crimes committed by young people—or "juvenile delinquents," as they were now being called—and comic books seemed an obvious explanation for this new phenomenon.

At the center of the case against comics stood psychiatrist Fredric Wertham's (1954) now notorious book, *Seduction of the Innocent*, in which he claimed that over-exposure to comics could lead young people into a life of crime. This book triggered the most sustained crusade against comics in the history of the medium—while ostensibly designed to ban the explicit sex, violence, and criminal behavior, on a deeper level it also involved issues of class, money, taste, education, religion, and politics (Hajdu 2008). More than a hundred acts of legislation were passed to curb the freedom of the comics industry, and in 1955 U.S. publishers were forced to form the "Comics Code Authority," a self-regulatory body that strictly controlled what comics creators were allowed to portray.

The anti-comics hysteria was an international phenomenon, with similar eruptions occurring in at least seventeen countries on three continents (Lent 1999). In many places, notably Britain and Germany, the moral panic took on a decidedly anti-American bent, with critics characterizing the post-war influx of American comic books as a campaign of cultural and ideological infiltration (Barker 1999; Jovanomic and Koch 1999). While this encouraged the development of an indigenous comics industry, it also strengthened prejudices against a medium that was increasingly considered to be solely for children and the uneducated. The comics industry appeared to be in terminal decline, a trend exacerbated by the increasing popularity of television.

Then, in the final years of the '60s, something rather unexpected happened in the U.S. to revive the moribund medium: artists rediscovered the potential of comics to speak to an adult readership. This development was noticeable to some extent even in the comics produced by the two dominant publishers of superhero comics, Marvel and DC, but the real revolution occurred outside the traditional publishing industry, in the underground comix movement, so named to emphasize the often X-rated, taboo-breaking content of the titles produced under its banner (Skinn 2004). Though the period was quite short-lived, from about 1968 to 1974, comix artists drew their subject matter from numerous sources such as the hippie movement, drug culture, and a new political awareness on issues such as civil rights, the environment, feminism, and the antiwar movement. Not surprisingly, most of them congregated in San Francisco, although New York and Chicago also developed their own underground comix scenes.

These artist's work was influenced by satirical comics aimed at the teenage market, especially humorous college magazines and Harvey Kurtzman's *Mad*, but creators were also reacting to the anti-comics campaigns of the 1950s, which many had experienced as children. Comix were humorous, artistically innovative, and deliberately outrageous, breaking every conceivable rule of "good taste" and decency to deliver a ferocious assault on conventional American values. Apart from horror, the main topic of comix was "deviant" sexual behavior, the more outrageous the better. This is particularly evident in the work of Robert Crumb, who is generally regarded as *the* pivotal figure of the comix movement.

Women had traditionally been excluded from the English-language comics industry, with all titles, even those explicitly directed at young girls, written and drawn almost exclusively by males. Now a number of female artists burst onto the scene, creating titles containing feminist stories by and for women. Unlike conventional comics, which still tended to be produced via assembly line, comix were created by individual artists in charge of the entire process and who retained copyright over their work. Indeed, many of them were self-published, taking advantage of cheap reprographic methods that had recently become available. For their distribution, comix relied on the network of hippie shops, or *head shops*, that had proliferated in most of the big cities in the U.S. and Canada, selling trendy clothes and drug paraphernalia.

Again, the response of conventional America was quick to follow. Newspaper articles attacking comix started to appear from the late '60s, and in the early '70s a new tide of censorship washed over the land. The U.S. Supreme Court accorded local communities the right to decide their own First Amendment standards with reference to obscenity, leading to the outlawing of many individual titles. Many head shops, which were already operating on the fringes of legal society, stopped selling comix or were closed down completely. Both in the U.S. and those European countries where the movement had had a strong influence, such as Britain and France, comix had more or less disappeared by the late '70s. This trend was exacerbated by the gradual replacement of the hippie movement by punk, which, according to Sabin (1996: 126), was "more of a howl of protest than a movement based on a coherent agenda."

Luckily, this did not spell the end of comics for adults. By this time, a strong fan and collectors' culture had developed, and specialist comics shops were emerging as the new retail network for comics. Unlike newsstands, these direct sale outlets did not return unsold copies, thus allowing publishers to cut costs radically and be more flexible and daring in their support of new titles. It is estimated that, at the end of the 1980s, there were about four hundred comics shops in Britain and four thousand in the U.S. (Sabin 1996: 157), while, by the mid-'90s, over 90 percent of all comics were sold through these channels. This new market catered mainly to the needs of the predominantly male fans of traditional superhero comics, but more unconventional and challenging works also found ready acceptance.

The direct sales network encouraged the emergence of independent publishers and a new type of more experimental, nonconformist titles for adults. These were typically of a satirical nature,[12] but they also included more serious, personal, or political works, often by the same creators who had begun in the underground movement. Initially, punk had the biggest impact on this type of comics, but later titles were influenced by other subcultures, such as rave, indie, and the traveling scene, as well as various artistic movements, both past and current. Several new anthologies emerged in this period, most notably *Weirdo* (1981) and *Raw* (1980) in the U.S., and *Escape* (1983) in the UK.

Since then, a veritable boom in comics for adults has swept America and Western Europe, with artists using the medium to explore new subject matter—from fantasy, science fiction, and erotic tales, to history, documentary, and biography, and, notably, autobiography. Many of these works have also been revolutionary in terms of the formal features and artistic styles they employ.[13] Japanese *manga*, for instance, with their use of deliberate, slow storytelling, and their focus on mood, have been an important inspiration to many comics artists. Following in the comix footsteps, these new, *alternative* comics are typically created by just one or two people rather than by a team, the publishers tend to be small companies, and the creators often retain copyright over their work. Perhaps the most striking development is that far more women are involved in the production of alternative comics than was ever the case in the mainstream industry.

The impact of the medium is being felt in film, fine art, design, and education (Talon 2004), and the academic world is also recognizing its potential as a literary and artistic form worthy of sustained attention. *Maus*, Art Spiegelman's retelling of his parents' survival of the Holocaust, gave enormous impetus to the growing reputation of adult comics, both through its subject matter and its experimental form. It received a host of awards, including a special Pulitzer Prize in 1992, and there is now a large body of scholarly writing specifically on this work (e.g., Geis 2003). Even long-established literary publishers are looking at the art form.[14] As a consequence, people who might previously have felt excluded from the closed world of the comics shop can now access these works easily through bookstores and the Internet. This may partly explain why alternative comics are attracting substantially more female readers than mainstream comics ever did, although the subject matter does, of course, also play a role.[15]

As Groensteen (2000: 30) points out, comic art seems to be rediscovering its roots, both in the sense that it is winning back its adult readership, and that it is returning "to its original form, the book." This newly acquired sense of respectability notwithstanding, comics still have to overcome a long history of marginalization by the political, cultural, and educational establishment. Although the various anti-comics campaigns differ in accordance with specific circumstances, certain facts are common to all. As a popular medium, comics were originally targeted at a predominantly working class readership, and among the other sections of society they often evoked strong class and occasional racial prejudices. There was also a suspicion that comics were subversive and harmful, both to individual readers and to society in general. Comics were easy to produce and distribute, creating a small-scale or even home-based industry that was hard for the authorities to control. The fact that many comics were produced by rebels and outsiders, and that they were implicated in counter-culture movements such as flower power and punk also did not endear them to mainstream society.

Some commentators believe it was the "hybrid" nature of this medium, "its failure to be either a real text or just a proper image" (Carrier 2000: 69), that caused some to view it with such suspicion and disdain: "We expect the world to fit our preconceived stable categories, and so what falls in between is easily felt, depending on our temperament and politics, to be either exciting or menacing. Hence the fascination with, and fear of, cross-dressing, androgyny, people of 'mixed-race,' comics, and other forms of in-betweenness" (pp. 70, 71).

However, hybridity is also a feature of, for instance, children's picture books and illustrated stories for young people, neither of which has ever attracted the same opprobrium as comics. Indeed, one of the most striking developments in the past few decades has been the proliferation of novel types of "multimodal" texts generated by digital means, where printed language is co-deployed with visual components such as layout, typography, color, and images of all kinds (Tyner 1998). While sections of the population may of course still have strong reservations about hybridity, it is certainly no longer anything exceptional, and postmodernism has even embraced it as a basic principle.

Rather, what seems to be at the root of the fear of comics is a more general suspicion of images. Particularly since the invention of print, the word-image distinction has been "freighted with value judgments" (Drucker 2008: p. 42) in Western culture, with writing being associated with high culture and learning, and images with popular culture and illiteracy. Groensteen (2000: 36) believes that many of the most powerful institutions in Western culture continue to privilege language over visual forms of expression. This attitude is reflected in some of the recent academic writings on visual communication, where the semiotic properties of images are still often expressed in terms of a *lack*. The conventional reasoning in these circles is that images are inherently unstable and ambiguous, which makes them unsuitable to the expression of precise meaning and accurate reasoning. Language, by contrast, is praised for its self-referential capacities and its ability to communicate all the sensory modalities (Messaris 1997; Ryan 2004; Stöckl 2004).

However, this logocentric attitude is beginning to be replaced with a more value-neutral view of the differences between words and images. Social semioticians, for instance, are uninterested in establishing the superiority of one mode over another, but instead focus on their distinct uses as "socially shaped and culturally given" resources for making meaning (Kress 2009: 54). Because of differences in the potentials and limitations of their material properties and the way they have been used over many generations in specific cultures and contexts, words and images have developed distinct ways of expressing similar meanings, as well as displaying a tendency towards specialization (Kress 2000; Lemke 2002). As a sequentially unfolding mode, written language is seen to be more suited to the representation of actions, while the spatial organization of images may lend itself more readily to the representation of relationships. The fear that the frequent exposure to images may contribute to illiteracy is also waning, with many theorists now arguing that the apparent transparency of pictures is often illusory and that they require specific reading skills (Jewitt and Kress 2003). Comics are increasingly recognized as a good way of fostering the love of all kinds of books in reluctant young readers and of enhancing the ability to understand the "often disjunctive back-and-forth of *reading* and *looking* for meaning" (Chute 2008: 452; see also Frey and Fisher 2008).

Contemporary social attitudes towards comics can thus be said to be deeply contradictory: on the one hand, they have to some extent maintained their marginal position. On the other hand, they are gradually acquiring a measure of social and cultural acceptance, and, in the case of individual works such as Spiegelman's *Maus*, they sometimes achieve recognition as outstanding examples of "high art."

Autobiographical comics: Respectable rebels?

Autobiography has become the genre that most defines the alternative, small-press comics production in North America and Western Europe today. However, it should be clear from the discussion above that neither the genre of autobiography nor the medium of comics can be defined in absolute terms nor pinned down conclusively. Instead, as I have argued, both must be seen in the context of the historical, economic, technological and sociocultural conditions under which texts are produced and consumed. Clearly, these conditions have changed since the first autobiographical comics appeared, and they are constantly evolving.

Although a few earlier experiments with autobiographical storytelling in the comics medium can be identified,[16] the roots of autobiographical comics are commonly traced to the underground "confessionals" of the American comix movement. Both Groensteen (1996) and Gardner (2008) pinpoint 1972 as the most plausible birth date of the genre. In that year, Robert Crumb wrote the aptly named "The Confessions of R. Crumb" for *The People's Comics* (reprinted in Crumb 1998), which was to be the first of many autobiographical works that focused on his often drug-induced male fantasies involving women with enormous breasts and thighs. Crumb had a dysfunctional family background, and felt lonely and alienated during his childhood and adolescence. When, as a young man, he moved to San Francisco and became a celebrity cartoonist, he suddenly found himself surrounded by attractive women, who were apparently only too willing to have sex with him. The more these women made themselves available to him, the more he despised them, so in his stories, the females were subjected to more and more indignities. Although Crumb's work is also savage in its portrayal of his own physical and moral shortcomings, there is little doubt it reflects a warped attitude towards women, a charge he does not deny: "I had this tremendous hostility towards everyone—but especially towards women. Sometimes now I look back and I'm shocked by just how violent and aggressive some of my cartoons are. But maybe that was my release. Who knows, if I hadn't have been a cartoonist, I might have been a psychopathic killer. Or else I might have killed myself, like my brother Charles" (Robert Crumb in an interview with Preston 2005). Crumb's outrageous and sexually explicit confessional comics had a lasting effect on the autobiographical comics genre, particularly in the U.S., where many graphic memoirists cite his work as a huge influence on their own artistic endeavors (e.g., Alison Bechdel in an interview with Chute 2006b).

The creation of Justin Green's *Binky Brown Meets the Holy Virgin*, which was also first published in 1972 (reprinted in Green 1995), undoubtedly constituted another pivotal moment in the development of the genre. The book recounts the torments of the author's alter ego, the adolescent Binky Brown, who suffers from an obsessive-compulsive fixation on various body parts, particularly his genitals. His strict Catholic upbringing leads him to interpret and express his obsessions in religious terms. Although *Binky Brown* is groundbreaking in its subject matter, it is also deeply indebted to the American superhero comics tradition. As Witek (2011: 230) points out, the many different incarnations of Binky "find an echo in the superhero's multiplying iterations of secret identities and mirror-image sidekicks, animal counterparts, and robot selves, all arrayed in the matching costumes that serve as the family livery." Green's book was thus a revelation to many readers and comics creators, revealing to them how the new graphic memoir genre could be used to bridge the gap between some of the old themes and conventions and the more ambitious, personal formats that were gradually emerging.

What these underground-inspired works have in common is the apparent desire of their creators to use brutally honest—even exhibitionist—accounts of personal experiences as a way of challenging puritanical American society and its concept of the "normal." At the same time, there is also a strong sense of guilt and self-flagellation in these early autobiographical works. This has had a lasting influence on graphic memoirs on both sides of the Atlantic, a large number of which have focused on transgressive behavior, often showing alter egos in an almost willfully unflattering light. Canadian Chester Brown (1992) and American Joe Matt (1999), for instance, both discuss their obsessive and guilt-ridden attitude to sex and pornography. Another example is the French comics creator Fabrice Neaud (1996), who has written a series of sexually explicit journals in comics form about his tortured life as a gay man.

Female comix creators also had a big influence on the early development of the graphic memoir. Artists such as Aline Kominsky and Phoebe Gloeckner used the comics medium to discuss the messy, intimate details of their everyday lives, including, in the case of Gloeckner, the effects of childhood sexual abuse on her adult relationships (see Chute 2010: 61–93). Unlike other comics genres, where female artists tend to be in a tiny minority, women continue to be influential in the field of autobiographical comics, creating some of the most striking and enduring work of this kind. While sexuality and transgressive behavior such as excessive drinking and drug-taking are still prominent subjects in the work of North American female artists in particular (e.g., Doucet 2004; Fleener 1996), the range of life writing by women in the comics medium is now vast.

Harvey Pekar was another artist who has had a lasting effect on the development of the graphic memoir genre.[17] His first collection of stories appeared in 1976 under the title *American Splendor*, with new issues appearing roughly every year since then. *American Splendor* was initially self-published, but was later taken on by established publishers and collected into trade paperbacks. In 2003 a film adaptation was released to critical acclaim. Harvey's work was groundbreaking in that it focused on mundane incidents from his life as a clerk and porter in a Cleveland hospital and on his anxieties about money, health problems, family, and friends. When he developed cancer, he and his wife Joyce Brabner told the story of his diagnosis, treatment and gradual recovery in *Our Cancer Year* (1994). Because Pekar has no particular skills as an illustrator, he wrote his stories in comic book format using stick figures, and then commissioned different artists, including his friend Robert Crumb, to draw them for him. Harvey Pekar demonstrated that autobiographical comics do not have to be about exceptional lives to be of interest to other people. The three volumes by Ariel Schrag (2008a and b; 2009), in which she chronicles her years at Berkeley High School in California, and the works of German comics artists Andreas Michalke (1999), Flix (2003; 2004), and Markus Mawil (2003) show a similar sensibility, focusing as they do on the rather unremarkable lives of ordinary people.

When such accounts of everyday experiences are linked to a journey or prolonged stay in a foreign country, the boundaries between autobiography on the one hand, and travel writing or reportage on the other, can become blurred. Thor Jensen (2007), for instance, describes travelling across the USA on a Greyhound bus with no money and no plans for the future. Although he offers us glimpses of the lives of the people he meets along the way, the focus is firmly on his own feelings and the way the rest of the world is filtered through them. Josh Neufeld's (2004) and Craig Thompson's (2004) accounts of their travels include more stories about the local sights, peoples, and cultures, while still maintaining a focus on their own responses to these encounters. By contrast, Guy Delisle's stories of his sojourns in North Korea (2006a, see Fig. 1.2) and China (2006b), Ted Rall's (2002) book about Afghanistan, and Joe Sacco's eyewitness accounts from Palestine (2003) and the Balkans (2004), are clearly concentrated on the circumstances and events they witnessed. Their work thus combines autobiographical elements with a highly personal and subjective form of reportage.

Another focus of autobiographical comics has, from early on, been on early childhood experiences and family life. An early example of this is British comics artist Al Davison's (1990) account of growing up with a severe form of spina bifida, *The Spiral Cage: An Autobiography*. Other trailblazers in this particular field come from the French tradition, particularly the works published by *L'Association* and *Ego Comme X*, small independent companies founded in 1990 and 1994 respectively.[18] David B.'s (2005) *Epileptic* (originally published in six volumes by *L'Association, 1996–2001*), for instance, tells the story of his brother's lifelong battle with a severe form of epilepsy. In the U.S., Craig Thompson's (2003) lightly fictionalized memoir *Blankets*, Alison Bechdel's (2006) *Fun Home*, Chester Brown's (1994) *I Never Liked You*, David Small's (2009) *Stitches*, and Miss Lasko-Gross's (2006) semi-autobiographical *Escape From "Special"* are further examples of works that focus on childhood experiences.

David B.'s work was also a major influence on Marjane Satrapi, who emigrated from Iran to France and later produced *Persepolis*, which chronicles her childhood and adolescence under the strict religious laws of war-torn Iran, her schooling in Vienna, and her temporary return to Iran as a young adult. This work provided the first real financial breakthrough for the graphic memoir genre in Europe, particularly when it was made into an animated film in 2007. There is no doubt that it inspired a host of other artists to tell their stories of exile and cultural difference through the comics medium. Indeed, Pasua Bashi, another Iranian artist, who now lives in Switzerland, explicitly refers to Satrapi in her graphic memoir *Nylon Road* (2009: 14), where she shows her younger self reading *Persepolis* and being bowled over by the discovery that such stories even existed.

Art Spiegelman's *Maus* is not primarily autobiographical, since large sections of the book are based on the author's father's recollections of the horrific experiences he and his wife went through as Polish Jews during World War II. However, this biographical material is always presented through the prism of Spiegelman's fraught relationship with his father, and there is a clear focus on how his parents' suffering has impacted upon the author himself.[19] The literary device of a parallel plot, in which autobiographical and biographical story strands are intertwined, is also used by David B.'s (2005) *Epileptic* and Bechdel's (2006) *Fun Home*, while in Emmanuel Guibert's (2008) *Alan's War*, an unrelated person's autobiographical narrative is reinterpreted through the perspective of the comics artist.

Self-referentiality, where the work comments on the process of its creation, has become an important feature of many autobiographical comics, particularly in France,[20] one well-known example of which is *Journal d'un album* ("Journal of an Album") (1994) by Philippe Dupuy and Charles Berberian, who have created many comics together, sharing both writing and drawing. As they demonstrate in *Journal d'un album*, collaboration has its own challenges but can also lead to inspired results, for instance, when the

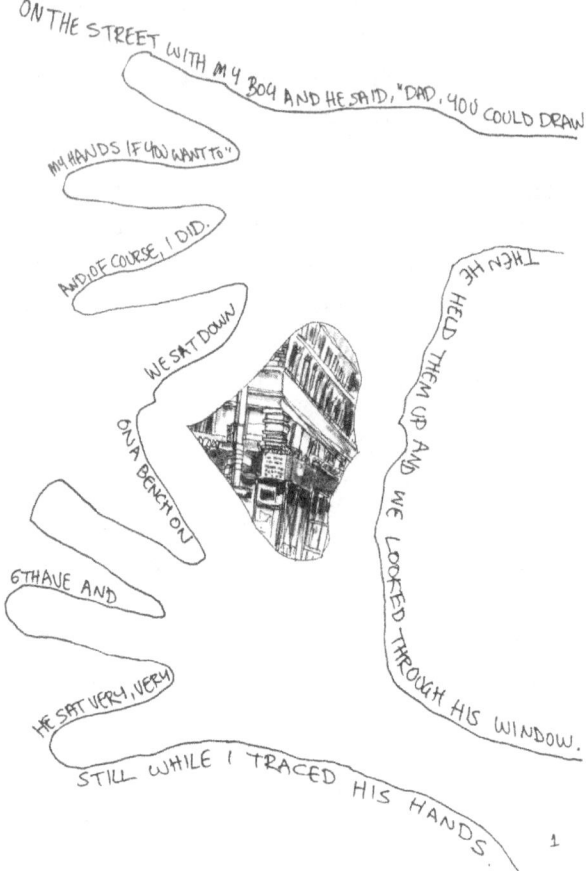

ON THE STREET WITH MY BOY AND HE SAID, "DAD, YOU COULD DRAW MY HANDS IF YOU WANT TO." AND OF COURSE, I DID. WE SAT DOWN ON A BENCH ON 6TH AVE AND HE SAT VERY, VERY STILL WHILE I TRACED HIS HANDS. THEN HE HELD THEM UP AND WE LOOKED THROUGH HIS WINDOW.

1

FIG. 1.3 Danny Gregory (2003) *Everyday Matters: A Memoir*, p. 1. Copyright © 2003 Danny Gregory.

same characters and situations are represented in a subtly different way by each artist. Eddie Campbell has also created two highly self-referential works: *Alec: How To Be an Artist* (2001) tells the story of his own development as a comics creator, by using the transparent conceit of addressing a number of useful tips to an imaginary budding artist. *The Fate of the Artist* (2006) takes self-referentiality to extremes: a mad kaleidoscope of different genres, texts, and voices, only some of which appear to bear any resemblance to the reality of

Campbell's own life, are used for a tongue-in-cheek exploration of the situation of comics artists in the modern world (see Chapter 4, Fig. 4.9). A scene from Danny Gregory's (2003) *Everyday Matters* (see Fig. 1.3) is another good example of a work which does not tell a coherent narrative, but instead focuses on the redemptive power of art itself.

Gregory's life was turned upside down when his wife was paralyzed from the waist down after falling under a subway train. Totally bewildered and traumatized, he turns to drawing as a way of reengaging with the people, places, and objects around him: "I only started drawing fairly recently. But I've found it has a power to change my life and the world around me so profoundly and I'd like to share it with you" (p. 3). Gregory has traced his son's hands (see Fig. 1.3) and drawn a small section of the townscape they could see when the boy held up his hands to form a "window." The reader is invited to share the unique vision of father and son in a particular place and moment in time. The verbal narrative retells this moment of creativity, and, by following the contours of the boy's hands, also demonstrates in a rather beautiful way how in comics words and images can become one on the surface of the page.

Gregory's work can also be regarded as belonging to the increasingly popular sub-category of autobiographical comics which, inspired perhaps by Brabner and Pekar's (1994) *Our Cancer Year*, tell the story of a crisis of some sort in the author's adult life. Engelberg (2006) and Marchetto (2006), for instance, both use the comics medium to portray their struggle with breast cancer. Further instances of this type of graphic memoir are provided by Swiss author Peeters's (2008) story of his love for an HIV positive woman, Penfold's (2006) portrait of her relationship with an abusive partner, Streeten's (2011) autobiographical story of coming to terms with the death of her baby son, and Cunningham's (2010) comic book about his work in the British psychiatric care system and his own mental health problems. For these artists, the act of writing/drawing explicitly or implicitly constitutes a form of therapy. They also often express a desire to provide help and comfort to readers who might be in a similar situation (see Chapter 5). Perhaps surprisingly for some readers, such narratives of crisis or illness are often told in a humorous tone. Brick's (2010) *Depresso, Or: How I Learned to Stop Worrying And Embrace Being Bonkers!*, for instance, mixes the tragic with the comic in a deeply irreverent way, an attitude epitomized in the author's postscript: "If you've been affected by any of the issues in this book, getta grip. It's only a comic!" (p. 263).

In the case of personal accounts of suffering, authors are often keen to establish the truthfulness of their work. By contrast, other graphic memoirists are much more interested in reflecting their feelings toward their own past in an authentic manner than in claiming to portray the "absolute truth," openly admitting that this necessarily involves diverging from the historical facts in some instances. The gap between the actual and the represented self is further emphasized in some works by the fact that the protagonist does not share the name of the author (e.g., Eddie Campbell 2000; 2001; 2006), or else through the deliberately "cartoonish" or "unrealistic" nature of the self-portraits (e.g., Lewis Trondheim in *Little Nothings;* see Fig. 1.4). A particularly playful way of orienting towards the issue of the truth is through the *fake* autobiography, the most famous examples of which are Judith Forest's (2009) *1h25* and Seth's (2007) *It's a Good Life, if You Don't Weaken* (see Chapter 4).

In sum, a huge range of works now exists by authors from across North America and Western Europe that can all be included under the amorphous category of autobiographical comics, although there is considerable overlap with other genres, such as biography, reportage, travel writing, and fiction. These works differ from each other not only in relation to their subject matter and the degree to which they lay claim to being faithful to the author's "real" life but also with regard to their visual style. Autobiographical comics creators are often particularly inventive users of the medium, constantly adapting its conventional formal features to suit their own narrative and artistic purposes. Individual works can look like conventional comics, but they can also be very unusual in style and layout, mixing a large number of different media in a highly eclectic way.

A case in point is Aline Kominsky-Crumb's (2007) volumi-
nous graphic memoir *Need More Love,* which combines comics
with photographs, longer prose texts, her own paintings, water colors, collages, photo-story parodies, and drawings by other artists,
including her husband, Robert Crumb. Many graphic memoirists
are established comics artists, but a growing number of creators
now come from a background of fine arts, graphic design, or book
illustration. There are also a few works by people who have no specific artistic training at all. The huge differences across all the works
that are labeled as "(semi-)autobiographical" thus emerge both
from the specific socioeconomic and cultural conditions under
which the books are produced, and from the motivations, interests,
and levels of training and experience of their creators.

According to Beaty (2009), one aspect common to creators of
autobiographical comics is that they deliberately set their work apart
from the fantasy element of traditional comics, because autobiography, as a more prestigious genre, offers them the promise of greater
legitimization and a way of asserting their own identities as auteurs.
However, as was discussed above, autobiography lost some of the
prestige it previously enjoyed when it was discovered by marginalized groups and expanded to include a range of discourse practices
not normally considered literary at all. Moreover, many graphic
memoirists do not seem to be particularly interested in legitimization. On the contrary, they appear to relish the countercultural
kudos associated with a medium that has, from its inception, regularly attracted the opprobrium of the establishment and been largely
ignored by critical reviewers, allowing comics creators the freedom
to "experiment and flex creative muscle" (Sabin 1996: 9).

Many creators of autobiographical comics seem well aware of
the ambivalent attitudes in wider society towards both the medium
and the genre in which they work. Indeed, some comics artists
address these tensions quite explicitly, often in a humorous manner.
In his autobiographical comic *Kunsttheorie versus Frau Goldgruber* ("Art Theory versus Mrs. Goldgruber"), Austrian comics creator Nicolas Mahler (2007) describes his attempts to convince Mrs.

Goldgruber, a tax officer, that his work constitutes a valid form of art. This is important because in Austria artists are taxed at a lower rate than other professionals. The dossier of exhibition catalogues that Nicolas compiles fails to impress her, but when she sees his strange, squiggly drawings she concedes that they do not look anything like the comics she knows and that they are unlikely to make him rich in any case: "Oh well, I suppose you could call it 'art'" ("Na das wird schon irgendwie 'Kunst' sein").

I will conclude this chapter with another example that demonstrates the tensions between the comic artist's self-perception as belonging to some kind of counterculture with his or her desire for recognition, as well as the genre's ability to address these tensions through the use of humor. Lewis Trondheim (born Laurent Chabosy) helped launch the graphic memoir genre in France when he began producing diaries in comics form in the early 1990s. These were later collected into albums under the apt title of *Approxima-tivement* ("approximately"), which conveys the idea that memory will always entail distortions and fictions. The themes of Trondheim's work remain resolutely on the level of the small triumphs and tribulations of everyday life, often with a strong dose of irony and self-deprecation. The fact that he always draws himself in the guise of a bird encourages readers from the outset to take his tales with a pinch of salt.

His work is also highly self-referential, in that he regularly addresses the process of writing comics and the lack of social status this typically affords him. He recounts (see Fig. 1.4) his response to winning the prestigious 2006 "Grand Prix" at the Angoulême comics festival in recognition of his outstanding contribution to the development of the medium. The prize is awarded annually by previous winners, reflecting the well-established auteur system in the French-speaking world. Here, Trondheim has drawn himself in a series of interviews, lamenting the fact that he has now become "the establishment, instead of being the troublemaker," and worrying that this may mean the end of his career. In the final image, however, he is shown walking along the street, grinning and

FIG. 1.4 Lewis Trondheim (2007) *Little Nothings: The Curse of the Umbrella*, p. 64 (original in color). © 2006 Trondheim; translation copyright © 2007 NBM.

chuckling to himself. The reader is clearly meant to understand that the author's pompous declarations regarding his anti-estab-lishment credo are bogus, and that he is in fact delighted by his newfound celebrity status.

Since all life writing inevitably involves a degree of fictionalization and imagination, it is pointless to attempt to isolate those features that make a text unambiguously autobiographical. Similarly, the borders between comics and other media, such as the strip cartoon, the artist's book, and the illustrated picture book, will always be fluid. For this reason, it makes sense to consider autobiographical comics as a loose category of life writing through the use of sequential images and (usually) words. Individual works differ greatly according to the specific historical, economic, technological, and sociocultural conditions in which they were created, and with every change in these conditions, new formats of graphic life writing will likely emerge. The following chapter homes in on the notion of the embodied self in graphic memoirs, exploring the consequences of having to depict one's own bodily identity over and over again in this genre.

Chapter 2

PICTURING EMBODIED SELVES

Alison Bechdel's (2006) graphic memoir *Fun Home* centers on her complicated relationship with her father, a funeral director, English teacher, obsessive restorer of the family's Victorian house, and, as it turns out, closeted homosexual, who has secret affairs with his male students. Despite—or perhaps because of—his own sexual preferences, he tries to bully his young daughter, much against her wishes and inclinations, into assuming a stereotypically feminine identity, telling her, for instance, to wear dresses and ribbons in her hair (see Fig. 2.1). The young Alison is filled with a deep sense of joy when she catches sight of a woman with a man's haircut and clothes while accompanying her father on a business trip to Philadelphia. To Alison, the stranger represents tangible evidence of the existence of alternative female role models, and it dawns on her that in the future she may be able to find a physical identity for herself that truly reflects her innermost feelings. Her father understands what is going through her head and reacts with anger and derision: "Is *that* what you want to look like?"

His response seems to have to do as much with his own troubled identity and repressed homosexuality as with his attitudes towards his daughter; to him, the butch woman embodies everything that is unacknowledged and "other." This interpretation is encouraged through the use of some clever visual devices: the shadowy outline of another person behind Alison's head can be read as a metaphor for her future self, and the man behind the counter bears

FIG. 2.1 Alison Bechdel (2006) *Fun Home*, p. 118 (original with color tint).
Copyright © 2006 Alison Bechdel.

a striking resemblance to Alison's father, in spite of his receding hairline, scraggy neck, crumpled uniform, and dejected demeanor. The woman and the waiter can thus be seen as representing a kind of mirror image of Alison and her father in the future.[1]

This excerpt from *Fun Home* points to something we all have in common, namely the perception of the self as constantly changing and inconsistent over time. It also reveals the important role of the body in giving us a sense of our own existence and identity. This idea, which is captured by the notion of "embodiment," has become a central concern of theorists from a wide range of academic disciplines, including philosophy, psychoanalysis, sociology, and cultural studies. Much contemporary autobiographical writing engages explicitly with the relationship between bodily identity and subjectivity. Particularly for women wishing to confront traditional cultural inscriptions of the female body, and people whose bodies have been radically changed through an accident or serious illness, corporeality tends to feature centrally in their life stories (Egan 1999; Smith 1993).

The body has also, from the very beginnings of the genre, been a key theme of many of the most influential graphic memoirs, including those by Justin Green and Robert Crumb, for instance. The centrality of the body in autobiographical comics is perhaps hardly surprising, since the requirement to produce multiple drawn versions of one's self necessarily involves some engagement with the body and body image. The autobiographical comics genre offers artists the opportunity to represent their physical identities in ways that reflect their own innermost sense of self, often by using a range of symbolic elements and rhetorical tropes to add further layers of meaning to their self-portraits (Mitchell 2010). I will refer to this process of engaging with one's own identity through multiple self-portraits as "pictorial embodiment."

I have discussed the author/artist's self as if it constituted an obvious and unproblematic entity,[2] but can we really say that Alison Bechdel has drawn "herself," for instance? As has already been mentioned in Chapter 1, Philippe Lejeune (1989) argued that the definition of autobiography depends on the presence of a referential pact, by means of which the author, explicitly or implicitly, affirms that the author, narrator, and protagonist are identical. However, the relationship between these roles is, in fact, much more complex than Lejeune's definition suggests, particularly in the case of autobiographical comics, where we are dealing with both verbal and visual representations of the self. For instance, some graphic memoirs are written and drawn by different people, and many comics creators use pseudonyms and/or deliberately give their autobiographical alter egos a different name. But even when, as in *Fun Home*, the referential pact is apparently being upheld, it often turns out to be illusionary upon closer examination. The living, breathing person who created *Fun Home*, for example, is clearly not identical with the narrator, the timeless, disembodied "voice" telling the story. The autobiographical protagonist is also a literary construct, which is made up of several earlier incarnations of the author's self, including the little girl (see Fig. 2.1). This young Alison clearly lacks the knowledge and benefit of hindsight the narrator enjoys; she does not know, for instance, that there are women who wear men's clothes and have men's haircuts, and she is also unaware of her father's motivations for being so hostile towards lesbians. As I argue in the first section of this chapter, the authorial self in autobiographical comics can thus be characterized as tacitly—or sometimes quite blatantly—plural (see also Hatfield 2005: 125; Ahmed 2009).

The balance of the chapter deals with different aspects of pictorial embodiment. Exploring the links between body and mind from a philosophical and (neuro-) psychological perspective, I address several of the key concepts to have emerged from these writings, with a particular focus on Drew Leder's (1990) twin terms "disappearance" and "dys-appearance," and apply them to the act of visual self-representation involved in the creation of autobiographical comics. I then draw on psychoanalytical theory in order to understand why mirrors feature so prominently in graphic memoirs, and why aspects of the body are sometimes portrayed as alien and monstrous. In the final section, I introduce sociological approaches to corporeality, and, in particular, their central argument that embodiment is an active, cultural process of rendering the body meaningful. The discussion first focuses on the way men and women are visually represented in autobiographical comics, before turning to the question of how dominant cultural inscriptions of the healthy/

sick body are reflected or challenged in graphic memoirs about the experience of illness and disability.

Multiplications of the authorial self

Narrative theorists typically insist on a clear distinction between the author, narrator, and protagonist of a story. The author is the "real," living human being who has created a particular work and who, at least while she is still alive, can travel around the world promoting her work. The term "narrator" is used to describe the voice that recounts the events in a narrative. The protagonist, finally, is the main character whose story is being told. While these three roles tend to be clearly distinguishable in the case of fictional texts, the boundaries between them become more blurred when we are dealing with autobiographical works.[3]

However, Lejeune's (1989) claim of a complete overlap in autobiography between the author, narrator, and protagonist can only be upheld if the self is construed as a coherent and unified entity, which remains more or less stable over the course of a lifetime. Such a view of the self is now generally considered to be inaccurate and misleading. According to Erwing Goffman (1969 [1959]), identity is an amalgam of the many different roles we all adopt in life in order to evoke the desired responses from our audiences. In this sense, there is no such thing as the one, true, coherent, and constant self (see Chapter 4). The young Alison sitting with her father in a diner in Philadelphia (see Fig 2.1), for example, is not identical to the girl she is when she is playing on her own, nor is she, both physically and in terms of her knowledge, attitudes, and behavior, the *same* person as the adult narrator or indeed the now middle-aged author. In this sense, the self in all life writing can be said to be tacitly plural, including a divergence between, at the very least, the *real-life I* (the author), the *narrating I* (the self who tells), and the *experiencing I* (the self told about) (Herman 2011: 233).

Authorship is a particularly complicated notion for works produced in the comics medium, because sometimes two or even more people cooperate in the process of writing and drawing a particular work. Indeed, in the more conventional comic book industry, a clear division of labor between writers, artists, inkers, and letterers is common. Although most autobiographical comics are created by just one person, there are several notable exceptions. Harvey Pekar, for instance, wrote all his books with just rough sketches and then commissioned different artists to complete the illustrations. This arrangement sometimes resulted in the same event in Pekar's life being retold in another book not just in a completely different narrative context but also in a radically different visual style (Versaci 2007). French artists Philippe Dupuy and Charles Berberian are another example of creative collaboration: unusually, they share both writing and drawing tasks. In their autobiographical *Journal d'un album* (1994), which describes the joys and challenges of this partnership, each has apparently written and drawn his own sections, although the exact nature of the division of labor is not made explicit anywhere in the book.

An even more complex interweaving of different levels of authorship can be found in *The Photographer* (2009), which recounts the trials and tribulations of French photographer Lefèvre in Afghanistan, where he documented a "Doctors Without Borders" mission in the mid 1980s (see Chapter 4, Fig. 4.5). This book is described as having been "lived, photographed, and told" by Didier Lefèvre, "written and drawn" by Emmanuel Guibert, and "laid out and colored" by Frédéric Lemercier (p. 6). In this case, the role of the artist is subdivided further, since different aspects of the visual design—the photographs, the illustrations, and the layout—were all completed by different people. The authorship of the book is also multiple, in the sense that it is based on the collaboration of Guibert, who wrote the text, and Lefèvre, who, before his death in 2007, recounted his experiences orally to his friend Guibert. The first-person narrative voice is thus supposedly that of the photographer Lefèvre, but we certainly cannot regard the author and narrator as being identical in this case.

One of the most basic distinctions in narrative theory, which goes back all the way to the ancient Greeks, is that between diegetic and mimetic storytelling. Diegesis refers to the verbal storytelling by a narrator, while mimesis is the act of showing a story, for instance in drama, the opera, or film. However, it is rare to find these kinds of storytelling in a pure form; the dialogue in a novel is mimetic, for example, while voice-overs in film may introduce a diegetic narrator. Most comics also contain elements of both, with the narrative voice typically contained in captions and text boxes, and mimesis provided by the pictures and the dialogue recorded in speech balloons (Carrier 2000: 35). Some comic books, such as Joe Matt's (2003) *Fair Weather* and Willy Linthout's (2009) *Years of the Elephant* (see Chapter 5, Fig. 5.2), use only mimetic storytelling and have no diegetic narration at all. In other cases, narrators are given a visual presence, which means that the narration may be conveyed through the words in speech or thought balloons as well. The following extract offers a particularly good example of such an "embodied" narrator.

Peter Kuper's autobiographical comic *Stripped* (1995) focuses on the author's disastrous sex life as a teenager and young adult. The story is told from the point of view of a middle-aged man in bathrobe and slippers, who is clearly meant to represent a deliberately humorous version of an older, wiser, more cynical Peter Kuper. This "narrating I" figure looks back on his life and contemplates the ridiculous antics of his younger self. Both his body language and words, which seem to emerge in puffs from the pipe he is smoking (see Fig. 2.2), indicate his utter contempt for the stupidity and naiveté of the young Peter.

As Currie (2007: 100) argues, "[t]here is always an element of self-distance in first-person narration in the sense that it creates a schism between the narrator and the narrated, though they are the same person, and in this schism, there is often a cooperation between temporal and moral self-distance which allows for the self-judgment of retrospect." In *Stripped*, the sense of distance from a former self involved in all autobiographical writing is taken

FIG. 2.2 Peter Kuper (1995) *Stripped*, p. 18 (excerpt). Copyright © 1995 Peter Kuper.

to extremes for humorous effect. In another scene, the young Peter and the narrator are shown together, with the former accusing the latter of being too judgmental about his drug-taking: "Hey! Aren't you forgetting a minor factor? It was *fun*! It made me *happy*! I actually had a *good time*! / Besides, what about all that coffee you drink—and that pipe you smoke?"[4] The narrator defends himself by pointing out that the coffee helps him to work, "so I can pay the bills around here and you know very well this pipe is only a prop" (p. 46).

Some scholars believe that the way in which a story is presented visually, for example in films or comics, should also be regarded as a form of narration (Chatman 1990; Baetens 2008). Miller (2007:

108) adopts the filmic notion of the *meganarrator* to capture the narrative process in comics, which, she believes, "works through both images and text." Similarly, Groensteen (2010: 4) distinguishes between the *recitant*, or verbal narrator, and the *monstrator*, "the instance responsible for the *putting into drawing* [*mise en dessin*] of the story." In the example discussed above, the depiction of the young Peter with rabbit's ears in two of the panels could indicate the monstrator's scornful attitude towards him, which would align the monstrator with the verbal narrator, the older, wiser Peter. However, this interpretation is undermined by the fact that the middle-aged Peter is visually portrayed in a way that makes him look fairly ridiculous in his outmoded bathrobe and slippers, which suggests he is not to be taken seriously either. We might thus conclude that the meganarrator of *Stripped* is contemptuous of both the young and the older Peter.

Such efforts to adapt the concept of the narrator, which was developed specifically for the modern novel, to other media and genres can sometimes feel rather strained and awkward (see also Hausken 2004). In my view, Wayne Booth's (1961) analytical concept of the "implied author" provides a more fruitful and straightforward way of addressing the effects of visual storytelling on meaning. The implied author is the reader's mental image of the person responsible for the selection and combination of events in a work. According to Chatman (1990: 82), this concept has the advantage of allowing the discussion of textual intent without recourse to biographism: "Rather than calling attention to the work as the product of a choosing, evaluating person, I see the work as a repository of choices—of already *made* choices, which can be considered alternatives to other choices that might have been made but were not."[5] If we adapt these ideas to the comics medium, we can discuss both the verbal and the visual features of a particular work in terms of a repository of choices made by an "implied author/artist." In the case of *Stripped*, for instance, we can describe the attitude of the implied author/artist towards both the younger and the older incarnations of Peter as distant and derisive, without being obliged to ascribe the same stance to the "real" creator of the graphic narrative, Peter Kuper.

The concept of an implied author/artist is particularly useful when discussing comics co-created by several different people. A good example is *Our Cancer Year* (1994), which was written by Harvey Pekar and his wife Joyce Brabner, and illustrated by Frank Stack. A key scene in the book (no pagination) shows Harvey, who is undergoing chemotherapy for lymphoma and is suffering terrible pain and insomnia, staring at his frail body in the bathroom mirror one night. Feeling totally disoriented, he turns to his wife and asks her for her reassurance: "Am I some guy who writes about himself in a comic book called American Splendor?" // " . . . or am I just a character in that book?" In the final panel of this sequence, Harvey's naked body is encapsulated, from the knees upwards, in a circular frame, which creates the impression that he is trapped in his portrait. These verbal and visual storytelling techniques were apparently chosen to convey the profound sense of distance and alienation that Harvey felt toward his own body. Since we have no way of knowing whether Harvey Pekar, Joyce Brabner, or Frank Stack was responsible for making these artistic choices, it seems more appropriate to talk about the intentions of the implied author/artist than to try and attribute these to any particular living person. However, in most cases it is possible to discuss the effects of verbo-visual storytelling techniques in graphic memoirs without the need to address authorial intention, or, indeed, without having to resort to such cumbersome notions as the monstrator or the meganarrator.

I will end this discussion with a scene from Joe Matt's *Peepshow*, which addresses the blatant multiplication of the autobiographical self in graphic memoirs in a particularly striking and self-referential manner. The author is shown sitting at his drawing board (see Fig. 2.3) complaining he is "sick of drawing so small!" and wants to "draw some teeth, goddammit!" The size of the panels, which in Matt's work are typically no more than an inch square, steadily increases, until his self-portraits become so large and detailed that

FIG. 2.3 Joe Matt (1999) *Peepshow*, p. 26. Copyright © 1987, 1988, 1989, 1990, 1991, 1992, 2003 Joe Matt.

they no longer fit neatly inside the panel frames. Panel five shows a monstrously oversized Joe threatening the tiny, cartoonish Joe of the first panel, who is desperately trying to escape by climbing out of the frame of the page. "Little Joe" is grabbed and devoured and ends up in the bowels of "Big Joe," where he is met by a devil figure, who orders him to get back to work. Both the giant and miniature Joe Matt, and the devil figure, represent humorous caricatures of aspects of the "real" author's self, and the depicted scene offers an intriguing metaphor for the acute sense of frustration and alienation the creative process sometimes involves.[6]

Appearances and dis/dys-appearances

The concept of "pictorial embodiment" also has an important philosophical dimension. In *Meditations*, René Descartes (2000 [1641]) insisted that it is consciousness and the ability to know through reason and radical doubt that defines human beings and places them above the rest of the material world. To him, the human mind was an indivisible thinking substance governed by entirely separate laws from those that rule the body. This assumption strongly influenced Western thought for more than three centuries, although it was repeatedly called into question by several schools of philosophy. For example, phenomenologists pointed out that it is via our physical sensations and actions that the world comes into being and reveals itself to us in a meaningful way. For this reason, as Merleau-Ponty (1962) argued, both consciousness and subjectivity should be regarded as inseparable from the *lived* body, the body that perceives, acts, reasons, and communicates. Such theories have since received strong support from neuropsychological studies, which suggest that all mental activities, including reasoning, decision-making, feelings, and social attitudes, involve both mind and body (Damasio 1994). It has been proved, for instance, that emotions are not nearly as intangible as they are often presumed to be. In fact, they are closely correlated with specific changes in different regions of the body, such as the functioning of the viscera, skeletal muscles, and adrenalin glands.

However, the relationship between the body and human consciousness is deeply paradoxical, as Leder (1990: 1) points out: "While in one sense the body is the most abiding and inescapable presence in our lives, it is also essentially characterized by absence. That is, one's own body is rarely the thematic object of experience." This absence, or "disappearance," of the body is a logical consequence of the way our conscious attention is always directed primarily towards the world: the organ used to perceive the world inevitably recedes from the perceptual field it discloses, in the sense that we do not see our eyes, smell our nasal tissue, or hear our ears. Moreover, the functioning of our inner organs is largely inaccessible to our conscious perception and active control. Leder (1990) suggests that it is only at times of dysfunction, when we are ill, in pain, or experiencing the physical changes associated with puberty, disability, or old age, that the body forces itself into our consciousness. The body is now perceived but is experienced as a "dys-appearance," the very absence of a desired or ordinary state, and as an alien force threatening the self (p. 91). In some cases, dysappearance can also be inaugurated by internalizing the attitudes of people who regard us not as autonomous subjects but as objectified "others," for instance, on the basis of a disability, different skin color, or gender.

Leder's theories offer a plausible explanation for why the author's own body features most prominently and explicitly in autobiographical comics that deal with physical changes or challenges of some sort. It is striking, for example, how many works focus on that acute awareness of the body that typically comes with puberty (e.g., Satrapi 2006; Schrag 2008a, 2008b, 2009; Weinstein 2006), particularly in cases where the young person is the victim of abuse (e.g., Gloeckner 1998). Many autobiographical comics also deal with physical and/or mental afflictions of various kinds (e.g., Engelberg 2006; Small 2009).

A good example of this is Jeffrey Brown's graphic memoir (2009) *Funny Misshapen Body*, which describes the mortifying physical symptoms the author suffered in his childhood and adolescence as a result of Crohn's disease. Soon after an operation on Jeffrey's abdomen, the wound has taken some time to heal, and the boy is distraught to discover it appears to be leaking (see Fig. 2.4).

FIG. 2.4 Jeffrey Brown (2009) *Funny Misshapen Body*, p. 105 (excerpt). Copyright © 2009 Jeffrey Brown.

While his mother is on the phone to the doctor, Jeffrey imagines his belly is about to split open. Once he has been reassured that such post-operative discharges are quite normal and that he should just make sure to keep the wound clean, he is rather intrigued by the "little hole" in his abdomen and shows it to his brother, who pronounces it to be "like an extra belly button." Jeffrey's medical problems and the operation have thus made him acutely aware not only of his damaged "outer" body but also of those inner organs not usually within a person's consciousness.

While the body apparently forces itself most urgently into our consciousness at times of physical or mental dysfunction or change, it also demands our attention whenever we are required to represent ourselves visually. Every act of self-portraiture entails a form of dys-appearance, in the sense that one's body can no longer be taken for granted as an unconscious presence. Graphic memoirists are in the unusual position of having to visually portray themselves over and over again, often at different ages and stages of development, and in many different situations. Thus, *all* autobiographical comics artists are, in the course of their work, constantly being compelled to engage with their physical identities.

Self-portraits are often considered to be able to express a person's subjectivity through the idiosyncratic style of the individual artist: "[W]hatever they show of the outer person, self-portraits speak of the inner self too in the character and choice of depiction" (Cumming 2009: 6). Jeffrey Brown's deceptively naïve and "cartoonish" style, for instance, seems to tell us as much, if not more, about his identity than the specific physical and facial features he gives himself in his drawings. However, while the possibility of a coming together of the self and the work in self-portraits seems tantalizingly achievable, it can never be completely fulfilled, since no image is ever identical with its living, breathing subject: "Even the self-portrait, while apparently closer to the making subject, cannot avoid this externalisation and objectification of the self, where the self confronts itself as an other while in the process of fabrication" (Doy 2005: 36).[7] Although probably all autobiographers are, to some extent, aware of this split, it is likely to be felt most strongly by people affected by trauma, where the self before and the self after a particular event are often experienced as radically different people.

Madison Clell's (2002) graphic memoir *Cuckoo*, in which the author tries to make her readers understand what it feels like to suffer from Dissociative Identity Disorder, can be seen as a particularly extreme example of the sense of otherness that Doy sees as integral to every act of self-portraiture. In her book, Clell describes her multiple personality states, each of which has its own name, history, personality, and voice. Either individually or in groups, these personalities episodically take control of her thoughts and behavior. Their distinct identities were formed as a result of the severe and recurrent sexual abuse she suffered as a child and adolescent, with each one representing a different coping strategy at various stages in her life. They make her feel part of a group of supportive friends rather than as an isolated, vulnerable individual.

When Clell is twenty-one, one of her other personality states, June, begins to take on a life of her own. Sitting in her boyfriend Jacob's car (see Fig. 2.5), Madison watches helplessly as June, with her childish concerns and seven-year-old "voice," assumes control and engages in an animated conversation with Jacob. The comics medium allows Clell to draw her different identities in the way she experiences them: "On the outside, we look like *me*, but we draw

FIG. 2.5   Madison Clell (2002) *Cuckoo*, p. 260. Copyright © 2002
Madison Clell.

how the body and brain *feels* at the moment" (p. 50). The little girl
is drawn in a thicker line and with a much more solid physicality than Madison's adult body, which seems to be fading into the
background. This visual technique powerfully conveys the sense of
different identities battling for supremacy in the same person.

A similar experience is described in Pasua Bashi's (2009) *Nylon
Road*, a graphic memoir of growing up in Iran, as seen from the
perspective of the author's current exile in Switzerland. Throughout the story, the autobiographical protagonist is confronted with

different incarnations of her younger self at various ages who engage her in heated debates about her past life and her current lifestyle. These younger alter egos are introduced not as a literary conceit but rather as actual physical presences. Not only do they appear unexpectedly and often at inopportune moments, they also have a "voice" and opinions apparently entirely beyond the control of the adult protagonist. The first of these specters is a little girl who looks remarkably like the author's own childhood self and suddenly turns up as the adult Pasua is having breakfast, causing great shock and consternation: "Since I am not an esoteric type, it was overwhelming to find myself in the same room with myself" (p. 16). In this book, the different versions of Pasua's physical self can be seen as an expression of the extreme sense of dislocation she experiences as a result of losing so many of her previous points of reference and moving to a radically different social and cultural environment.

Mirrors and monsters

The relationship between the body and the mind has always been a central concern of psychoanalytic theory, both in terms of how the libido shapes our motivations and behaviors, and how the psyche relates to the physical processes of the brain (Bersani 1986; Shalom 1985). Building on Sigmund Freud's writings, Jacques Lacan (1977) put forward a highly influential theory about the relationship between our sense of self and perceptions of our own body. According to this theory, the so-called "mirror stage" from the age of six to eighteen months represents a vital phase in every human being's development. This is when we first perceive our bodily reflection in the mirror as an integrated and whole "me," as opposed to the "inner" self, which is fractured, volatile, and which constantly threatens to dissolve completely. The ideal of a complete, stable self is thus an imaginary construct, which is founded on a fundamental illusion. In Lacan's theory, the body of the mirror double remains throughout life an object of desire, but it is also a source of alienation, as it embodies our futile craving for a self under our complete control. The unconscious desire to possess this elusive mirror image also motivates our desire to gaze at other people's bodies. When mirrors are used in self-portraits, they can form a potent visual metaphor for the ambiguity involved in seeing something that both is and is not "me," as well as for our inability to pin down our fluctuating sense of self:

> Everyone's mirror is the site of repeated stand-offs between hope and disappointment, confidence and frank incredulity, between yesterday when things were looking up and the cold light of today. This unsteadiness is not just a function of the mirror, of course, for it occurs within our selves. But the mirror becomes a metaphor for this appalling mutability, its slipperiness reflecting our inability quite to grasp, or even clearly see, our ever-shifting selves. (Cumming 2009: 148)

This connotative meaning potential may well explain why mirrors and mirror images feature so prominently in a large number of graphic memoirs (e.g., Satrapi 2006: 53, 293; Schrag 2009: 94–105). In a key scene in *The Spiral Cage*, British author Al Davison's (1990: no pagination) account of growing up with a severe form of spina bifida, the adult protagonist catches sight of his semi-naked body in a full-length mirror as he is dragging himself out of bed. Initially he recoils from the image, sinking to the floor in desperation as he remembers all the vicious verbal and physical assaults he has had to endure over the years, as well as the many times he was told— wrongly, as it turns out—that he would never learn to walk. His sense of alienation from the reflection in the mirror is thus reinforced by other people's negative and stigmatizing attitudes towards his body, which he has gradually incorporated into his own self-image. This experience of utter dejection forms a pivotal moment in Al's life as he suddenly realizes that it is up to him to decide how he wants to perceive himself and be perceived by others. On a double-page spread we see him violently destroying and disposing of his walking stick, crutches, orthopedic boots, and support braces. In the final strip he is shown from behind, silhouetted against a bright sun, as, freed from his various walking aides, he steps across the threshold of his house into the outside world, and, by implication, into a more self-confident future.[8]

Cancer Vixen (2006) by socialite New Yorker cartoonist Marisa Acocella Marchetto also uses a mirror as a metaphor for the unsteadiness of self-perception. Marchetto works as a cartoonist and illustrator in New York, and she is, by her own admission, obsessed with her physical appearance and glamorous consumer lifestyle. After having been diagnosed with breast cancer, the autobiographical protagonist accuses her former self in the shape of her mirror image of having caused all her problems by being more interested in her looks and wardrobe than in sorting out her health insurance. Her specular image stares back at her with an expression of shock and disbelief, and the scene ends with Marissa hurling the telephone at the mirror and smashing it to pieces. "Had she been alive," the narrator comments, "my grandmother would be shattered; this vanity was her favorite piece" (p. 69). This example conveys the mysterious sense we often have that mirrors can preserve within their depths the presence of all the people who have peered into them, including our own past incarnations.

Mirrors also feature prominently in David Small's graphic memoir *Stitches* (2009), which focuses on the author's traumatic childhood in 1950s Detroit.[9] At the age of eleven, David develops a large growth on his neck, and initially neither he nor his parents are aware of the lump, despite his father's medical background. Instead, it is his mother's glamorous female friend, the object of David's bashful adoration, who notices the swelling and begs the parents to have it checked (pp. 116–19). As David studies his reflection in a mirror (see Fig. 2.6), the sense of alienation the young boy feels towards his own image is conveyed effectively by showing ever smaller parts of his face and neck as his attention zooms in on the area of the growth. In his imagination, the lump swells up to a hideous size, and he pictures a malicious embryonic creature curled up inside it. This monstrous

FIG. 2.6 David Small (2009) *Stitches: A Memoir*, p. 147 (excerpt). Copyright © 2009 David Small.

figure—half man, half alien—has been haunting David's dreams and imaginings since he was six years old, when, while wandering around the semi-deserted wards of his father's hospital one evening, he chanced upon a display of aborted fetuses, the largest of which appeared to him to come alive, pursuing him through the nightmarish hospital building (Small 2009: 37–41).

The monstrous fetus is a good example of the unique hold on our imagination of what Julia Kristeva (1982) calls the "abject." She suggests that anything that crosses the boundaries of the body, such as waste material and bodily fluids, is perceived as unsettling, because it is neither completely separate from nor entirely part of the illusive ideal of a "clean and proper self." The "abject" confronts us with those fragile states where we stray onto the territory of the animal and where we are confronted with our own mortality: "It is thus not lack of cleanliness or health that causes abjection but what disturbs identity, system, order. What does not respect borders, positions, rules. The in-between, the ambiguous, the composite" (p. 4). Because of their childbearing functions, women's bodies are particularly closely linked to the abject. Kristeva (1982) believes that the relationship between mother and child is marked by conflict, as the child struggles, through the paternal symbolic order of language, to break free from the maternal body, while also constantly craving to return to the safety of a complete union: "It is a violent, clumsy breaking away, with the constant risk of falling back under the sway of a power as securing as it is stifling" (p. 13). The abject both repels and fascinates: on the one hand it offers a constant reminder of the vulnerability of the subject, but on the other hand it can provide the pleasure of challenging norms and breaking taboos.

According to Shildrick (2002), the abject is symbolized most powerfully by those "monstrous," liminal bodies that are neither wholly self nor wholly other. Monsters may be fictional creations, but "real" bodies, particularly those of women and of people with particular kinds of diseases or disabilities, are also sometimes perceived in this way. These bodies come to epitomize the trace of the abject within, provoking responses that are more complex and disturbing than those accorded the absolute "other": "[W]hat we see mirrored in the monster are the leaks and flows, the vulnerabilities in our own embodied being" (p. 4). Although the human ideal of corporeality is based on the idea of the singular and unified, nature actually has a "startling capacity to produce alien forms within" (p. 10), as for instance in pregnancy, or in the case of malignant tumors, which also seem to develop a life of their own and threaten the bodily order from within.

The fetus may also sometimes be regarded as abject, not just because of the way it combines human characteristics with those of less-evolved species in the evolutionary chain, but also because it symbolizes the threat of an incomplete separation from the mother.

Therefore, it is perhaps not surprising that "unnatural" forms of procreation and monstrous embryos are frequently invoked in horror films.[10] Such visual representations not only help to *fix* our free-floating fears of abjection—in this case, the abjection associated with pregnancy—they also allow us to indulge in the voyeuristic desire to gaze with impunity at monstrous bodies (Manguel 2002; Robins 1996). By representing the most terrifying of his past body images in his drawings, David Small can thus be seen as retrospectively exorcizing his own worst fears, as well as perhaps allowing his readers to do the same.

The abject and the monstrous are common themes in many autobiographical comics, but they are seldom approached with the same sense of terror as in *Stitches*. Indeed, many comics artists show a distinct lack of disgust, or even a sense of pleasure and celebratory exuberance, in their portrayal of the abject. Graphic memoirs by female cartoonists such as Julie Doucet, Ariel Schrag, and Mary Fleener, for instance, often transgress the boundaries between the self and non-self deliberately, offering explicit, shameless representations of bodily functions such as menstruation, sexual intercourse, and miscarriage (see also Miller 2007: 229–41). The example of Jeffrey Brown's discovery of his leaking abdomen (see Fig. 2.4) also illustrates an ambiguous attitude towards that which should be inside but which threatens to become the outside: although he is initially appalled by the hole in his belly, he is then shown to be captivated and even rather amused by it.

Psychoanalytic approaches to humor propose that jokes can function as a welcome release from the constant need to repress our socially unacceptable desires. These theories would predict humor to be particularly prevalent in those areas of life governed by strict social norms and taboos (Freud 1976 [1905]; see Chapter 5). One of the most extreme examples of this kind of humor is Joe Matt's (1999) *Peepshow*, in which the autobiographical narrator positively wallows in the abject, describing and showing his reluctance to wash regularly and his dirty habit of biting his toe nails and eating his own snot and scabs. He dedicates a whole page of his book to the question of "how to quietly take a shit" (p. 66), drawing obvious delight from the breaking of every conceivable taboo and the imagined discomfiture of some of his readers by depicting himself in the act of defecation and including cartoon drawings of feces and a host of onomatopoeic words which create the illusion of an accompanying "soundtrack."

The comic strip from *Peepshow* (see Fig. 2.3) recalls Bakhtin's (1984) notion of the "grotesque" body, which used to play a central role in the folk humor and carnival festivities of pre-industrial European society. The grotesque body was often depicted with a hugely exaggerated nose, mouth, belly, and genitals, and it was typically shown to be engaged in the act of eating and drinking, which, according to Bakhtin, symbolized man's triumph over the world: "The limits between man and the world are erased, to man's advantage" (p. 228). In complete contrast to the classical ideal of the body as strictly limited, closed, and individualized, the carnivalesque body is "continually built, created, and builds and creates another body" (p. 233). Joe Matt's drawings show how cartooning, with its inherent tendency towards the carnivalesque hyperbole, can provide a potent means of conquering through humor the "cosmic terror" (Bakhtin 1984: 237) we all experience in the face of the limitless vulnerability of the self, by offering artists a way of constantly inventing and reinventing themselves through their multiple playful self-portraits.[11]

Cultural inscriptions of the body

Over the last few decades, the body has also become the central focus of a wealth of work by sociologists, cultural theorists, art historians, and feminist and queer theorists. These writings often draw on psychoanalytic theory but they tend to emphasize the sociocultural aspects of embodiment, conceiving it as an active process—performed both by the self and by others—through which the body is rendered meaningful (Butler 1993; Waskul and Vannini 2006).

According to this view, our bodies do not constitute a prediscursive, material reality; rather, they are constructed on the basis of social and cultural assumptions about class, gender, sex, race, ethnicity, age, health, and beauty: "To do, to dramatize, to reproduce, these seem to be some of the elementary structures of embodiment" (Butler 1997: 402). The cultural assumptions underlying the performance of bodily identity, in turn, are reflected in, and influenced by, the body images we all carry around in our heads and the actual bodies and pictures of bodies we are constantly confronted with in our everyday lives. As Gail Weiss (1999) points out, this means that the body is necessarily a fluid and unstable concept:

> Put simply, there is no such thing as "the" body or even "the" body image. Instead, whenever we are referring to an individual's body, that body is always responded to in a particularized fashion, that is, as a woman's body, a Latina's body, a mother's body, a daughter's body, a friend's body, an attractive body, an aging body, a Jewish body. Moreover, these images of the body are not discrete but form a series of overlapping identities whereby one or more aspects of that body appear to be especially salient at any given point in time. (Weiss 1999: 1)

Far from leading to a fractured identity, Weiss suggests, this multiplicity of body images is what allows us to adapt in a constructive, flexible way to the many different situations we encounter in our everyday lives. However, some members of a culture are always accorded more freedom than others to determine how their own bodies are defined. The concept of the individual as a rational, universal subject, which has dominated Western thought for many centuries, can only be secured by using the body as a kind of sorting mechanism in setting various normative limits of race, gender, sexuality, and class. These practices of social exclusion can be seen as a collective form of abjection, where the boundaries between the inside and the outside relate to the cultural practices that construct some social identities as "other" and in need of "regulation through expulsion" (Stacey 1997: 76; see also Cohen 1994; Smith 1993). While white, socially privileged men are thus still, at least to a certain extent, able to define themselves as unencumbered by their physicality, those whose bodies are constructed by the powerful majority as culturally "other," such as women, and the socially or racially marginalized, become more closely associated with their physicality. Similarly, people with a serious illness or disability are often forced to become more "fully body" through the way in which they are perceived by others. Every time autobiographical comics artists draw themselves and those around them, they cannot avoid engaging with the sociocultural models that underpin body image, including categories of sex, gender, health, and beauty. Pictorial embodiment is thus always a profoundly social and political activity.

Gendered bodies and the "gaze"

In the scholarly literature, the different cultural attitudes towards male and female bodies are often discussed by means of the notion of the *gaze*. This concept, which was originally developed by Lacan, was later adapted by film theorists and art historians as a way of trying to explain the pleasures that audiences derive from looking at the bodies of other people on screen or in pictures. The most influential of these writings was feminist film theorist Laura Mulvey's (1973) essay on "Visual pleasure and narrative cinema." In it, she suggests that the womb-like circumstances of the theater auditorium, where people sit in the dark and stare with impunity at the bodies on screen without being seen themselves, encourage regression and with it the illusionary sense of owning these other bodies. There are three kinds of looking in the movies: from the camera to the scene, from the spectator to the screen action, and from one character to another in the film. In classical Hollywood films, Mulvey claims, all three types of looking are strictly gendered, in the sense that they typically involve male, voyeuristic patterns of gazing at female bodies. The viewer, whether male or female, is thus forced to align, as subject, with this voyeuristic, controlling, sadistic gaze, or else to identify masochistically with the woman as object. Mulvey's theories have since been criticized for overlooking the complex patterns of gaze that characterize even the most traditional Hollywood films and for ignoring the active role that individual movie viewers play in deciding how to see the bodies on the screen and with which patterns of gaze to align (Sturken and Cartwright 2001: 82–93). Nevertheless, theories of the gendered gaze still enjoy some influence in feminist and cultural studies, and it is thus worth considering their value in trying to understand the pictured embodiment of men and women in the graphic memoir.

It is undoubtedly true that Western art has traditionally been geared towards the male viewer, with many oil paintings featuring naked female bodies for the delectation of the mostly male art collectors and their associates. In the classic female nude, the individual woman is reduced to her physical self, and her body is arranged in a way that puts it on display for the male gaze; often she is shown lying down or in another powerless pose, and she is either looking away or looking back with calculated charm (Berger 1972; Nochlin 1991). Sometimes, the woman is also admiring herself in a mirror, thereby offering the spectator the chance to condemn her for her vanity while simultaneously deriving pleasure from ogling her naked body.[12] Men, by contrast, have always tended to be pictured as active, powerful subjects: "We learn, visually, that males and females are utterly different, with self-absorbed males defined primarily by superior strength. This strength [. . .] connotes dominance, both physical and social" (Caputi 1999: 59). The long history of encouraging gendered patterns of looking and being looked at, has, according to Berger (1972), had a profound influence on men and women's attitudes towards their own bodies and those of the other sex. Women, in particular, are encouraged to look at themselves through the implied gaze of others and to survey themselves constantly: "*[M]en act* and *women appear*. Men look at women. Women watch themselves being looked at. This determines not

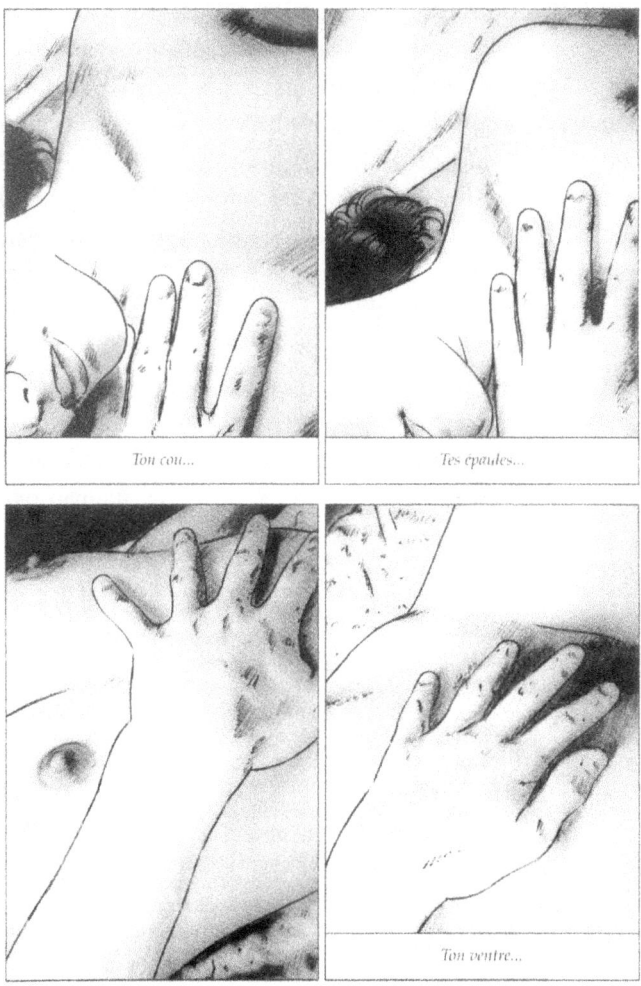

FIG. 2.7 Frédéric Boilet (2001) *L'épinard de Yukiko*, p. 55. Copyright © 2001 ego comme x.

only most relations between men and women but also the relation of women to themselves" (p. 47).

Some graphic memoirs by male comics artists seem to invite traditional, heterosexually gendered patterns of looking through the way they depict themselves and the women in their lives. A good example of this is Frédéric Boilet's (2001) *L'épinard de Yukiko* ("Yukiko's Spinach"), which describes the author's passionate, but short-lived love affair with the young Japanese woman of the book's title. The story is dominated by his obsessive concentration on the most intimate details of her naked body, which is depicted over and over. On pages 51–59, the autobiographical protagonist symbolically takes possession of Yukiko's body by placing his hand on and naming those parts of her body that strike him as particularly beautiful, including her shoulders, neck, stomach, and navel (which he, in his faltering Japanese, mispronounces as "spinach"). Apart from his hand, the rest of Frédéric's body remains invisible most of the time (see Fig. 2.7). The subjective point of view in the drawings more or less forces the reader to join Frédéric in his survey of Yukiko's physical attributes. The way her body is visually broken up through the panels into its component parts is characteristic of the fetishistic gaze, which is totally captivated by what it sees and which makes physical beauty an object in itself.

There is a widely held belief that all of us, regardless of our background, know instinctively who is or is not beautiful. This belief has been emphasized and strengthened by popular science writers like Nancy Etcoff (1999), who claims that our sense of ideal beauty is based on natural selection and that what was biologically advantageous gradually developed into a universal aesthetic preference. However, there is a lot of evidence that the ideal of perfect beauty has, in fact, changed radically over time, and that different cultures have divergent ideas about what is considered beautiful. While there may well be a biological basis to perceptions of attractiveness, the notion of ideal beauty is always socially and culturally constructed. It is a myth that has been validated by art since antiquity, and which is now being fed by the millions of digitally enhanced images constantly being circulated across an increasingly globalized market. Such images play an important role in encouraging ever-greater levels of consumption by inviting comparisons and offering "constant reminders of what we are and might with effort yet become" (Featherstone 1991: 178; see also Laneyrie-Dagen 2004; Mitter 2000).

Naomi Wolf (1991) suggests that there is a deliberate gender bias in the way the contemporary version of the beauty myth is interpreted and applied. According to her, it was invented at the beginning of the Industrial Revolution as a means of keeping women in their place at a moment in history when, at least in the West, they were gaining increasing social and economic independence. As women gradually liberated themselves from established myths about motherhood, domesticity, and chastity, the ideal of the perfect female form thus provided a new way of prescribing their behavior: "Inexhaustible but ephemeral beauty work took over from inexhaustible but ephemeral housework" (p. 16). It also served, and continues to serve, the purpose of making women feel "worth less" in comparison to men, so that they acquiesce more readily to their continuing discrimination in the workplace.

Notions of beauty often intersect with attitudes towards other ethnic groups and cultures. For instance, Western culture has a long, shameful history of taking the superior beauty of white skin for granted and of presenting African facial and bodily features as "primitive" and "ugly," but also, more implicitly, as sexually arousing. Similarly, Eastern and Middle-Eastern societies have, for several centuries, been imagined by Western scholars, authors, and artists as the exotic "other," and attributed qualities of exoticism and barbarism. As part of this "Orientalist" (Said 1979) discourse, Asian women still tend to be portrayed as submissive and highly sexualized.

In *L'épinard de Yukiko* there is certainly a strong sense of Yukiko's body being presented not just as beautiful but also as culturally "other" and thus exotic and arousing. This attitude becomes particularly clear in a sex scene that takes place at a traditional Japanese guesthouse (pp. 116–24). In a sequence of panels that echo those mentioned above (see Fig. 2.7), we see Frédéric's hand as it gradually unwraps Yukiko's body from the kimono she has donned after bathing naked in the shallow outdoor baths. The young woman's submissiveness is also emphasized in one of the very few scenes in the book where Frédéric's body is depicted as well. It starts with a full-frontal view of the couple as they are gazing into the mirror while brushing their teeth (pp. 88–96). Eventually, Frédéric carries Yukiko to the bed, removes most of her clothes and performs oral sex on her, while he himself remains fully clothed throughout. Readers get the sense that they are watching the whole scene from the fixed perspective of the mirror into which the couple was previously gazing, and, as before, they are invited either to assume a male, voyeuristic viewpoint, or else perhaps to identify with the utterly passive and objectified Yukiko.

Another example of a traditional cultural inscription of the female body is Edmond Baudoin's (1995) *L'éloge de la poussière* ("In Praise of Dust"), where the autobiographical stories are interspersed with a great number of erotic life drawings of the women the author has loved. In many cases these pictures seem to be inserted into the text at random, with no apparent link to the narrative context. The only instance in the book where Edmond is depicted naked is a double-page spread of jumbled-up scenes of him and his girlfriend engaged in passionate love-making, and even here the focus is always clearly on the woman's physicality, with his own body drawn sketchily and without much detail.

At first sight, Jean-Christophe Menu's (1995) *Livret de phamille* ("F[ph]amily Record Booklet") seems to follow a similar pattern of subjecting the female form to the male gaze. When the artist draws himself, he does so mostly through the use of a cartoonish figure. His wife, by contrast, is often represented in a much more realistic style, and the book includes many life drawings of her naked and highly pregnant body.

In the small number of realist images of Menu himself, he is generally engaged in the act of drawing, which seems to emphasize his role as storyteller rather than as a character. There is also a depiction of him reflected in the shop window of a women's fashion store as he waits, with the sleeping baby in harness, for his wife to complete her purchases. Miller (2007: 236) believes that this self-portrait can be regarded as reflecting "Menu's desire to merge into the female space of the mirror image," and that it provides evidence of a more complex and multilayered attitude towards established gender roles and patterns of looking than a superficial reading of the text would suggest. She points out that the cartoon version of Menu is in fact highly embodied, in the sense that it has hangovers, suffers pain, and bleeds copiously when it cuts itself. Moreover, the drawing style of the artist, and particularly the "frenzied immediacy of jagged lines" (p. 236) that characterize the sections describing the frustrations of everyday life, can perhaps be seen as a physical inscription on the page of the artist's embodied emotions.

Although theories of the gendered gaze thus still have some value as a means of understanding the way men and women are visually portrayed in graphic memoirs, it is becoming increasingly clear that the social conditions of spectatorship have shifted and become much more complex in recent years. This is partly due to profound changes in Western societies of traditional gender roles, with more women defining themselves through their work rather than simply in relation to men. Conversely, male bodies are now also increasingly subjected to the dictates of the beauty industry, although there seems to be a marked difference in the way men are portrayed for heterosexual and homosexual audiences: "The male presented as an erotic object for heterosexual women seems largely to be the reasonably attractive but distinctly average man. Males offered as erotic objects for homosexual men are idealized, rendered unusually handsome, virile, dominating and phallic" (MacKinnon 2003: 48). This would seem to support the argument that it is social and economic power relations, rather than any straightforward gender differences, which determine the extent to which both women and men are embodied and open to the scrutiny of others (see also Morgan 1993; Nixon 1997).

It is possible to find many examples in contemporary Western cultures of images that deliberately defy dominant subject positions, either by inverting traditional gender roles or by presenting bodies in ways that deflect a possessive gaze or that are respectful and non-objectifying. Moreover, we must remember that meanings are never simply and straightforwardly encoded into an image by its producer; instead, they arise from the encounter, in particular sociocultural contexts, of individual viewers with the image. Even when a picture of a woman presents her in conventionally objectifying ways, it is thus likely that some contemporary viewers will reject the "preferred" reading that is apparently encoded in the image and instead regard it from a "negotiated" or "oppositional" point of view (Hall 1993). Indeed, as the example of Jean-Christophe Menu's (1995) *Livret de phamille* indicates, it is often extremely difficult, if not impossible, to determine unambiguously what the "preferred" meaning of an image is. Even Menu himself is unlikely to be able to tell us with any certainty whether he intended his depictions of himself and his wife to reflect or to challenge established gender roles, since his pictures are likely to encode a range of contradictory meanings, some of which he may not even be aware of at a conscious level.

That there are now far more female photographers and artists than in the past is also likely to impact cultural practices of representation. There is certainly evidence that female comics creators are increasingly challenging traditional cultural inscriptions of the gendered body and claiming the right to represent their own physicality and that of their male partners in a way that truthfully reflects their own experiences. Aline Kominsky-Crumb is a particularly interesting example of this phenomenon. She is married to Robert Crumb, who is notorious for his misogynistic cartoons in which he submits a whole string of women with grotesquely large buttocks to various forms of what can only be described as more or less consensual sexual assault (see Chapter 1). As Aline explains in her book, *Need More Love* (2007), when she joined the comix movement in the 1960s and 1970s, many of her fellow feminist cartoonists were contemptuous of her relationship with Crumb, interpreting it as a sign that she was prepared to submit to his unreconstructed male sexual fantasies. Since then, husband and wife have collaborated on a number of autobiographical comic strips, in which each is responsible for drawing him- or herself. Several of these comics tackle head-on the issue of Crumb's reputation as a sexual predator, using humor and irony as a means of overturning the stereotypical notion of women as powerless victims.

FIG. 2.8 Aline Kominsky-Crumb (2007) *Need More Love: A Graphic Memoir*, p. 223 (excerpt, original in color). Copyright © 2007 MQ Publications Limited; text and illustrations copyright © 2007 Aline Kominsky-Crumb.

On one page, for example, both artists have drawn themselves in a characteristic way (see Fig. 2.8), with Crumb calling attention to his odd, lanky physique, and Aline drawing her body in a way which emphasizes the physical qualities that her husband apparently so admires in women, most notably the large, powerful buttocks and thighs. In a panel that strongly recalls some of the scenes in his notorious comix (e.g., Crumb 1992, 1998), Robert is shown quite literally pouncing on her in a frenzy of lust. In the third panel, the aggressive undercurrent of their relationship is made even more explicit through Robert's admission that he fluctuates between "wanting to *kill*" his wife and "having the tenderest feelings" towards her. Aline is clearly unfazed by all this, admitting that she rather enjoys being "subdued" by him. In a meta-narrative commentary, Aline complains that "Robert had the nerve to touch up" her self-portrait in panel three, a charge Robert answers by pointing out that it was "too minimal." In response to both his aggressive sexual advances and his interference in her artistic freedom to depict her own body, Aline reminds him that she can always bounce him off "with only minimal effort," a threat she carries out with gusto in the final panel.

In *Need More Love* Aline (2007: 151) claims she is actually much more attractive in real life than what she calls her "hideous" self-caricatures suggest, a claim she substantiates implicitly by including in her graphic memoir a great number of rather flattering photographs and portraits of herself by fellow artists, including one by her husband, which uses a more realistic and less cartoonish style than most of his other artwork (p. 337). In it, Aline is again represented as a powerful and self-confident woman. The drawing includes speech balloons, in which the sitter is instructing the artist to "Play down all the wrinkles an' stuff." The fact that this picture was included in the book would suggest that it was indeed to some extent a collaborative venture and that the author was certainly not displeased with the way she is portrayed in it. Overall, *Need More Love* may be regarded as a particularly clear example of a female comics artist taking complete control of her own pictorial embodiment, and rejecting any attempts by her husband, readers, other artists, or wider society to impose extraneous body images on her.[13]

Apart from a reassessment of the shifting power relations between men and women, in recent years there has also been a greater recognition of the possibility of the pleasures that female viewers can derive from looking at male bodies, and of the gay and lesbian gaze. In Alison Bechdel's (2006) *Fun Home*, for instance, the author draws her own body and that of her female lover with a great deal of tenderness. Although some panels show them engaging in explicit sexual acts, the focus is always on the women's emotions rather than just their bodies, thereby conveying a sense of equality and mutual respect.

In apparent contrast to this, French comics creator Fabrice Neaud's (1996) *Journal (1)* seems to reflect the widespread fixation on physical good looks in the male gay community. When he depicts his promiscuous sexual relations with the men he meets while cruising for sex along the ramparts of his hometown, these furtive encounters are often depicted in pornographic detail, with an extreme emphasis on the genitals and an almost clinical eye for physical imperfections. When Fabrice first meets Stéphane, for whom he develops obsessive and largely unrequited feelings of passionate love, he initially sees him as just another sexual conquest, and he is represented as a literally faceless stranger whose features become more and more blurred and indistinct as they negotiate the terms of their sexual encounter (pp. 24–25). However, after their first and only night of passion, which is represented in the book through a large, white panel, empty but for the single word "together" (p. 26), there is a noticeable change in the way the artist depicts his lover. Although he draws him again and again and from different angles, the focus of these portraits is always on Stéphane's individuality and face, not on his body. Indeed, there is not a single drawing of Stéphane's naked body at all in the whole book.

In a scene after an unexpected meeting between the two men in a gay bar, Stéphane has just had his hair cut, and, rather reluctantly, he allows his former lover to feel his cropped head. Fabrice is shown lying in the grass (see Fig. 2.9), his eyes closed and an intense look halfway between agony and ecstasy on his face. This suggests that he is recalling the precise sensation of touching Stéphane's hair and feeling both the pleasure and pain of his unrequited love. The fact that Fabrice's slender, half-naked body is seen from a bird's eye view and that it is laid out diagonally across the panel, with his head facing towards the bottom left-hand corner, conveys a strong sense of his vulnerability. This self-portrait certainly cannot be said to conform to the traditional convention of depicting the male body as active, powerful, and strong. Instead, it shows a determination on the part of the (implied) author/artist to reject established sociocultural models of sex, gender, and beauty, and to replace them with

FIG. 2.9 Fabrice Neaud (1996) *Journal (1)*, p. 46 (excerpt). Copyright © 1996 ego comme x.

his own unique and constantly shifting conceptions of his body and
the bodies of his lovers.

Healthy and diseased bodies

As I mentioned above, a large number of autobiographical comics deal with physical illness or disability, another area of social life
where powerful social discourses of "normality" and "abnormality"
exist. Featherstone (1991) believes that Western consumer culture
has deliberately fostered a particular attitude toward the body that
encourages individuals to monitor themselves constantly for bodily
imperfections and to adopt responsibility for combating any signs
of disease, deterioration, or decay. The beautiful, healthy body is

taken as a sign of a person's discipline and self-control, while para-doxically offering the promise of a more desirable, hedonistic life-style: "Within this logic, fitness and slimness become associated not only with energy, drive and vitality but worthiness as a person; like-wise the body beautiful comes to be taken as a sign of prudence and prescience in health matters" (p. 183). Conversely, signs of aging are associated with moral weakness, and ill-health tends to be blamed on the patients themselves. As a consequence, Western mainstream society is both acutely health conscious and obsessed with disease: "both are expressions of a powerful cultural mandate that individu-als control their bodies" (Couser 1997: 9).

Carol Lay's (2008) *The Big Skinny: How I Changed my Fattitude* is a perfect example of how these ideas can translate into the comic book form. The author uses her own experience of a lifetime of futile dieting and her final discovery of a successful way of shedding excess pounds to tell readers how they, too, can gain control over their body. The book starts with a fabulously slim Carol being asked by the hostess at a dinner party how she has managed to lose so much weight. When she responds by saying that she counts calories and exercises daily, the hostess is visibly stumped and disappointed. What the woman—and, by implication, the reader—clearly wanted to hear, the autobiographical narrator muses, was that there was some new, radical form of dieting that would offer a miracle solu-tion to obesity. Instead, she promises to tell readers "how I lost weight and maintain that loss by taking total responsibility for my own choices. The stories and information in these pages may help you find the courage to lose old habits and make new, healthy ones" (p. 6). A large part of the book is given over to practical information and instructions, including detailed descriptions of exercise rou-tines, calorie charts, and menus for low-calorie meals.

Marisa Marchetto's (2006) autobiographical comic about breast cancer, *Cancer Vixen: A True Story*, also deals with the costs of maintaining a fit, beautiful body, as well as with the con-sequences of suddenly discovering she is no longer completely in control of her physical health. She starts her story with a long string

FIG. 2.10 Marisa Acocella Marchetto (2006) *Cancer Vixen: A True Story*, p. 73 (original in color). Copyright © Marisa Acocella Marchetto 2006.

of tongue-in-cheek descriptive labels for her pre-cancer self: "What happens when a shoe-crazy, lipstick-obsessed, wine-swilling, pasta-slurping, fashion-fanatic, single-forever, about-to-get-married big-city girl cartoonist (me, Marisa Acocella) with a fabulous life finds . . . a lump in her breast?!?" (p. 1). Significantly, she discovers the lump while swimming, which indicates that her hedonistic lifestyle is supported by a regular regime of body maintenance.

Feeling despair and self-pity after she is told the tumor is cancerous (see Fig. 2.10), Marisa retires to bed to consult her mother and some of her best friends about what to do. When she depicts herself and her equally stylish friends and family, every verbal description and visual detail—from the clothes, hairstyles, and spectacles, to the telephones and jewelry—tells us something about the people Marisa likes to be associated with and, by implication, how she herself wishes to be seen. All these characters are white, middle-class professionals who clearly invest a lot of time, money, and energy on maintaining their bodies to fit the dominant cultural ideal.

Throughout the book, Marisa constantly reiterates her sense of having to preserve her good looks so as to ward off all the attractive young women who have designs on her fiancé, a successful entrepreneur. She also recalls the research she conducted for a women's magazine that had asked her to create a comics reportage about how much it costs to be an "It" girl (pp. 15–21). After having sampled the services of a phalanx of "experts" in the field of body enhancement, including the most sought-after plastic surgeon, dermatologist, personal trainer, "hairtailorist," manicurist, and dentist in New York, Marisa comes to the conclusion that "in this town you're either a nobody or a great body and it already costs $179,546 and I'm not even done with it" (p. 19). The protagonist's sense of revulsion at such a shallow, consumerist view of a person's value is increased after her cancer diagnosis. However, this overtly critical attitude is somewhat undermined by the artist's drawings, which reveal a much more ambivalent attitude towards the beauty myth. As a comparison of her self-portraits with a photograph of her on her wedding day (p. 127) reveals, the former are clearly designed to make her look much younger and more conventionally attractive than her actual forty-three-year-old self.

Even in a panel that is supposed to show the protagonist at a moment of deep anxiety and despair (see Fig. 2.10), her cartoon alter ego looks a little pale and disheveled, but still pretty by conventional standards. The circular bubble shape around Marisa indicates the sudden sense of isolation she feels after her involuntary acquisition of a new body image: that of the cancer patient. The views expressed by Marisa's friends and family reflect the idea that it is her responsibility to take charge of her own recovery—with the aid of various highly paid professionals, of course. Marisa is shown to be utterly overwhelmed by the flood of well-intentioned, but basically unhelpful and often ill-informed advice of her friends, which are all delivered in a tellingly uncompromising form ("You have to . . . "). On the following page (p. 74) she is hiding under her duvet and the seven people shout the same message at her in unison, a message written in huge, red capital letters across the whole page: "When are you going to start fighting this thing?"

The responses of Marisa's friends and family to her disease are indicative of the dominant attitude towards physical ill health in Western consumer societies identified by Featherstone (1991) and others. People suffering from cancer, for instance, are often seen as causing their own illness either through an unhealthy lifestyle or by repressing their emotions. Susan Sontag (1991) famously argues that cancer is steeped in harmful metaphorical meanings, with patients being encouraged to "fight" the symptoms of the disease and to "take charge" of circumstances over which they have, in fact, little or no control. She believes that the war metaphor, in particular, has had a pernicious influence on the way people view cancer:

> The metaphor implements the way particularly dreaded diseases are envisaged as an alien "other," as enemies are in modern war; and the move from the demonization of the illness to the attribution of fault to the patient is an inevitable one, no matter if patients are thought of as victims. Victims suggest innocence. And innocence, by the inexorable logic that governs all relational terms, suggests guilt. (Sontag 1991: 97)

At the time *Cancer Vixen* was created, the author's cancer was in remission. The title and the drawing on the cover of herself administering a lethal martial-arts-style kick to an invisible enemy reinforce a reading of her story in terms of a "victory" against all the odds. Therefore, it fits in well with the deep-seated desire in contemporary Western culture for illness narratives that provide "coherent stories of success, progress and movement" and that are apparently preferred to those which acknowledge the chaos and randomness of real life: "Loss and failure have their place but only as part of a broader picture of ascendance. The steady upward curve is the favoured contour" (Stacey 1997: 9).

However, the constant critical references in *Cancer Vixen* to the possible environmental causes of soaring cancer rates and the exploitation of cancer victims by the U.S. profit economy counterbalance the reading of Marchetto's work as a simple story of individual triumph over ill-fortune. For instance, Marchetto (2006: 34–35) uses a mock "Cancer Guessing Game" to lambaste the way cancer patients are encouraged to feel responsible for having caused their own illness. The game looks like a monopoly board, with some frames containing questions about all the known and surmised risk factors associated with cancer, such as smoking, taking the pill, and living near a nuclear reactor, and other frames featuring the conflicting claims of so-called experts. All the frames contain instructions to move up, down, or (most frequently) back by between one and twelve spaces, which signals the utterly futile nature of this particular "game" (see also Tensuan 2011).

Although Joyce Brabner and Harvey Pekar's *Our Cancer Year* also has a "happy end," its authors take an even more critical attitude towards triumphalist discourses of victory over an enemy. The blurb on the book cover uses several war metaphors, describing the story as "a true and unflinching account of two people battling cancer" and saying of Harvey that "he had a better-than-average chance to beat cancer and he took it—kicking, screaming and complaining all the way." However, the concept of a "kicking, screaming and complaining" patient hardly paints a particularly heroic picture and is clearly meant to be at least somewhat ironic. Moreover, Harvey's stubborn determination to complete his course of chemotherapy in the shortest possible time and his refusal to take any sick leave from his work as a hospital clerk are shown to cause him and his wife a lot of unnecessary additional suffering. Stack's visual portraits of

Harvey also underline his increasing fragility, thereby undercutting the sick man's belligerent posturing. The story of Harvey's cancer is interwoven with a record of what happens to seven young activists from some of the most troubled regions in the world, whom Joyce befriends at a student peace conference. The narrative text in the very first panel of the book sets up an explicit analogy between the mistaken belief that the most radical physical cures are always the most appropriate and the equally misguided conviction that aggression can solve political and economic problems: "This is a story about a year when someone was sick, about a time when it seemed that the rest of the world was sick, too. It's a story about feeling powerless, and trying to do too much . . . " (no pagination). Together, these different narrative devices serve to undermine the idea that a sick body must be treated as an enemy.

Al Davison's (1990) *The Spiral Cage*, which has already been mentioned above, also explicitly deals with the question of how much control people have over their bodies and body images, particularly when suffering from an illness or disability. The artist often draws himself naked, showing himself at his most vulnerable, helpless, and depressed. It is notable that none of the fragments of black and white photographs of Al on the first page of each chapter of the book are of his whole body. Instead, they show just his head and shoulders at various stages in his life, and in them he is always looking cheerful and full of life. As Scott (1999: 237) points out, photographic portraits tend to evoke strong anxieties in some people, and act as a focus of their self-love, self-hate, and alienation from past incarnations of themselves. This is because the camera seems to require of us a coherence and control of the self which, in fact, we do not possess.[14] Sontag (2005 [1977]: 10) goes as far as to liken the taking of someone's photograph to an act of violation: "To photograph people is to violate them, by seeing them as they never see themselves, by having knowledge of them they can never have; it turns people into objects that can be symbolically possessed."

Photographs of disabled people's bodies are thus liable to appeal to some viewers' prurient interest in the "monstrous" and to provoke stereotypical responses. Self-portraits, by contrast, can be used to show how the artist actually feels about his or her own body and to challenge some of the cultural inscriptions that are commonly imposed on them.[15] The cultural stereotypes of the disabled are particularly difficult for men to contend with, as dominant definitions of masculinity are based on the ideal of a strong, autonomous body. Many of the stories in *The Spiral Cage* deal with how Al uses Buddhist meditation and martial arts training to develop greater control over his body and mind, and to build up the physical strength he feels he needs to defend himself and to counteract the view others have of him as a helpless victim:

> He refuses to be still, to be inactive, to lack mobility, to be confined by aids to mobility, and he refuses to be bullied by men who take it upon themselves to embarrass him, to manhandle him, to terrorize him in public places and institutions. He "writes/draws back" his own developing vision of masculinity through conflict, a successful transition from boy to heterosexual man. (McIlvenny 2003: 254)

As the example of *The Spiral Cage* demonstrates, the requirement by autobiographical comics artists to produce multiple portraits of themselves and of other people in their lives provides the opportunity for them to engage explicitly with their own body images and with the sociocultural assumptions and values that render bodies meaningful. The graphic memoir genre's unique capacity for what I have termed "pictorial embodiment" may even provide entirely novel ways of understanding the body, both for the graphic memoirist him-or herself and for the wider reading public. Al's self portraits in *The Spiral Cage*, for instance, are a far cry from the images of disabled men we frequently see in the media. Similarly, Fabrice Neaud's (1996) *Journal (1)* presents the reader with a whole range

of different ways of visualizing the male body, many of which challenge and subvert the more conventional body images that are
circulated within the gay community and in broader society. The
following chapter will explore the ways in which comics creators
use the graphic memoir to remember their past experiences and, in
some cases, to imagine a better future.

Chapter 3

COMMEMORATING THE PAST, ANTICIPATING THE FUTURE

Blankets is Craig Thomson's (2003) autobiographical account of his fundamentalist Christian upbringing in a small town in the American Midwest, where his sensitive nature and creativity are greeted with incomprehension and ridicule. In one sequence Craig is being severely reprimanded by his English teacher for writing a poem about people eating excrement. By way of explaining to the reader why he wrote the poem, the autobiographical narrator recalls an earlier memory of how he failed to protect his little brother from sexual abuse by their babysitter. The narration has returned to the events that took place in the English class (see Fig. 3.1), but Craig's memory of the abusive babysitter is just as present to him as his teacher and jeering classmates. The merging of two different moments in time through the association of the intense feeling of shame common to both is conveyed by placing representations of both scenes into the same narrative space of the classroom and onto the same page of the book.

In Western industrialized nations, time is commonly conceptualized as something linear, regular, and measurable. However, as this example suggests, our actual experience of temporality is much richer and less reassuring than this. When we are enjoying ourselves, for instance, time seems to fly by, whereas embarrassing moments are typically experienced as painfully slow. In our

FIG. 3.1 Craig Thompson (2003) *Blankets*, p. 32. Copyright © 2003, 2004, 2005 Craig Thompson.

memories, time acquires a further dimension, often skipping certain events completely, while preserving an exact record of seemingly unimportant details, or combining two different moments in unexpected ways. It is this idiosyncratic experience of subjective time, with its irregularities, circularities, overlaps, and gaps, which graphic memoirists typically want to "commemorate," or share with their readers, and which are the focus of the first two sections of this chapter.

The aforementioned scene also demonstrates the importance of a sense of temporality to our ability to tell stories. As will be explained in the third section of this chapter, time has always been a central concern of narrative theorists, who like to draw a distinction between the chronology or duration of events in a story ("story-time") and the way these are re-arranged in the process of their telling ("discourse-time") (Bal 1985; Genette 1980). I argue that this traditional structuralist approach to narrative time is unable to capture adequately the fluid time structures that characterize life writing, as it is based on several flawed assumptions about the nature of our temporal experience.

In the fourth section of this chapter I identify some of the many resources that exist in comics for the evocation of temporal meaning. Indeed, the medium seems to be particularly well suited to the task of conveying the human experience of time, since many of its formal features follow patterns that reflect the way memory itself works. Examples include the gaps—both between verbal and visual meaning, and between individual panels—that characterize comics, as well as the fact that in this medium meanings often emerge through associative links across a page or even a whole work (Groensteen 2007). As the example above demonstrates, the spatial nature of the comics medium also makes it possible "to spatially juxtapose (and overlay) past and present and future moments on the page" (Chute 2008: 453). These different formal resources, and the multiple ways in which they interact, provide autobiographical comics creators with a wide range of means for representing their unique experience of time.

Clock time and subjective time

Recurrent cyclical events such as the rising and setting of the sun, the phases of the moon, and the seasons have always played a central role in how human civilizations experience the passage of time and the sequencing of events. The invention of mechanical timepieces afforded more refined ways of quantifying these intervals—clocks and watches allowed urban, industrial societies in particular to develop complex sociocultural practices based on a linear understanding of time as a series of precisely measurable units. However, these standardized conceptualizations of time do not always accord with our actual, subjective experiences of it, which are influenced by shared attitudes within our own culture. Individual cultures appear to differ greatly from one another in how they value time and in whether they are primarily oriented towards the past, the present, or the future (Hall 1973; O'Sullivan 1994; Kövecses 2005). The specific situations in which we find ourselves can also have an impact on our time perceptions. For instance, if we are bored and restless, time will take on a different shape for us than if we are completely absorbed in an enjoyable activity or enduring moments of acute embarrassment or terror:

> Lived time, the time of our lives, is obviously not devoid of meaning. It is not a mere succession of neutral now points, a formal grid transparent with respect to the content of experience. On the contrary, lived time seems to be in strict accord with the present meaning of experience. In other words, our sense of time changes with the significance of our experience. (Kerby 1991: 17)

The distinction between clock time and time as we know it from direct experience was also central to Henri Bergson's philosophy (Bergson 1889; Kolakowski 1985). Bergson argued that we tend to think of time as a kind of space, consisting of a set of abstract, homogenous, infinitely divisible segments that together form an indefinitely long line. *La durée*, or "psychic" time, by contrast, is what we know intuitively, from our actual experience. It is a single, indivisible entity, made up of an accumulation of individual moments each of which carries within it the entire flow of the past. Bergson believed that we find it easier to talk about clock time than to express our experience of *la durée*, which seems to require more poetic forms of expression.

It would be wrong, however, to create an overly simplistic dichotomy between measured time and psychic time (Currie 2007). Clearly, both clock time and more subjective experiences of time are available to our human consciousness. As Hartman (2002: 232) points out, on the one hand, the ordinary, everyday flow of time often appears to be "a banal matter of record," but, on the other hand, "an emotional stopwatch punctuates life with traumatic or near-apocalyptic effect," creating much more idiosyncratic perceptions of temporality. Examples of events that suddenly interrupt our comfortable sense of linear, regular time are, on a collective level, natural catastrophes or terrorist attacks, while on a personal level it can be the "now" moment of falling in or out of love.

Frederik Peeters's (2008) graphic memoir *Blue Pills* serves as a poignant example of the complex and multifaceted nature of the human perception of time. The autobiographical protagonist has been dating Cati for several weeks, and in a sequence after she reveals to him that both she and her son are HIV positive, Frederik is stunned by this news. For what is, in fact, no more than "one full second" but what clearly feels to him like an interminable length of time, he does not know how to react or what to say. Waves of contradictory thoughts and feelings wash over him, while outwardly he remains utterly still and unperturbed. Clock time—indicated through the verbal narration and the "click, clack" of a ticking clock (see Fig. 3.2)—is juxtaposed with the young protagonist's subjective experience of the moment. A portrait of his face and upper body in the exact same pose is repeated in three panels of equal size. In the first of these images, three words that express Frederik's thoughts and feelings are emerging from his head like plumes of smoke, in the second one they have multiplied and are filling up most of the upper part of the panel, and in the final image they are gradually drifting away again. The panel borders look as if they are in the process of dissolution, offering a powerful visual metaphor for the way in which, in Frederik's perception, individual moments merge to become a single, indivisible entity.

Of course, in this example we are dealing not with Frederik Peeters's perception of a current moment in time but rather with

FIG. 3.2 Frederik Peeters (2008) *Blue Pills: A Positive Love Story*, p. 35 (excerpt). Copyright © 2008 Frederik Peeters; English translation © Anjali Singh.

his subsequent memories of it. All forms of life writing—including journals, where the events recounted tend to be closer in time to their actual occurrence—entail a degree of reinterpretation and reconfiguration of the past through the filter of memory. Autobiography also invites individuals to relate past experiences to their present circumstances and imagined futures.

Memory, commemoration, and anticipation

The complexities of human memory have attracted the attention of researchers in a whole range of academic disciplines, including neurophysiology, psychology, psychotherapy, cultural theory, and literary criticism. Despite the different theories and perspectives these distinct fields of inquiry have brought to the debate, there now seems to be broad agreement that memory is not limited to the straightforward storage and retrieval of past moments (Wägenbaur 1998). Rather, the work of memory involves a highly complex and self-referential system of selection and interpretation in which constant choices are being made, mostly at a subconscious level, about which information to retain and which to discard. Indeed, forgetting is an essential function of memory, because it allows the system to avoid sensory overload and to adjust to ever-changing situations.

The remembering of past events can occur in many different forms. They may be recalled voluntarily, or resurface unbidden and unexpectedly, evoked for instance by an image, a word, a smell, a taste, a place, or a strain of music. Memories of traumatic events have a distinct quality. Psychoanalysis has shown how those events or situations that are so overwhelming that they cannot be fully assimilated into the totality of a person's experience tend to remain timeless, fixed permanently at a certain moment in the traumatized person's life (van der Kolk and van der Hart 1995). As Caruth (1995: 153) puts it, the traumatic experience "literally *has no place*, neither in the past, in which it was not fully experienced, nor in the present, in which its precise images and enactments are not fully understood." Patients suffering from Post-Traumatic Stress Disorder are haunted by repeated intrusive flashbacks, dreams, hallucinations, and behaviors, which, while surprisingly literal and absolutely "true" to the original event, are inaccessible to the person's conscious recall and control. While traumatic memory thus "has no place" in time, it does often attach strongly to physical locations. In many forms of trauma, such as life-threatening accidents or rape, memory is also often stored in the body.[1]

As soon as we begin to describe our memories to ourselves or to others, we turn them into stories, reconstructing "the events of a life in the light of 'what wasn't known then,' highlighting the events which are now, with hindsight, seen as significant" (King 2000: 22). We also tend to make connections between experiences that were originally separate in time and space, and that initially were not perceived to be causally linked. It is impossible to know, for example, whether the close association in Craig's mind between his brother's abuse by their babysitter and the essay he wrote about excrement (see Fig. 3.1) was already established at the time the events occurred, or only retrospectively, when the adult author was remembering his childhood and trying to make sense of his life. Our recall of painful periods in our lives, in particular, tends to be confused, unstructured, and "full of gaps, condensations and substitutions" (Stacey 1997: 98). Inevitably, the process of turning memory fragments into stories will thus involve a degree of imaginative projection, which settles "into the gaps left vacant by recollection, such that we can no longer be certain of the difference between them" (Kerby 1991: 25). This phenomenon can help to explain why, for example, siblings often remember the same events from their childhood in such strikingly different ways, particularly if those experiences were traumatic.

Life writing is like ordinary, everyday memory in that it involves similar processes of joining together voluntary and involuntary memories and fictional elements in order to form a more or less coherent narrative. Unlike more private acts of remembering, however, autobiography is also a deliberate and self-conscious act of *communication*, whereby the events of a life are made public in order to be shared with others. The communicative purpose of life writing impacts the manner autobiographers attend to their memories in the first place, as well as affecting how they select, interpret, and combine their memories into stories. The resulting accounts of a person's life are then actively recreated, and sometimes challenged and contested, in the minds of individual readers. I will use the term "commemoration" to describe this collaborative remembering by autobiographers and their readers.

One of the main differences between private memory and commemoration is that the latter typically entails a greater measure of self-reflexivity on the part of autobiographers. According to Currie (2007: 88), autobiography involves a process of moving forward in time by working backwards into the author's own past, with the time of the narrative functioning "as the site of self-conscious reflection both on past events and on the nature of writing about them." In many autobiographical works, the author's interest in reconstructing for his or her readers a chronology of events and anchoring them in historical time is thus constantly competing with the desire to reflect on the workings of memory. When people try to grasp and articulate the specific ways in which they remember, King (2000: 9) suggests, "metaphor seems inevitable." Perhaps not surprisingly given the nature of the medium they are using, many autobiographical comics artists seem to favor visual analogies of memory. Edmond Baudoin (1995: no pagination), for instance, uses the following evocative image to describe the fleeting nature of the act of remembering: "Memory is contained in a shell. When it opens a crack, the glimmer of a pearl appears for an instant" ("La mémoir est dans un coquillage. Quand il s'entrouvre, la lueur d'une perle apparaît un instant").

Photographs are particularly closely associated with memory. Indeed, the visual impact of photographs may be so powerful that we sometimes cannot be sure whether our memories are based on witnessed events or on photographs of the events we have seen (Haverty Rugg 1997). Rosalind Penfold's (2006) graphic memoir of living with and finally escaping from an abusive marriage, *Dragonslippers*, uses the analogy of photography to address the malfunctioning of memory when faced with unbearably hurtful experiences (pp. 229–31). Rosalind's therapist explains that good memories are stored as part of a coherent narrative, just like the pictures in a photo album, while traumatic memories resemble a bag full of jumbled-up negatives. This analogy is emphasized visually as well: The panels in which Rosalind and her therapist are shown discussing positive memories are drawn with photo corners, as if they represented part of an ordered display in a photo album. In contrast to this, the section in which Rosalind's traumatic memories are addressed ends with a panel that resembles a fragment of a roll of undeveloped film.

Like Penfold, Lynda Barry conceptualizes memory in terms of visual images of various kinds. In her playful and creative comic book *What It Is* (2009: 33), which explores the inner and outer realms of imagination and creativity, the question "What is a memory?" is addressed through the use of several scraps of fabric, printed texts, drawings, and a class photograph from an elementary school, in which most of the children's faces and bodies have been painted over, giving them a ghost-like appearance. "When an unexpected memory comes calling," one of the verbal labels reads, "who answers?" "An image which travels through time," is the somewhat cryptic answer.

Another important dimension of commemoration is our human propensity to see the present as teetering on the brink of becoming the past, most notably during significant moments in our lives, such as our wedding day or that once-in-a-lifetime holiday, which we already know will become extremely important to our future memories and self-representations. For people who keep a diary, and for those embarking on an autobiographical project of some sort, the awareness of the potential of the present to become a narrative is likely to be particularly strong: "If, in order to look back at what happened, we tell a story, we must also know that the present is a story yet to be told" (Currie 2007: 5).[2] In some cases, this awareness may even lead to a situation where "an event is recorded not because it happens, but it happens because it is recorded" (p. 11). Ariel Schrag's (2008a and b; 2009) chronicles of her high school years, for instance, are full of verbal and visual representations of events that seem to have been staged deliberately by the author because of their potential for making a good story. A good example of this is the highly elaborate and, as it turns out, disastrous plan she hatches to lose her virginity to her boyfriend just before her seventeenth birthday, despite her dawning realization that she is actually much more attracted to girls than to boys (Schrag 2008b, chapter 4). Schrag also generates new material by showing her work to her friends and family members and then recording their responses (e.g., Schrag 2008b: 42). I refer to such forms of the self-conscious intervention by an author in his or her life story as "premeditated commemoration."

German comics artist Dirk Schwieger provides an even more extreme example of premeditated commemoration. He used his webcomic blog while living in Tokyo to invite people from all over the world to submit specific "tasks" for him to perform and then report on in a weekly comic strip. The exact wording of this invitation is included in the front of the published version of his weekly webcomic blog: "This is Tokyo—Maybe you have heard of a *place* I should go to or you know a *person* I should (try to) meet up with or you're just interested in a *topic* that's somehow related to my new home town. Just drop me a short line via info@eigen-heim.com and I will *do* it, no questions asked and whether I like it or not. So send a mail and read about it next week!" (Schwieger 2008: no pagination). Examples of the tasks he was set include going on a rooftop rollercoaster, meeting a local band, and spending a night in a pod hotel. Each "assignment" thus became an actual experience and then a commemorated narrative event, which was posted on the blog and which often triggered new suggestions by his followers.

Although life writing is, by its very nature, primarily concerned with retrospection, anticipation also plays a crucial role in many autobiographical works. Again, the ability to construct fantasies and imagine alternative situations is inextricably linked to our capacity for storytelling, which constitutes "our chief means of looking into the future, of predicting, of planning, and of explaining" (Turner 1996: 4, 5). Frederik Peeters's (2008) *Blue Pills*, for instance, ends with the autobiographical protagonist lying in bed and joyfully anticipating his journey to Bangkok the following day. Cathy and her little boy are due to join him three days later: "I see her arriving in the hall, with her adorable worn face . . . her head full of worries and desires . . . / . . . and her bag full of little blue pills . . . " (p. 190). The drawings on this final page are sketchy and frameless, suggesting a merging of the past, present, and future in Frederik's mind as he drifts off to sleep.

Held ("Hero") (2003), by the German comics creator Flix, offers a particularly interesting example of the human ability to anticipate the future by imagining alternative storylines. Almost half of this work, which was originally created as part of the artist's dissertation for his degree course in Communication Design, is dedicated to the depiction of the future life of his autobiographical alter ego, Felix. This anticipatory section starts with a description of Felix's successful graduation and his subsequent feelings of satisfaction and relief at having accurately predicted his own triumph. He hopes that the whole life story he has created for himself may turn out to be equally true: "In that case, how reassured I would feel as I went through life . . . Given that I had written myself *such a beautiful happy end*" ("Wie beruhigt könnte ich dann durchs Leben gehen . . . Denn ich hatte mir doch *so ein schönes Happy End* geschrieben") (p. 66). Then Felix presents to the reader the three possible professional trajectories of the newly qualified Design graduate.

The three vertical columns represent the alternative routes that are now open to him (see Fig. 3.3), with column a and b illustrating what would happen if Felix decided to work for a large and a small company respectively, and the final column showing life as a self-employed artist. The drawings in the first three rows from the top describe some of the different outcomes this decision would entail; for instance, how it would affect his working environment and how much money he could expect to earn. However, in the two rows at the bottom of the page his future prospects are shown to be remarkably similar: In each case, the protagonist is shown as suffering from "burnout," either as a result of pressure from others (a and b) or his own zeal (c), so that he always ends up suffering a heart attack.

The following page shows Felix struggling to meet the demands of a large number of contractors, while also trying to care for his wife and children. In the final panel, the narrator confirms what readers will have guessed already by the time they have reached the bottom of the page: "I had opted for *c* . . . " ("Ich hatte mich für *c* entschieden . . . ") (p. 68). He then proceeds to tell the story of the

FIG. 3.3 Flix (2003) *Held*, p. 67. Copyright © 2003 Carlsen.

remainder of Felix's future life, including his increasingly fruitless attempts to juggle work and family life, his near-death experience after succumbing to the inevitable heart attack, his decision at the age of fifty to give up his cushy job at the university and fulfill his life-long dream of living in Spain, the death of his beloved wife and, finally, his own demise at a ripe old age. At one point the narrator observes that, contrary to what he expected when he was younger, the world in the future is much the same as it always was, apart from the considerable influence of Japanese culture on everybody's lifestyle: "This enthusiasm for Japanese culture was initially aroused by Asian manga . . . Tsk! And for so long people thought that comics had no cultural relevance at all . . . " ("Ausgelöst wurde diese Japanbegeisterung durch asiatische Manga . . . Ts! Und dabei dachte man lange, Comics seien ohne kulturelle Relevanz . . . ") (p. 94). *Held* represents a curious mixture of satire and the more serious attempt by the author to transform the frightening chaos of an unknown future into a reassuring story for public consumption. The book makes it clear that, just like our memoires of the past, our future hopes and projections are also always underpinned with story and fantasy.

Narrative time

As we have seen, stories play a central role in the way we organize and understand our experience of time, including our ability to remember the past and anticipate the future. Conversely, narrative cannot function without temporal structuring; as Berger (1997: 6) puts it, "narratives, in the most simple sense, are stories that take place in time" (see also Ricoeur 2004).

In traditional structuralist accounts, temporal structure is generally seen as susceptible to a double ordering: "Story-time," or narrated time, consists of the sequence, duration, and frequency of events pertinent to a narrative, whether they are recounted explicitly or not. "Discourse-time," or time of narration, by contrast, refers to those temporal qualities of events as they are presented in a particular text (Genette 1980; Culler 2004). In contrast to time-based media such as film or theater, where the presentation of a story has a literal sequence and duration, in written narratives discourse-time can only be deduced indirectly from the spatial arrangement of elements and the number of words, lines, or paragraphs taken up for their recounting. As Genette (1980: 34) concedes, this means that discourse-time in printed texts is actually a "pseudo-time" that derives its temporality metonymically from its own reading: "the written narrative exists in space and as space, and the time needed for 'consuming' it is the time needed for crossing or traversing it, like a road or a field."

Genette (1980) offers a detailed account of the many ways in which the sequence and duration of events in story-time can differ from the way in which they are experienced in discourse-time (see also Bal 1985). For instance, story events are often anticipated in the narrative ("prolepsis"), or else they are temporarily withheld and only recounted after they have logically already occurred in the story ("analepsis").[3] Story-time and discourse-time can also be compared and contrasted with regard to relations of repetition: thus, it is possible to tell n times what happened n times, to tell n times what happened once, and to tell once what happened n times. Finally, different relations can pertain between the duration of an event in the story and the time it takes for an audience to watch or read about the same event. "Ellipsis" refers to cases where an event of a particular duration is simply not present at all in the narrative, while a "pause" describes the opposite phenomenon, namely where the story is interrupted by a section of extratemporal description by the narrator. "Scenes" are sections where the speed of the story is roughly equivalent to the speed of telling the same, and the "summary" is when events are condensed into just a few words. According to Genette (1980: 95), "slow motion," where acts or events "are told about more slowly than they were performed or undergone," is also possible, although he believes that genuine cases of this device are rare in the novel.

There are several problems with this approach. One difficulty concerns the idea that, in the case of printed texts, the *sequence* of events in discourse-time can be inferred from the order in which they are recounted in the book or on a page. In fact, the reading of a printed text is not necessarily strictly sequential and linear: We do not always start a text at the title page or indeed at the top of each page, and often our eyes are attracted to different points of salience (Lemke 2002; White 2005). Comics, as Genette (1980: 34) himself acknowledges, have even more pronounced spatial characteristics than purely verbal texts, simultaneously inviting a "successive or diachronic reading," and "a kind of global or synchronic look." Although they are typically read from the front to the back, and by following the panels from the upper left to the lower right corner on each page (Cohn 2008), in some cases the reading path is less regulated, even anarchic, leaving the individual reader to decide in which sequence to view the panels on a page or across a double-page spread. The order in which the eye is expected to take in the various elements within each individual panel is typically even less clearly indicated. All this makes the relationship between temporal and spatial sequence in comics more complicated and exciting than in traditional literary texts.

A similar issue arises with regard to the *duration* of events in discourse-time. Narratologists have tried to compensate for the lack of any actual temporal duration in novels by comparing the number of lines used to describe different events.[4] The obvious equivalent in the case of comics would be to count the number of illustrations or panels dedicated to each event. In a scene from *Blue Pills*, for instance, one second in story time is represented in the discourse by four separate frames (see Fig. 3.2), thus creating a sense of what Genette would call "slow motion." However, as will be discussed in more detail below, the pace at which a comic book is read depends not only on the number of panels on the page but also their format, size, style, and arrangement—and the amount of text and detail contained within each panel. Moreover, the reading pace is likely to vary hugely from one individual to another, depending, for instance, on their prior experience with the comics medium, their available time, and their interest in a particular story.[5]

Another weakness of Genette's approach is its understanding of time as an objective, measurable sequence of events of a particular duration that can then be rearranged in a story. More recently, narrative scholars have begun to challenge this assumption. Cognitive narratologist Herman (2002: 211–61), for instance, criticizes the structuralist account of narrative time for neglecting the phenomenon of "fuzzy temporality." He suggests that some narratives employ a form of polychrony, where it is difficult or even impossible for readers to assign a place on a timeline to particular events, or where events are anchored in multiple temporal frameworks, so that competing ways of sequencing are possible. Such deliberate disruptions of linear chronology can be used to draw attention to the "always unfinished work of memoralization" (p. 232), or to show how traumatic events "resist being modeled in the form of a chronological series" (p. 239). As will be shown in the discussion below, a number of autobiographical comics are characterized by just such a "fuzzy" representation of the temporality of painful events as they are captured and reshaped by memory.[6]

Herrnstein Smith (2004) is also critical of traditional conceptions of narrative time. Strongly refuting the idea that story-time exists independently of its narration, she argues that events only acquire a particular sequence and duration in and through their telling. This is most obviously true in the case of fiction, but the same argument, she believes, also applies to narratives that report "real" happenings, such as historical accounts or autobiography. Our memories of past events tend to be in the form of vague and often inconsistent recollections, verbal information, and visual, auditory, and kinesthetic impressions. These will be "organized, integrated, and apprehended as a specific 'set' of events only in and through the very act by which we narrate them as such" (p. 109). For this reason, Herrnstein Smith believes, scholars should concentrate on describing the means by which readers of a narrative are encouraged to infer a sequence of events that is not already given. As part of the normal process of engagement with a narrative, readers will construe a particular chronology and duration of events, drawing on their awareness of the temporal qualities of the described events either in real life or in other known versions of the narrative, shared expectations regarding the logic of temporal and causal sequence, and a familiarity with the relevant conventions of language, style, and genre.

Following Herrnstein Smith, my examination of narrative time in graphic memoirs will focus on the means by which readers are encouraged to infer a particular sense of temporality from the storyworld. However, I would like to suggest that in this process readers are likely to draw not only on their knowledge of clock time, but also on the universal experience of subjective time. For instance, we all know that, depending on the circumstances, time can expand and contract and skip backward and fast-forward, and that our memory of the past and our fantasies about the future may add another layer of temporal meaning, deleting whole chunks of experience and dwelling on seemingly unimportant details. It is this active process of collaboration between the graphic memoirist and the reader in the construction of narrative temporal meaning that I have tried to capture by the notion of "commemoration."

Temporal cues in the graphic memoir

The following discussion will identify some of the ways in which a particular sense of sequence and duration can be conveyed to the reader through the semiotic resources available to the comics creator, many of which are unique to the medium. My discussion of these different "temporal cues" is organized into four subsections, each of which focuses on one of the tensions identified by Hatfield (2005, 2009; see Chapter 1): between the written and the pictorial code, the single image and image-in-series, sequence and layout, and between text as narrative and text as material object. Comics artists have a vast array of temporal cues in different combinations at their disposal. Consequently, they are able to convey many different experiences of time, including clock time and subjective time, remembered time, and anticipated time.

The written versus the pictorial code

All the eighty-five graphic memoirs I consider in this book combine words and images, with each semiotic mode fulfilling different functions with regard to temporal structuring. Generally speaking, the words in captions tend to anchor events in a particular moment and to order them chronologically, while the focus of the visuals is more on the subjective experience of time. I agree with Witek (1989) that prose is generally able to present information about measured, historical time more clearly and efficiently than images can. A good example of this is provided by the scene from *Blue Pills* (see Fig. 3.2), where the verbal commentary indicates precisely how long it took Frederik to respond to his girlfriend's shocking revelations, while the visual images offer a moving portrayal of how he perceived this key moment in his life.

Apart from providing a narrative voice, words in comics can also represent ambient sound, diegetic text, and, through the unique convention of the balloon, the speech and thoughts of the different characters in the story. By calling to mind "that which can only exist in time—sound" (McCloud 1994: 95), speech balloons convey their own sense of duration, and, if there are several balloons in a panel, of sequence as well, as normally one utterance logically follows another. The same is also to some extent true of thought balloons, although thoughts are not linked quite so clearly to a specific duration.

In the case of the example from Thompson's *Blankets* (see Fig. 3.1), the teacher's words are split into two separate bubbles on either side of the drawing of the boy, which, when read in the traditional order of left to right, create a sequence of events: first she tells him off, then she realizes that he is crying, and this makes her even more annoyed. The regular, handwritten typography does not increase in size or boldness, suggesting that she restrains her anger and does not raise her voice. The onomatopoeic rendering of the sound of the school bell, by contrast, is written in large, thick, irregular capital letters that are tightly packed together and cover the whole of the bottom edge of the page. This gives the impression of a loud, intrusive sound that continues alongside the teacher's utterances, the other students' derisive responses, and Craig's attempt to hide behind his desk. The transcription indicating the sound of the bell ringing persists along the top edge of the following two panels as well, providing a sense of temporal continuity, although the decreasing size of the words and the increasing gaps between them indicate that the sound gradually fades as Craig leaves the building and heads home.

Just as implied sounds can suggest a particular sequence and duration, implied silence can have the effect of removing a panel from any specific time span, creating a powerful sense of what Carney (2008: 198) calls "the silence of time passing," which, depending on the narrative context, can feel dreamy and peaceful, or agitated and oppressive. A good example is a full-page panel from *Persepolis*, Marjane Satrapi's graphic memoir about growing up in Iran during the 1970s and '80s (see Fig. 3.4).[7] This full-page splash shows the approximately six-year-old Marjane at the moment when she loses her faith in God after her beloved uncle has been executed by the Islamic regime, although, as a Marxist, he originally supported the revolution. From early childhood, Marjane has seen herself as the first female prophet and imagined herself having regular friendly chats with a bearded, fatherly God-figure. Her religious fantasies are eclectic, incorporating elements from Islam, the Old Testament, Christianity, Zoroastrianism, and the revolutionary literature lying about the house. Marjane's loss of faith is an extremely traumatic and disorienting experience, which is conveyed through the image of the little girl floating in outer space, arms outstretched in an attitude of crucifixion. The narrative voice in the text box makes it clear that in this case the "silence of time passing" and the associated sense of placelessness is experienced as something distinctly

FIG. 3.4 Marjane Satrapi (2006) *Persepolis*, p. 71. Copyright © 2002, 2003 L'Association; translation copyright © 2003 L'Association and 2004 Anjali Singh.

unsettling: "And so I was lost, without any bearings . . . What could be worse than that?"

This rhetorical question is apparently answered by the words in the speech balloon in a ragged star-shape, which intrude on and seem to shatter the sense of being outside of ordinary, historical time. In a movie theater, sound is normally matched carefully with image in projection, but it is also possible to have sounds or voices from an earlier or later point in the story than the events currently visible onscreen (Bordwell and Thompson 1993: 313–16). Similarly, in comics, speech and thought balloons are typically attached to specific characters in the here and now of the story conveyed by the images, but in some cases a disembodied "voice" can intrude on an earlier or later space/time dimension. In the panel from *Persepolis* (see Fig. 3.4), the words in the speech balloon ("Marji, run to the basement! We're being bombed!") are not attributed to a specific speaker, but from the context we can surmise that they are spoken by Marjane's mother or father. Together with the caption running along the bottom edge of the panel ("It was the beginning of the war"), they introduce the next section of the book, which discusses the weeks leading up to the Iran-Iraq war, several years after the death of Marjane's uncle.

In effect, this panel thus represents a time-span of roughly four years, but it also stands for the loss of episodic memory that can follow a traumatic event—and the feelings of senselessness associated with it. The parent's voice, by contrast, belongs to a specific historical moment and begins the narration of a new period in Marjane's life, which, although also difficult and frightening, at least can be given a narrative form, and thus a sense of meaningful temporal progression. As Witek (1989: 43) points out, something that the comic book can do that prose alone cannot is to "keep previous scenes physically before the reader after the narrative has moved on." In this example, the haunting image of the little girl adrift in cosmic space conveys a potent sense of horror and foreboding, which colors the following account of the family's experience of the Iran-Iraq war.

Some events can be so traumatic that no visual representation can properly do them justice. In such cases, comics artists sometimes employ a "blind" image, a panel that is entirely white or black or grey (Carrier 2004; see Chapter 4). As Groensteen (2010: 11) suggests, this typically signals a loss of consciousness or sight, but it may also indicate "a refusal to show the surrounding world." A good example of this can be found in a later scene in *Persepolis*: After a bombing raid on Tehran, the adolescent Marjane rushes back to her house, terrified it may have received a direct hit. In fact, it is the neighbor's house that has been completely destroyed. As she walks past, she catches sight of her friend Neda's turquoise bracelet protruding from a pile of rubble. An image of Marjane's shocked face, her hand covering her mouth, is accompanied by the following caption: "The bracelet was still attached to . . . I don't know what . . . " (p. 142). In the next "silent" panel she is shown covering her eyes, and this is followed by a completely black panel with just the following text in a narrow box along its bottom edge: "No scream in the world could have relieved my suffering and my anger." Thus, Satrapi's memory of this experience from her life as a young girl is shown to be so horrific that it resists any subsequent attempt to represent it, be it in a verbal or a visual form.[8] Instead, it invites readers to project their own imagined version of this scene onto the blank space, which encourages them to engage emotionally with Satrapi's experiences and perhaps, by extension, the plight of all people living in warzones (see Chapter 5).

The single image versus the image-in-series

Comic book artist and theorist Will Eisner (1985: 39) suggests that comics work by cutting up the continuous flow of experience into separate segments of "frozen" scenes, which are normally enclosed by a frame. The reader is then invited to bridge the gaps between the panels by drawing on his or her experience of real life to fill in the intervening moments. Eisner's concept of "frozen" scenes is somewhat misleading, however, as it suggests an immobility and temporal stasis that is not actually characteristic of most comics panels. As Saraceni (2003: 7) remarks, every comics panel represents a portion of the narrative, "where something actually takes place and takes time." These portions of time can be of variable duration:

while some panels may well show just one precise moment in time, it is possible to find many others "into which moments, hours, even days, are compressed" (Hatfield 2005: 58). Indeed, as the example from *Persepolis* (see Fig. 3.4) discussed above indicates, the time span conveyed by a single comics frame can even extend to several years. It is important to remember, however, that in this medium the single panel never functions in isolation, as it always forms part of a larger sequence of panels. Following Hatfield, I will thus argue that a sense of time in comics emerges in the tension between the single image and the sequence conveyed through a series of contiguous images.

Much of the debate about the relationship between time and the single image has centered on photography. Through its indexicality, the photograph gives us the illusion that it can hold the recorded moment "in stillness," thereby seemingly capturing "a trace of something lost": "In this sense, the photograph confronts us with the fleeting nature of our world and reminds us of our own mortality" (Kuhn and McAllister 2006: 1; see also Maynard 2001). It is this strange ability of the photograph to make the "has been" present by re-presenting it in all its visual detail that Roland Barthes (2000 [1980]) described as its particular force or *punctum*. But unlike photographs, drawings are independent of the moment of depiction and the resulting images do not lay claim to being a direct trace of the past (see Chapter 4). In this respect, comics panels are much more closely related to traditional arts such as painting and lithography than they are to photography.

A good place to begin the discussion of time in the traditional visual arts is with Gotthold Ephraim Lessing's 1766 essay "Laocoön: An Essay on the Limits of Painting and Poetry" (cited in Steiner 2004). In it, Lessing made the often-quoted claim that space is the domain of painting, while time belongs to the domain of poetry. He also put forward his theory of what has become known as the "pregnant moment," which describes the way in which a visual representation may, by depicting the moment that precedes the absolute climax of a dramatic event, suggest both the preceding and the succeeding actions. In this case, the passing of time is contained *in potentia* in the depicted moment. Many paintings belonging to the genre of post-Renaissance history painting, which represented scenes inspired by historical events, mythology, poetry, or religion, may be described as functioning in this way. Here, the appreciation of narrative will depend to a large extent on viewers' awareness of the stories or real-life events that underpin the representations.[9] This has lead Steiner (2004: 161) to suggest that history painting is only "weakly narrative": "it could imply or call to mind a narrative but not represent a narrative in all its unfolding richness."

Steiner (2004) distinguishes such "weakly narrative" paintings from those she considers to be truly narrative in the sense that they are able, through specific visual techniques, to suggest a particular sequencing of events. She describes a number of such techniques that have evolved over the course of European art. The Hellenistic period, for example, saw the invention of the "continuum" (or "continuous") narrative, in which several individual episodes, each including the same central characters, are shown in a single setting or landscape. Medieval painters were particularly creative in developing new ways of conveying consecutive moments, including the orientation of figures so that each one is looking towards the next event in a series, and the arrangement of events along a path or in various rooms in a building.

Comics artists have apparently rediscovered some of these medieval narrative techniques. In *Persepolis* (2006: 36), for instance, Satrapi uses a single long panel stretching across the whole width of the page, which shows five people arranged in a line. Starting from the left-hand side, each character whispers something into the ear of the person next to him or her. The narrative context makes it clear that the same piece of gossip is being told and retold at different moments in time. A good example of the continuous narrative technique can be found in David B.'s (2005) *Epileptic*. In a large square panel on page 127, the autobiographical narrator depicts his brother, Jean-Christophe, who suffers from debilitating epileptic seizures, going to the supermarket without telling anyone.

Discovering his absence, the mother drives off to try and find him. In the meantime, Jean-Christophe has set off back home, but, while suffering a violent seizure, he falls by the roadside, where he is not visible to his mother as she drives past. To indicate the two separate strings of events, both Jean-Christophe and the mother in her car are represented twice in this one panel.[10]

The difficulty with Steiner's distinction between truly and weakly narrative single images is that the static image can never *depict* time, but can only *represent* it. This means that *all* still images rely on the viewer's active contribution to the process of constructing temporal meaning, although this may be more or less strongly suggested by the form and content of an image and may involve conscious interpretation to a greater or lesser extent (Abbott 2002; Le Poidevin 2007). The genre conventions associated with a particular image, the context in which it is encountered, and the knowledge and predispositions of the individual viewer will also play an important role in determining whether or not the image is seen as telling a story. Many of the medieval and early Renaissance paintings Steiner presents as paradigmatic of truly narrative images are only likely to be understood in this way by contemporary viewers if they are familiar with the conventions of medieval art and prepared to spend time and effort constructing a story from the clues in the painting. In the case of comics, on the other hand, the narrative purpose is likely to be at the forefront of any reader's mind, so that he or she is likely to be highly receptive to any features of the individual panel that are able to invoke temporal meaning.

There are also other ways in which pictures may appear to be "activated" in some way, for instance by portraying figures in an unstable or asymmetric position, or depicting movement that is "frozen in the instance of representation" (Schirato and Webb 2004: 87). In the comics medium, animation is also commonly implied through the use of various kinds of "motion lines" (Horn 1998: 136) leading to or from a moving element, or else through so-called "polymorphic" or "stroboscopic" images (Cohn 2006), which show a single entity repeated in multiple positions of an action within a frame.

According to social semioticians Kress and van Leeuwen (1996: 43–78), what distinguishes narrative from non-narrative images is the presence of real or virtual "vectors," strong, often diagonal lines connecting elements in a picture, which function as the pictorial equivalents of action verbs. The "Actor" is the visual participant which, in whole or part, forms the vector or from which the vector emanates. If there are two participants in a visual narrative, then one is the "Actor" and the other the "Goal," that is, the entity at which the action is directed. For example, in the panel showing the babysitter and the brother (see Fig. 3.1), the babysitter's arms and legs form a vector shape, which is further emphasized by the diagonal lines of the open door. The action in this panel could thus be verbalized as something like "the babysitter is leading the brother out of the room." The babysitter's closing of the door could be seen as another action process, which anticipates the abuse he is about to perpetrate on the brother and which thus conveys a deep sense of foreboding.

However, as the image of Marjane floating in outer space (see Fig. 3.4) demonstrates, it is also possible to convey a subjective experience of time by visual means without suggesting any sense of motion or action. Indeed, in this example, it is the very *lack* of concrete activity that invites the reader to conjure up a sense of the passage of time, which, through the terror of meaninglessness, feels as if it will never end. A pertinent example from German comics creator Markus Mawil's (2008) graphic memoir *We Can Still Be Friends* also conveys a strong sense of temporality without insisting on any particular sequence of actions or events. The book describes a camping trip taken by the autobiographical protagonist and his friends. The boys meet a group of young women staying on the same campsite, and they end up sharing light-hearted banter and flirtation over a leisurely picnic (see Fig. 3.5). The scene is shown from a distorted bird's eye view, so that some of the characters are upside-down on the page. The desultory talk in the balloons is not clearly attributed to specific speakers, and it does not follow any logical order, just as the various actions that the young people are

FIG. 3.5 Markus Mawil (2008) *We Can Still Be Friends*, no pagination. Copyright © 2003, 2008 Markus Mawil Witzel.

shown to be performing—eating, smoking, pouring a drink, lifting the lid of a saucepan—are not tied to any particular sequence or duration. This conveys the sense of amorphous time, which is so characteristic of long, pleasurable meals in the company of friends and which, retrospectively, acquires a certain dream-like quality.

Another notable feature of this example is that, while it clearly shows one, unified scene, it is divided up through a grid of blank spaces into nine squares of equal size, thus occupying an ambiguous position somewhere in-between the single image and seriality. McCloud (1994: 70–72) identifies six possible transitions that can exist between panels in a series: moment-to-moment, action-to-action, scene-to-scene, subject-to-subject, aspect-to-aspect, and, finally, the non-sequitur. Only the first three of these transitions are temporal, with subject-to-subject and aspect-to-aspect conjunctions being of a more comparative or spatial nature.[11] He uses the notion of closure to explain the—largely subconscious—process whereby individual panels are combined in the reader's head into a coherent sequence by filling in the "gutter," the blank spaces in-between panels.

In the camping scene mentioned above (see Fig. 3.5), the grid lines running through the scene do not indicate any relationship of transition, neither temporal nor spatial, between the different segments of the picture, nor do they seem to invite a conscious process of closure. Instead, a sense of continuity is conveyed by the fact that the gutters and the margins of the page are partially overlapped by several objects and speech bubbles, giving the impression of a scene that is "bleeding" into the world of the reader and escaping into "timeless space" (McCloud 1994: 103). The formal properties of this page can thus be seen to symbolize the inevitable gaps in our recollection of past experiences, as well as suggesting that memory often focuses on atmosphere and emotions rather than on strict sequences of specific events.

According to Claire Painter (2007: 53), who has explored temporality in children's picture books, we share a cultural understanding of how particular actions typically combine into sequences, which makes it possible to represent these actions at greater or lesser levels of detail: "When the pace speeds up, a sequence of actions may be encapsulated in a single image as a single action; when the pace slows down, a "single" action is represented as a series of images, visually expanding the action into a sequence." She suggests that it is generally possible to identify a norm or "baseline pace" for depicting activity sequences in a particular text.[12] Picture book narratives tend to "slow down" when there are fewer words to support the interpretation of visual meaning, and this slower pace is often used to encourage readers to conjure up a sensuous experience of the depicted actions.

Several comics scholars have similarly tried to establish the pace of comic book narratives by comparing the number of panels dedicated to particular actions (e.g., Eisner 1985).[13] However, the speed at which a comic book is read and the pace we attribute to the actions and events in the story are not strictly related to the number of panels on a page. The size, directionality, and shape of panels on a page can, for instance, strongly influence our perception of the flow of time, as can reiteration, overlap, and changes in perspective (Dittmar 2008; Groensteen 2007; Schneider 2010). Moreover, as Wolk (2007: 181–202) suggests, the pace of reading may be influenced by introducing abrupt changes in time, geographical locations, and perspective from one panel to the next, so that readers are constantly forced to pause for reflection in order to make sense of the story. Most importantly, the narrative context will always have an impact upon the reader's perception of time in a comics story.

The following example is drawn from *Can of Worms* (2000), Catherine Doherty's autobiographical story of her discovery as an adult that she was adopted and of her long and arduous search for her birth mother. Once Catherine has established her mother's surname, Maheu, she spends many months in the local records office going through all the references she can find to people with this surname. In the book, her initial search is represented over five pages, starting on page 17, which features just four square panels arranged in a perfect square in the middle of the page. They show an over-the-shoulder view of Catherine sitting in front of a microfiche screen reader, a close-up and then an extreme close-up of her face reflected in the screen, and finally her hand over the "copy" button on the screen reader. Over the following pages, her activities in the registry office are represented again and again, while the number of panels per page steadily increases. As the various actions

FIG. 3.6 Catherine Doherty (2000) *Can of Worms*, p. 21 (original with color tint). Copyright © 2000 Fantagraphics Books; all contents copyright © 2000 Catherine Doherty.

become more and more condensed and the number of panels multiplies, each page simultaneously comes to stand for a longer time period, with more and more of Catherine's life being elided. Page 20 represents a break in this general pattern, as it features just one image of Catherine's hand switching off the alarm clock. On the facing page the number of individual panels has increased to sixteen (see Fig. 3.6), while their size has decreased proportionally. We can tell from the repeated activities and the changes in temperature indicated by the way Catherine is dressed (see panels 1/4, 2/4, and 4/2, for instance)[14] that we are dealing with her routine activities performed again and again over many months. The repetition of visual motifs with only minor variations, the regular arrangement of panels with small gaps between them, and the inclusion of three pictures in an indistinct, light blue wash means that readers are discouraged from focusing on each image separately and from reading them in any particular order. Rather, the individual panels seem to merge together and form one unit, which emphasizes the numbing sameness of Catherine's search.

Despite the obvious variation in the size and number of panels used to describe Catherine's activities in the records office over the five pages, it would thus be inaccurate to describe this in terms of a simple speeding up or slowing down of the pace of the narrative. Instead, the natural tension in comics between the single image and the image-in-series is used here in order to convey both a sense of repetitive activities performed over a long period of time and the subjective experience of time that passes sluggishly because of boredom and the frustration of not attaining the desired outcome.

The way comics artists use the number and arrangement of panels on the page to indicate temporality is sometimes compared to musical notation and more specifically to rhythm (Eisner 1985; Groensteen 2007; Hatfield 2005). Rhythm is normally understood to mean the cycles that consist of "an alternation between successive sensations of accentedness and non-accentedness" and which are repeated within time intervals that are equal or at least perceived as equal (van Leeuwen 1985: 217). Human beings have the natural propensity to perceive rhythmic alternation in any successive stimuli, which suggests that rhythm is "a basic biological given" (van Leeuwen 2005: 181).

As comics do not unfold over time, it only really makes sense to talk of the rhythmic qualities of individual works in relation to the reader's perceptions. For instance, rhythmic cycles in comics could be perceived on the basis of sequences of actions in the storyworld, or else of material units such as the page or double-page spread. Principles of repetition and accentuation may then be experienced with regard to visual stimuli, such as the number, size, shape, placement, color, and style of panels, and/or the implied aural stimuli of speech balloons and onomatopoeic words. Catherine Doherty's description of her activities at the records office could thus be described through the metaphor of a musical score, with each page representing one bar and each panel a beat. The first panel on every page would be naturally stressed, and further accents might be perceived through the repetition of certain visual motifs—for instance, the three panels in a lighter shade (see Fig. 3.6), and through the "soundtrack" accompanying her activities ("click," "slap," "snip snip"). However, individual readers' perception of rhythmic qualities in comics is likely to depend on their familiarity with the medium—their ability to read the "score," as it were.

Sequence versus layout

As was suggested in the discussion of the sixteen-panel page above, the shape and arrangement of panels on the page is at least as important as sequentiality when it comes to readers' perceptions of the temporal structure of comics. Several comics artists and scholars have noted the unique potential for spatializing time in this medium (Chute 2010; Miller 2003; Vice 2001). McCloud (1994: 100) puts this most succinctly when he writes that, in comics, "time and space are one and the same." For instance, the size and width of panels often change as time accelerates and decelerates, as does the space between panels. The close association in comics between time and space chimes with conceptual metaphor theory and its claim that there is a universal tendency to think and talk about time in terms of space, with the future in front of us, the present right by us, and the past behind (Lakoff and Johnson 1980: 41–44; Lakoff 1993).

A scene from David B.'s graphic memoir *Epileptic* presents a good example of the crucial spatial dimension of temporality in the comics medium. When the autobiographical narrator's brother, Jean-Christophe, has reached young adulthood, he is encumbered by his illness and the resulting disabilities and struggles to find a

purpose to his life. The sequence recounts his desire to return to the center where he spent some time as an adolescent and the par- ents' attempts to dissuade him from his impossible plans (see Fig. 3.7). The first panel shows the father begging his son not to make a scene, followed by the mother's reassurance that, "None of that stuff matters, you know . . . ," and then Jean-Christophe's dismissive response ("Pfff . . . "). Every utterance implies a moment of a particular duration, each following from the other in logical succession.

Panels 1/2 to 2/2 represent a unified conversation, with each scene showing immediately consecutive moments in time. The orientation and size of the depicted participants change from one panel to the next, but this only emphasizes the antagonistic nature of the discussion, rather than indicating either a slowing down or speeding up of the pace of events in the story. The narration in the text boxes suggests an indefinite temporal lapse between the conversations represented in panel 1/1 and panels 1/2 to 2/2, and then again between Jean-Christophe's outburst in panel 2/2 and the scene depicted in 3/1, which are separated by the time it takes for the young man to buy a train ticket and for his mother to talk him out of his plans. The final panel is not allocated any fixed place in chronological time, functioning instead as a timeless representation of Jean-Christophe's enduring feelings of hopelessness.

The spatial characteristics of the page also impinge upon the reader's perception of time in the storyworld. The page has a three-dimensional, layered quality to it. Individual panels have irregular, wavy edges and are overlaid on a black background, and they are enclosed and partially overlapped by the awkward, twisted, and elongated shape of Jean-Christophe's broken body. This framing device continues over six pages (p. 296–302), on the last of which the young man's body has morphed into the shape of a monster. The inherent tension in the comics medium between the sequence of panels and the surface of the page is thus exploited by the artist to convey both a vague impression of linear, chronological time and the more subjective experience of being trapped in an aimless day-to-day existence, a form of "temporal claustrophobia."

Comics are also unique in the way that it is possible for every panel to have a potential relationship not just with other panels on a double page, but with every other panel in the book as well, forming complex strands of correspondences through what Groensteen

(2001; 2007) has termed *tressage*, or "braiding." These links can be established through various plastic or semantic similarities.[15] In the page which shows Catherine's activities in the records office, for instance, the repetition of virtually identical scenes, shown from the same perspective, create various patterns of relationships between the sixteen panels on the page, as well as with similar panels on the preceding pages (see Fig. 3.6).

In *Epileptic*, the image of a snake-like monster with a dragon's head occurs again and again throughout the book as a metaphor for Jean-Christophe's illness and the impact it has on family life. This image is again brought into play in the scene discussed above, where in the first four panels on the page the monster remains in the background (see Fig. 3.7), like a giant shadow, but in panel 3/1 it forms a circle around Jean-Christophe and his mother, conveying a powerful sense of entrapment. In the final frame the young man's body is visually engulfed by the monster, and he is curled up in a way that implies a return to an embryonic state of development. The fact that the monster and its "fetus" are oriented towards the left-hand side, which, in the Western tradition, tends to be associated with the past (Huxford 2001), visually reinforces the verbal comment that "the only escape he can envision is a return to the past" (*Epileptic*, p. 301). The brother's future life is thus not imagined as something exciting and full of endless possibilities but as something frustratingly circular and regressive.

Another good example of visual echoes creating semantic links throughout a work can be found in Satrapi's *Persepolis*. On page 6 a panel shows Marjane as a baby, lying on a rug with outstretched arms, a beaming smile, and a faint halo around her head. This panel, captioned, "I was born with religion," is clearly meant as an ironic allusion to popular representations of baby Jesus. It starts a four-page sequence about her religious fantasies as a six-year-old. Sixty-four pages later, on the page that recounts Marjane's response to the execution of her beloved uncle, she is shown lying on her bed in an identical position, only this time she is about six years old, she is crying, the "halo" has disappeared, and her outstretched arms now recall Christ's crucifixion rather than the nativity scene. On the opposite page (see Fig. 3.3) the same visual motif is repeated yet again. These visual echoes create associative connections across the time of the story and, through the allusions to extratextual representations of Jesus's life, into historical time as well.[16] The result is a fascinating portrayal of the workings of memory not as a filing cabinet of separate "incidents," but as fragments of experiences, thoughts, and emotions that may run in parallel, feed into each other, or occasionally even merge completely. Clearly, Satrapi is not simply recording her private memories as they enter into her mind; rather, she is engaging in a deliberate act of commemoration, revealing connections between experiences that initially were most likely not perceived to be causally linked, and drawing parallels between her own life and the life of Jesus in order to make an ironic point about the iconography of suffering.

As was shown in relation to the example from Thompson's *Blankets* (see Fig. 3.1), the collision of memories from various periods of development of a person's life may also be represented explicitly by placing visual representations of these moments into the same picture.[17] This technique of depicting an "impossible and provocative at-onceness" (Hatfield 2005: 51) is often used by graphic memoirists to capture the unique qualities of traumatic memory, which involves the intrusion of the past into the present in the form of repeated flashbacks, hallucinations, and dreams. This visual technique serves to pull the reader backwards or forwards in time, conveying the sense of "a present which cannot avoid returning to a particular time in the past to make sense of itself" (Vice 2001: 54).

Another obvious way in which layout can impact upon the reader's perception of the story-time is by juxtaposing images on the same or on facing pages to represent a relation of simultaneity. Although the reader must still focus first on one and then the other, the sense of them co-occurring at the same moment is much more powerful when they are matched up visually. It is possible, for instance, to split the page vertically or horizontally down the middle, with each half showing activities being performed in parallel by different characters, usually in different locations. When the same person occurs in each of the parallel time-strands, this logically indicates alternative trajectories rather than simultaneity. On the page from *Held* (see Fig. 3.3), for instance, the three parallel vertical columns represent the different professional routes that are open to the autobiographical protagonist after his graduation.

Text as narrative versus text as material object

So far, the discussion has centered on those aspects of comics that relate to their functioning as narrative texts. However, the materiality of the comic book is also an important semiotic resource that may impact upon readers' perception of time in the story, both through their physical, embodied engagement with the book as an object and their awareness of the production process. As Carrier (2000: 62) points out, "there is a distinction in kind between arts where other people's presence constitutes part of the viewing experience and those art forms, like comics and the novel, where it does not." Comics are usually read by one person, who holds the book close to his or her body and who is generally in complete command of the order in which the book is read and the pace at which the pages are turned. Readers are also likely to be at least partially aware of a book's thickness and weight and the quality and feel of its pages. Thus, a thick tome in a hard binding, such as Aline Kominsky-Crumb's *Need More Love*, which consists of 383 pages, is more likely to give us the sense of a full, long life than *Belly Button Comix*, the thirty pages of autobiographical stories in a magazine-format created by Aline and Robert Crumb's daughter, Sophie.

For many readers, comics are likely to trigger nostalgic memories of their own early reading experiences as children and adolescents (Jacobs 2008; Whitlock 2006). In a foreword to Joe Sacco's (2003) *Palestine*, for instance, Edward Said recalls the strict ban his teachers and parents imposed on comics when he was growing up in the post World War Two Middle East, and the sense of thrill and elation he felt every time he manage to evade this prohibition.

When, many years later, his son brings home a copy of *Palestine*, Said is "plunged directly back into the world of the first great intifada (1987–92) and, with even greater effect, back into the animated, enlivening world of the comics I had read so long ago. The shock of recognition was therefore a double one" (p. iii). The recognition Said describes is intimately connected with the comic book's status as a material and social object, that is, with the look, feel, and smell of it, and the role it played for him in developing his own identity as a teenager.

Several writers have explored the idea that the path of the eye traveling across the page can be seen as a spatial metaphor for time passing (e.g., Groensteen 2007). McCloud (1994) suggests that the panel the reader is currently looking at is experienced as the present, with the panel(s) that went before representing the past and those after indicating the future:

> Wherever your eyes are focused, that's now. But at the same time your eyes take in the surrounding landscape of past and future! Like a storm front, the eye moves over the comics page, pushing the warm, high-pressure future ahead of it, leaving the cool low-pressure past in its wake. (McCloud 1994: 104)

The way the eye is encouraged by the layout to move across a page may well affect our perceptions of the storyworld generally as well as of the specific quality of the time experienced within it. The very regular, almost rigid arrangement of the sixteen panels from Catherine Doherty's (2000) *Can of Worms* (see Fig. 3.6), and the repetition of similar elements is likely to encourage readers to take in the whole page and to try and make sense of connections between panels, rather than reading them in the usual order from the upper left to the lower right corner. This may affect the way they understand Catherine's experience of time and memory, encouraging them to see it as a jumbled-up collection of "snap-shots," rather than a linear succession of specific events.

In contrast to this, Mawil's depiction of a picnic with friends (see Fig. 3.5) seems designed to entice readers to linger on the page, letting their eyes wander over the various elements without any sense of haste. In order to study the drawings and read the speech bubbles in the lower half of the page, readers are invited to turn the page upside down, which involves a particularly strong physical engagement with the book as a material object. This may be seen as encouraging readers to share the depicted characters' experience of a slow, pleasurable moment.

The action of turning the page may also be associated with temporal meaning. In her memoir about her treatment for breast cancer, Marisa Marchetto (2006) explicitly refers to the analogy between turning a page and repeating an experience. On the page preceding her detailed description of the medical procedures and mundane anxieties and irritations involved in radiation therapy, she has drawn a large grey door with a sign saying "Danger. Radiation" and an arrow with the instruction to the reader to: "Turn page to open door and do it 33 times" (p. 195). Although readers are actually unlikely to follow these instructions, they may nevertheless be enabled to empathize more readily with the sense of boredom and frustration that radiation treatment involves.

When we read comics, we are generally aware of the drawing process as something not as instantaneous as snapping a photo, but which takes a certain amount of time. Most comics are drawn in multiple phases, generally starting with script and/or "dummy" pages and going through several stages of alterations and refinement (Eisner 1985: 122–38). These different phases leave traces in the finished product, which can be exploited by those comics creators who, for whatever reason, want to draw attention to the creative process. In Linthout's (2009) autobiographical comic about a man facing the trauma of his son's suicide, for instance, all the original sketch lines are still clearly visible beneath the darker outlines of the final pencil drawings (see Chapter 5, Fig. 5.2). This can be read as a metaphor for the gradual process of trying to come to terms with the pain of bereavement by transforming these feelings into artistic forms of expression.

In many autobiographical comics the physical changes of the main protagonists over time are reflected in the way they are portrayed. Some artists, such as Al Davison (1990) and Jim Valentino (1995), use different drawing styles to represent themselves at different moments in their lives. Sometimes these stylistic variations reflect the artist's increasing experience and creative development over the period in which a work was created, so that different periods of his or her life are drawn in markedly different ways. A good example of this is Lauren Weinstein's (2006) graphic memoir, *Girl Stories*, which, on the page facing the table of contents, includes the following author's note: "These comics were done over a period of seven years. During that time I experimented with many methods and materials. So you'll see the same characters drawn differently throughout the book" (p. 2). Weinstein has drawn some of the diverse tools and materials used to produce the book the reader is currently holding in his or her hands. She also includes two small sample drawings of herself from five different periods in her life, which demonstrate her increasing skill and maturity as an artist. Her self-ironic comments about these diverse styles ("lots of hatching and stippling," "learned how to digitally color," etc.) emphasize the imperfect work-in-progress that she clearly considers her memoir to be. Ariel Schrag, who has published four autobiographical comic books about her high school experiences, also possesses a style that evolved noticeably over the years.

Graphic memoirists thus have a vast array of temporal cues in different combinations at their disposal in order to convey as vividly as possible their subjective experiences of time, to commemorate events in their lives, and imagine possible futures. Indeed, the specific formal and material qualities of the comics medium seem to make it particularly well suited to the telling of life narratives, especially those involving painful or traumatic events, which are often remembered in the form of associative impressions and fragments of narrative. The vagaries of human memory, which were stressed again and again throughout this chapter, are also considered in the following chapter, which deals with the issue of "truthfulness" and "authenticity" in graphic memoirs.

Chapter 4

PERFORMING AUTHENTICITY

Edmond Baudoin (1995) starts his autobiographical comic *L'éloge de la poussière* ("In Praise of Dust") with a picture showing him sitting on the pavement in war-torn Beirut, drawing a beautiful building opposite (see Fig. 4.1). He is so absorbed by this activity that he fails to notice the car pulling up on the opposite side of the road and the young soldier approaching and looking over his shoulder to see what he is doing. Having previously been warned of the danger posed by the trigger-happy young men who roam the streets in 4x4s, Edmond is initially petrified, but his terror soon turns to astonishment when the man passes him a photo of his fiancée and asks him to draw her picture. A black panel is followed by one that shows a close-up of the photograph, gently held between the soldier's thumb and index finger. The handwritten text in the final panel reads: "Only seven years have gone by since then. Did this boy survive the war? Does he still love his fiancée? Did he really have this face? This story is slowly sinking into unreality. I sometimes find I'm no longer sure that I really experienced it" ("Sept ans seulement se sont écoulés. Ce garçon a-t-il survécu à la guerre? Aime-t-il toujours sa fiancée? Avait-il ce visage-là? Cette historie s'enfonce doucement dans l'irréalité. Il m'arrive de n'être plus tout à fait sûr de l'avoir vécue").

This example may serve to remind us that life writing has a more complex relationship with the truth than explicitly fictional work. As was discussed in Chapter 1, the question of whether

FIG. 4.1 Edmond Baudoin (1995) *L'éloge de la poussière*, no pagination. Copyright © 1995 L'Association.

autobiography must, and indeed whether it ever can be entirely truthful, has for a long time been a hotly debated subject in literary studies. Under the influence of postmodernism, the concept of a single, straightforward Truth has been dismantled in favor of a view of the "truth" as multiple, fractured, and shaped by each individual's unique perspective and partial recall. Moreover, memory is generally conceptualized as a constant process of reinterpreting the events of a life in the light of what, with hindsight, is seen to be significant (see Chapter 3). There now seems to be almost universal agreement both among scholars and in the wider community that "there is no such thing as a 'uniquely' true, correct, or even faithful autobiography" (Bruner 1993: 39).

Readers have no way of knowing, for example, whether the incident involving the soldier really happened the way Baudoin chose to tell it, and the author/narrator himself admits he cannot be sure how faithful his representations are to the historical facts. Indeed, like most other contemporary memoirists, Baudoin does not seem to be particularly concerned with establishing the absolute truthfulness of his account.[1] The powerful cultural conventions governing the construction and interpretation of works labeled as autobiographical will nevertheless lead many authors to aspire to—and their readers to expect—some kind of special relationship between a narrative and the life it purports to represent. This "special" relationship, I argue, is best captured through the notion of "performed authenticity."[2]

As I show in the first section of this chapter, authenticity is typically associated with being realistic, genuine, and true to the essence of something. One such essence is the "self": "An authentic person or self is one who is in touch with his or her real phenomenological and emotional experience and who reveals his or her own true thoughts, feelings, and actions" (Gubrium and Holstein 2009: 124). The concept of authenticity also applies to the visual field, where it can be defined very loosely as any image that lays claim to a privileged, transparent relationship to its object of representation (Wortmann 2003: 14). Visual authenticity can be based on picture-immanent features, but it is more often contextual, drawing its power from the myths surrounding the individual images or types of images or from the "performed" integrity of the image producer(s).

However, authenticity is a notoriously slippery concept, and notions of the authentic self, the authentic self-narrative, and the authentic image are always, and inevitably, socially constructed and deeply evaluative (van Leeuwen 2001). My approach is strongly influenced by dramaturgic conceptions of authenticity that stress the fact that we all adopt multiple roles depending on the social contexts in which we find ourselves. In this sense, being authentic is not about being as true as possible to a coherent and stable inner self; rather, it is something that is performed more or less convincingly and either accepted or rejected by an audience. The purpose of this chapter is thus not to try and define what makes a graphic memoir essentially authentic or inauthentic, but rather to identify the distinctive strategies of authentication, both verbal and visual, which appear to be operating across the works being analyzed.

In the second and main part of this chapter I consider some of the most common strategies graphic memoirists use to signal to the reader their intention to be frank and genuine about their own memories, experiences, and emotions. Visual cues seem to play a particularly important role in conveying authenticity. By deliberately diverging from the stylistic conventions associated with more traditional, fantastical comic book genres, the creators of autobiographical comics can stress the truthful nature of their accounts. Baudoin's stark, angular, black and white drawings, for instance, certainly do not look anything like the visual styles commonly found in science fiction, adventure, or superhero comics. Many creators of graphic memoirs also incorporate photographic images, or pictures that visually resemble photographs, into their work, thereby drawing on the mythical status of photography as a particularly authentic medium.

However, it is not the case that a sense of authenticity in autobiographical comics always increases in accordance with the level of stylistic realism, as Kress and van Leeuwen's (1996) notion of "naturalistic visual modality" seems to suggest.[3] Indeed, paradoxically, comics creators sometimes try to enhance the perceived genuineness of their accounts by adopting an ostentatiously *naïve* cartoonish drawing style or by employing deliberately incongruous elements and thereby drawing attention to the artistic forms and narrative techniques they employ. When, for instance, Baudoin uses a black panel and crossed-out words in the final text box to address the limits of his own memory and the impossibility of entirely faithful representation, this may come across to the reader as a particularly sincere form of authenticity.

A dramaturgic approach to authenticity in graphic memoirs

According to Hartman (2002), contemporary Western society is characterized by a deep yearning for the genuinely authentic. This yearning, he believes, has been intensified by the dismantling of the concept of a singular Truth and the proliferation of pictorial constructs of all kinds through the Internet, which has led to a widespread anxiety that "nothing is what it appears to be, that everything, eventually, will turn out to be deceptive, manipulated, counterfeit" (p. 61). Although the quality of experience referred to by the term "authenticity" is thus obviously highly valued in many areas of contemporary life, it makes little sense to try and come up with a conclusive definition of the authentic. Instead, it may be regarded as "a set of qualities that people in a particular time and place have come to agree represent an ideal or exemplar" (Vannini and Williams 2009: 3), or else as a kind of "rhetorical touchstone for constructing and responding to the real in relation to persons, actions, and events" (Gubrium and Holstein 2009: 136). Indeed, some scholars now prefer the term "authentication" to "authenticity," because it "foregrounds the processes by which authenticity is claimed, imposed, or perceived" (Bucholtz and Hall 2004: 498).

Several different uses of the term have been identified, including the authentic as something that is genuine in respect of origin or authorship, which bears the stamp of approval of an authority, or which is reliable, trustworthy, in accordance with the facts (Coupland 2003; Montgomery 2001). Another meaning of authenticity commonly referred to in contemporary society is that which relates it to the notion of a unique inner self, which we are ethically and morally obliged to nurture and realize in the conduct of our lives (Taylor 1989). However, conceptions of the authentic self differ according to which particular notion of personhood and identity they are based on, with some conceiving the self as centered and integrative, and others as decentered and antagonistic (Ferrara 2009).

Dramaturgic approaches to authenticity reject the idea that we all possess a unique, true, unchanging inner self, which can then be expressed "authentically" in our everyday interactions. Such approaches often draw their inspiration from Goffman's (1969 [1959]) *The Presentation of Self in Everyday Life*, which describes structures of social interaction from a theatrical point of view. Goffman argues that whenever we are in the presence of others, we perform particular strategic roles in order to evoke the desired responses from our audience and to shield ourselves from embarrassment or failure. Our performance involves two different kinds of expressiveness: expressions "given," and expressions "given off." The former involves communication in the traditional, narrow sense of verbal language, whereas the latter involves a wide range of non-verbal actions (e.g., body language, facial expression, quality of voice) perceived by others to be less directly under the actor's control and thus treated as symptomatic of his or her "true" interests, motives, and identity:

> As members of an audience it is natural for us to feel that the impression the performer seeks to give may be true or false, genuine or spurious, valid or "phony." So common is this doubt that [. . .] we often give special attention to features of the performance that cannot be readily manipulated, thus enabling ourselves to judge the reliability of the more misrepresentable cues in the performance. (Goffman 1969 [1959]: 66)

In fact, skilled social actors are able to manipulate these non-verbal expressions as well, but most people are less conscious of their effect. According to Goffman, authenticity is thus not so much about choosing a role that readily accords with our one, true, "innermost self"; rather, it lies in the choice of the most appropriate roles for the different types of social interaction in which we engage, and in our ability to perform these roles convincingly and with the expected standards of dexterity and coherence. As Schwalbe (2009) points out, however, not everyone is equally free to manage their performance of self. Particularly for some subordinated groups in society, such as black men in the U.S., there are obvious restrictions on the repertoires of identities that are available to them.

Another important distinction Goffman makes is that between front- and backstage behavior. Backstage is where performers can withdraw from their audiences to relax and be "out of character"; the kitchen in restaurants, for example, or the bathroom in a typical home. It is also the place where performances are constructed and practiced, and where "stage props and items of personal front can be stored in a kind of compact collapsing of whole repertoires of actions and characters" (Goffman 1969 [1959]: 114). Not surprisingly, given our need to manage the impression we want to make, access to backstage areas tends to be much more tightly regulated than to the front regions.

One way performances are judged to be authentic or not relates to the social norms governing the expression of emotion in particular situations and in particular cultures (Shweder 1991): crying, for instance, can sometimes be seen as sincere and appropriate, and other times as false and manipulative. The dominant modern culture of emotion in Western societies, McCarthy (2009: 241) suggests, regards feelings both as integral to self identity, and as a key for unlocking the true, inner self. According to this concept, authentic selfhood can be regarded as "an intensely sentimental (i.e., suffused with emotion) type of discourse; it is a way of speaking about who I am, my *identity*, which in its modern manifestation is an intense experience (and pursuit) of myself as I truly am." In recent years, the manifestation of strong feelings and emotions has apparently moved outwards into a more public forum, with many individuals seeking large audiences for their display of joy or grief at sporting events or memorial services for celebrities, for example.

The notion of subjective experience is also likely to be at the center of any assertion of personal authenticity. Scannell (2001: 406) argues that an experience is perceived to be authentic to the extent that it belongs to the individual and forms part of the inner self: "An authentic experience is so because I own it, and thus I can claim it as my own experience and not anyone else's." On the one hand, the authentic experience depends on having been there and having witnessed it directly, which means that it is not fully transferable. On the other hand, in some respects we are all just like everyone else and thus able to share at least some aspects of our experiences with others.

A dramaturgic approach to authenticity in graphic memoirs may seem counterintuitive, since we are not dealing with actual embodied performances and audiences. However, graphic memoirists may be regarded as presenting themselves to their readers in a mediated form of social interaction in which the authenticity of their subjective memory and experience is at stake. Authenticity in autobiographical comics thus becomes a matter "not of verifiability but of trustworthiness," which has to be earned in a process of constant renegotiation between the artist, the materials, and the reader (Hatfield 2005: 150). Instead of judging an author's sincerity from his or her spoken words and actions, readers will be looking for signs of the authentic or inauthentic in the text, and sometimes the "paratext" (Genette 1997) as well. Since autobiographical comics tell *and* show events from someone's life, the issue of authenticity in this genre applies not only to the verbal narration but also to both the content and the style of the visual representations.

The assumption of an intimate link between seeing and believing is deeply rooted in our cultural consciousness, an assumption reflected in such common phrases as "a picture is worth a thousand words" and "the camera does not lie."[4] Wortmann (2003) suggests that human beings have always longed for visual forms of representation able to convey reality in a completely transparent and reliable way, despite, or indeed because of, our awareness that such mediation can never be absolutely transparent. Apart from promising viewers a pure, unadulterated experience of reality, the authentic image also fulfills certain emotional needs, for instance, by facilitating identification with the people depicted and enhancing the feelings of pity, suspense, expectation, excitement, and happiness that can result from this (Schierl 2003; see also Chapter 5).

The search for authentic images can be traced back to antiquity. It assumed particular significance during the Enlightenment, when scientific advances encouraged the belief in the possibility of representing reality "as it is" by technological means. Some authentic images are claimed to have emerged without corrupting human intervention, either by miraculous means (as in the case of the Byzantine *acheiropoietos*), or else by means of a supposedly transparent medium (such as the camera). The notion of an authentic image is thus a chimera, which is always being formulated anew in response to representational practices that threaten to disrupt the status quo. From the 1970s onwards, Schierl (2003) believes, "producer-oriented" forms of authenticity, which rely on the performed integrity of the image creators, seem to have become particularly influential. This development coincides with the growing influence of postmodernism and with a concomitant recognition of the subjective nature of the "truth." As the following discussion will demonstrate, producer-oriented authenticity certainly seems to play a central role in many autobiographical comics.

Performed authenticity in graphic memoirs

As a distinct genre, the graphic memoir is likely to have developed its own "preferred senses of the genuine" (Gubrium and Holstein 2009: 131), at least some of which will be governed by the formal and informal rules of institutions such as publishers and book sellers. As it is not possible to present an exhaustive list of all the different ways of performing authenticity in graphic memoirs, I will just pick out some of the most common and relevant ones, with a particular focus on visual cues. Some of these authentication strategies will be explicit, deliberately "given," whereas others are more implicit, "given off," for instance, through the visual style in which a comic is drawn. A sense of authenticity may also be created by deliberately giving the reader access to the backstage regions of a performance; in other words, by revealing some of the formal and narrative "props" used to construct a particular work. Finally, a few graphic memoirists have published mock or fake autobiographies, which openly challenge and subvert the very notion of the authentic in life writing.

Explicit authentication

Miriam Engelberg's (2006) graphic memoir about suffering from breast cancer, *Cancer Made Me a Shallower Person*, may serve as an example of some of the more explicit verbal and visual signs commonly used to perform authenticity in this genre. Engelberg was an American computer trainer and part-time writer who, at the age of forty-three, discovered comic art as a "lifeline" to help her through the experience of being diagnosed with metastatic breast cancer.[5] In Goffman's terms, explicit claims to authenticity are expressions "given," and they are thus less likely to be taken at face value by the reader than expressions "given off." Indeed, they may sometimes even alert people to the possibility of deceit or insincerity (Gubrium and Holstein 2009: 125). Perhaps for this reason, graphic memoirists tend to use them quite sparingly and often in combination with more subtle and ironic authentication strategies.

One of the most obvious ways of claiming authenticity is through genre classification, which represents an avowal of truthfulness and factuality backed up and "authorized" by the public endorsements of editors, publishers, the book industry, critics, and academics. The genre of *Cancer Made Me a Shallower Person* is clearly indicated in the subtitle (*A Memoir in Comics*), and it is also reiterated several times on the back cover, where the book is described, for instance, as a graphic memoir in the tradition of Art Spiegelman's *Maus*.

Graphic memoirs also sometimes contain a range of direct verbal claims to authenticity, which may appear either in the text itself, in the "peritext," such as the book cover, title page, and prefaces, or the "epitext," which includes interviews, press releases, and reviews (Genette 1997). In the introduction to her book, for instance, Engelberg declares her intention to share all the details of her experience of illness with her readers:

> We all have issues that follow us through life, no matter how much therapy we've had. The big one for me is about feeling different and alone—isolated in a state of Miriam-ness that no one else experiences. That's what drew me to read autobiographical comics, and that's why I hope my comics can be of comfort to other readers who might be struggling with issues similar to mine. When I was first diagnosed, I felt pressure to become someone different—someone nobler and more courageous than I was. But maybe nobility and courage aren't the only approaches to life with an illness; maybe the path of shallowness deserves more attention! (Engelberg 2006: xiii)

This quote addresses in a highly explicit way the paradoxical nature of experience as something that is both utterly unique and, at least potentially, universal and shared (Scannell 2001). It also reveals her desire to be as open and sincere as possible about her reactions to her illness, some of which, she admits, are not particularly admirable. The narrative itself also refers to many incidents that show Miriam behaving in very ordinary, non-heroic ways. The panel from a page entitled "Hilarious never before heard jokes," shows Miriam telling a joke which, as readers are clearly meant to recognize, is actually not particularly funny or original (see Fig. 4.2). The strip is thus intended as an ironic and self-deprecating commentary on Miriam's desperate attempts to make light of her frightening experiences, a strategy that implicitly reinforces the author's claims to authenticity by showing her willingness to be painfully honest.

FIG. 4.2 Miriam Engelberg (2006) *Cancer Made Me a Shallower Person*, no pagination (excerpt). Copyright © 2006 Miriam Engelberg.

As mentioned in Chapter 1, Lejeune (1989) famously proposed a straightforward textual criterion by which authors signal that they are prepared to uphold the "autobiographical pact," namely the fact that the author, the narrator, and the protagonist share the same name. While this criterion clearly applies in Miriam Engelberg's case, quite a few graphic memoirists use pseudonyms or give their autobiographical alter egos a different name. Phoebe Gloeckner's comics, for instance, often feature a child protagonist named Minnie, who apparently shares many of the author's physical and personality traits and who has had similar traumatic experiences. In a letter addressed to an imaginary reader, Gloeckner warns against the temptation to assume that she and Minnie are the same person:

> Dear Reader, I am not Minnie Goetze. Please don't take
> offense—your confusion is no surprise. She does look like I
> did at one time, and has had many of the same experiences.
> To declare that she and I are not the same must seem to make
> me a prevaricator, or, worse yet, an out-and-out liar. But I am
> neither. (Gloeckner 2011: 179)

This quote suggests that not all autobiographical comics creators are prepared to commit to the referential pact by engaging in the explicit authentication strategy of a shared name. Gloeckner also implies that the authenticity of a graphic memoir is often judged (wrongly, in her view) on the basis of the degree to which the drawings resemble the actual, real-life people they are supposed to represent. On some level, readers do seem to expect graphic memoirists to be reasonably honest about their own appearance. Many would probably feel cheated upon discovering that an author who describes and draws himself as tall, slim and strikingly handsome, is actually short, overweight and unattractive. Discussing her meeting with Swiss comic book creator Frederik Peeters, for instance, journalist Elizabeth Day (2008) is delighted because she is able to recognize him immediately from the self-portraits in his graphic memoir *Blue Pills* (2008): "The same solid angles, slightly hunched shoulders and skewed, quiet smile. The only difference is that he wears spectacles in the drawings and contact lenses in person; rather charmingly, he apologizes for this when we meet." In Engelberg's (2006) book, there is a black and white portrait photograph and a brief biography of the author on the very first page of the book, which means that readers are able to compare her self-representations with her photographic image. Despite her simple, naïve drawing style, Engelberg's self-portraits bear an obvious resemblance to the woman in the photograph.

However, graphic memoirists are typically concerned less with trying to capture their outer appearances as accurately as possible and more with expressing character traits and shifting states and emotions. As Cumming (2009) points out, a self-portrait always reveals something "deep and incontrovertible" about the inner self of the artist and how he or she hoped to be seen. In this sense, self-portraits specialize in a "special class of truth, this pressure from within that determines what appears as art without, that leaves its trace in every self-portrait" (p. 4). Engelberg's cartoon drawings of herself, for instance, are able to convey much more effectively than realistic self-portraits the devastating effects of the cancer treatment on her physical health and her fluctuating states of mind.

In contrast to conventional self-portraits, which are often more flattering or deceitful than the portraits produced by others, many self-portraits in autographics are deliberately ironic and self-deprecatory, with some comics creators even reverting to overt caricature. Lewis Trondheim, for instance, always depicts himself as a gentle and rather fragile-looking cockatoo (see Chapter 1, Fig. 1.4), which, comics scholar Miller (2007: 219) notes, still somehow manages to retain a "curious resemblance" to the actual model. Such brazen departures from the realist tradition of conventional self-portraits may prod readers to reconsider the importance of likeness as an indicator of autobiographical truthfulness. Cartoon drawings can, after all, sometimes reflect the "authentic" self more successfully than a photograph or a highly realistic portrait ever could: "Those who need a truth deeper than similarity ('he is himself' rather than 'he is like himself') will need to avoid the illusoriness, the blinding, which likeness produces, and approach their prey through the 'unlike like'" (Scott 1999: 236; see also Chaney 2011).

Authentication through detail and quoted dialogue

When people recount their experiences, they often try to lend additional credibility to their tales by mentioning lots of details and quoting snatches of dialogue, which, according to Gubrium and Holstein (2009), is an effective way of emphasizing "that the talk did, in fact, take place, and was not imagined or fabricated" (p. 129). Tannen (1989: 139) agrees, arguing that the marked use of detail of any kind may reinforce the hearer's or reader's "sense of the vividness of the memory, and therefore its reportability and authenticity." Even if someone else's words are reported accurately, it is in fact impossible to achieve a complete match between an original utterance and its representation in a narrative, since language is always changed by the new context.[6] Indeed, often the material presented as dialogue probably never occurred in that form at all. However, this does not change the fact that reported speech appears genuine and that it may be taken by readers as a sign of authenticity "given off" rather than "given" deliberately.

As we can see from the panel where Miriam tells the joke, *Cancer Made Me a Shallower Person* typically focuses on the minutiae of personal encounters and the humdrum of everyday life. Like other graphic memoirists writing about their experiences of cancer (Brabner and Pekar 1994; Fies 2006; Marchetto 2006), Engelberg offers detailed accounts of the various medical procedures she must undergo and the effects these treatments have on her physical and mental well-being. She also exposes the wide range of reactions she gets from other people, including her friends and family, medical professionals, fellow sufferers, and strangers.[7] A lot of this information is imparted to the reader by reproducing her inner monologues and the many conversations she has with others.

The centrality of reported speech to Engelberg's storytelling technique is not unusual for artists working in the comics medium, where speech balloons offer such a straightforward means of including direct quotations into a narrative. The example introduced above is particularly remarkable (see Fig. 4.2) in that the speech bubble attributed to Miriam contains a direct self-quotation embedded within another self-quotation (" . . . So then I said, 'My haircut? Oh that's courtesy of chemo!'"). The genuine nature of the verbal exchange between Miriam and a fellow cancer sufferer is emphasized through the use of linguistic features characteristic of conversational language, including abbreviated words ("chemo"), repetition as a signal of participation ("My haircut?"; "'Courtesy of chemo?'"), non-standard word order ("I *never* would have thought of that"), and words indicating expressions of amusement ("snort," "guffaw"). Furthermore, the visual appearance of the hand-lettered words in the balloons suggests the irregularities of tone and pitch that are characteristic of the human voice (van Leeuwen 2006), thereby reinforcing the sense that this conversation actually took place and was not simply imagined or invented.

Visual style and authentication

Performed authenticity in comics is a matter not only of visual "content," but also of stylistic features. As Carney (2008: 195) points out, the particular style of illustration of each comic offers "a constant visual reminder of the hand of the illustration artist, much more so than the writer's traces." In these stylistic features the reader may seek to discover evidence of "graphiation," the idiosyncratic gesture that produced a particular work (Marion 1993, discussed in Baetens 2001). Although the visual style of comics is, at least to some extent, under the control of the artist, it is likely to be considered a sign "given off" rather than "given," and therefore a more reliable cue to authenticity than some of the more explicit claims discussed above.

It is noticeable that graphic memoirists often use a style of drawing that quite openly and deliberately diverges from the styles commonly associated with conventional comic books. In this way, artists can indicate their clear intention to tell a different, and, by implication, more genuine and truthful, kind of story. Witek (1989) suggests that a realistic, quasi-photographic style, in particular, tends to cue non-fictional comics genres. Although I will later challenge Witek's claims, I admit that it is certainly possible to find some examples of graphic memoirs that appear to support his theory. Fabrice Neaud (1996), for instance, mostly uses a realistic style based on the techniques of photo reference and life drawing to portrait his experiences of life as a young homosexual (see, for instance, Chapter 2, Fig. 2.9), although particularly emotional or harrowing moments are often represented through more symbolic images (Beaty 2007). When telling stories from their own life, Craig Thompson and Max Cabanes also use more realistic drawings than they employ in their fictional work.

Max Cabanes is a French artist who has worked with several different visual genres, including Disney postcards and book illustrations. *Heart Throbs* (see Fig. 4.3) is an unsentimental and, according to the blurb on the book cover, "partly autobiographical" account of a childhood and adolescence spent in the South of

FIG. 4.3 Max Cabanes (1991) *Heart Throbs*, p. 69 (excerpt, original in color). Copyright © 1989 Casterman; UK edition © 1991 Xpresso Books.

France. It is divided into separate sections relating to sexual experiences at different ages, and in several of the stories he tells, reality seems to merge seamlessly with the young protagonist's anxieties and fantasies. The story is rendered in a fairly realistic style, which combines line drawings and watercolor painting.

Although we may feel that we know what is meant when someone talks about a drawing style being "realistic" or "unrealistic," it may sometimes be useful to analyze these qualities more precisely. McCloud (1994: 30) attempts to show the difference between a (photo-)realistic image and a cartoon by describing the latter as a form of "amplification through simplification," where unnecessary detail is left out in order to allow a focus on the essential. However, his use of the term "iconic abstraction" to describe a scale stretching from the most realistic images to the most "iconic" form of representation, namely written words, may be more confusing than helpful, as it diverges from Peirce's original terminology.

In Peirce's (1960) semiotic theory, words and images are seen as fundamentally different kinds of signs. Words are "symbols," based on an arbitrary connection between a signifier and a signified; their meaning is completely dependent on convention. Images, by contrast, are "icons," which are founded on a close physical resemblance between signs and their meaning. "Index," finally, refers to a sign that relies on a direct physical or causal relation between itself and what it signifies: for instance, smoke is an index of fire. Peirce suggested that signs are generally not interpreted exclusively as symbols, icons, or indexes, but rather on the basis of all three, in different proportions. Photographs are both iconic, in that they tend to closely resemble what they portray, and indexical, because, as the products of chemical processes occurring in the same space and time as the recorded event, they seem to offer a direct, unmediated record of reality. According to Peirce's definitions, cartoon drawings lack the indexical quality of photographs, and they are also generally less "iconic" than photographic representations in that they do not resemble the represented objects quite so closely (see also Magnussen 2000). The more simplified a drawing is, the more it acquires "symbolic" (and not, as McCloud claimed, "iconic") qualities, in the sense that its meaning starts to rely more heavily on cultural conventions than on a material likeness.

The social semiotic concept of "visual modality" also promises a way of describing the extent to which an image resembles its objects of representation. What makes this approach particularly attractive for our purposes is that it suggests a way of addressing the relationship between such stylistic features and perceptions of truthfulness. Social semiotic theory is based on the application of Systemic Functional Linguistics to non-linguistic modes (Hodge and Kress 1988; van Leeuwen 2005). The central argument is that these modes are able to fulfill the same communicative functions as language, but in their own distinctive forms. The concept of modality, for instance, which is used by Halliday (1994: 75–91) to describe the different linguistic means whereby speakers express their judgment of the probabilities or the obligations involved in what they are saying, can, according to Kress and van Leeuwen (1996), also be applied to visual meaning. Visual modality relates to the degree to which an image is to be taken as true or real and to the resources image producers use to express this. Modality is thus closely connected to the notion of authenticity (van Leeuwen 2001: 396).

There are, social semioticians suggest, particular historically evolved visual conventions for expressing a distinction between fact and fiction, real and fake, reality and fantasy, and these, at least within particular social contexts, act as reasonably reliable guides to the truth of visual messages. These so-called "modality markers" include the degree of detail rendered, the presence or absence of background and depth, color differentiation, saturation and modulation, light and shadow, and brightness (Kress and van Leeuwen 1996: 165–67; Van Leeuwen 2005: 167). All these markers can be increased or reduced independently of each other, resulting in a vast number of possible "modality configurations" both within and across particular visual genres. The authors emphasize that there are no fixed correspondences between points on these scales and modality judgments. Instead, the truth value of a given configuration depends on how reality is defined by the social group for which a representation is intended. At the moment, the dominant standard by which we judge visual modality in Western societies is, according to Kress and van Leeuwen, a form of naturalism that assesses reality on the basis of how much an image corresponds with what we would see with the naked eye. In naturalistic modality, images are most "truthful" when they are about two thirds up on the scales outlined above.[8]

As art historians and cultural critics are fond of reminding us, *what* and *how* we see is always socially and culturally constructed (Berger 1972; Gombrich 1977; Staniszewski 1995). Although traditionally a main way of understanding images has been "to think of them as referring to, or depending upon, objects in the real world" (Wells 2000: 310), across different cultures and historical periods people have developed completely different standards as to what constitutes a "naturalistic" rendition of reality. This means that there are no necessary or sufficient rules of correspondence between pictures and their real-world referents. Indeed, even the most faithful painting or photograph is two-dimensional and will generally not be life- sized, thus requiring some familiarity with the relevant conventions in order to be perceived as "realistic." Realism is thus not something that is self-evidently given, but rather "something our perceptual culture has educated, or persuaded, us into" (Scott 1999: 9).

While acknowledging the way in which our concept of reality is bound up with technologies of representation and reproduction and our attitudes towards them, Kress and van Leeuwen (1996: 163) suggest that we still define naturalistic modality on the basis of the standard 35mm color photograph. By drawing a photo-realistic, or, in Kress and van Leeuwen's terms, a "naturalistic" representation of a scene, the creators of comics should thus be able to give their readers the sense that they are being presented with something that actually happened. A lower level of naturalism, by contrast, would indicate that the depicted scenes are to be taken as "less real," or entirely fictional.

Using the markers identified by Kress and van Leeuwen, we can describe the differences between the artistic styles of Engelberg (see Fig. 4.2) and Cabanes (see Fig. 4.3) in a systematic way. Although they depict similar scenes, each showing the protagonist in the company of his or her friends or acquaintances, they could hardly look any more different. Cabanes's artwork is fairly detailed and relies heavily on literal resemblance, although there are a few abstract elements as well. For instance, the facial proportions of the semi-autobiographical protagonist in the bottom left-hand corner are slightly distorted and exaggerated. The speech balloon represents an even more abstract intrusion into an otherwise quite realistic-looking image, since it translates speech or thought into a visible form. The drawing depicts depth and background to a degree that is only a little less articulated than what we would expect if we were to look at this scene with our own eyes. The artist has used an almost full palette of quite finely nuanced and medium-saturated colors and quite realistic degrees of articulation of tone, light, and shadow.

Engelberg's drawing is clearly much lower on all these dimensions than Cabanes's artwork. Here, details are limited almost to the bare minimum, and her style tends towards abstraction in that she uses the "universally accepted scribbles that stand in for what mouths and noses and motion and sweat look like" (Wolk 2007: 120), rather than trying to make them resemble these features as closely as possible. There is no background at all, and the drawing is also not highly articulated in terms of depth, although the third dimension is suggested through overlap and the placing of two of the figures higher up on the picture plane. There is also an elementary use of linear perspective. It is a black and white drawing, which uses no light and shadow and no shades of grey at all. According to Kress and van Leeuwen's criteria, Engelberg's style is thus much less visually "naturalistic" than Cabanes's, which would suggest that the former is intended to be taken as less "truthful" than the latter.

In fact, as we have seen, Engelberg's book makes much stronger claims that the story is based on real-life experiences than Cabanes's does. Therefore, it would appear that, at least in the case of autobiographical comics, stylistic realism is not the most common cue to authentic intention. Although the visual style of a comics artist *is* an important authentication strategy, it often draws its power less from its iconic resemblance to reality than from the indexical clues it seems to offer about the artist's genuine characteristics and intentions. In the case of Engelberg's book, for instance, the simple, child-like drawings can be said to "authentically" reflect her lack of artistic background and training, as well as suggesting the artlessness associated with spontaneous "writing-as-therapy." But it is not only amateur cartoonists like Engelberg whose work is characterized by a naïve, unrealistic drawing style. Carney (2008: 196) believes that many skilled alternative comics artists "infuse their work with a sense of the handmade and personal that deliberately evokes the 'subartistic' and 'amateurish' as a means of endowing an aura of the authentic and personal to the image and to the narrative voice of the comic." Jeffrey Brown's (2005; 2009) autobiographical work (see Chapter 2, Fig. 2.4) and Spanish illustrator Miguel Gallardo's comic book about his relationship with his autistic daughter, *María y yo* ("Maria and I") (2010), are good examples of the use of a consciously assumed amateurish style.

Other graphic memoirists use a drawing style that gives the impression of being intentionally and overtly spontaneous, thus allowing them to suggest that they are acting as relatively neutral channels of their own authentic thoughts and feelings. In an interview with the British Sunday newspaper *The Observer* (Day 2008), for instance, Peeters explained that he drew the story of his relationship with an HIV positive woman directly in ink and consciously did not go back and correct his work: "This was something I wanted to do to let go of the thoughts in my head" (see Chapter 3, Fig. 3.2). The only panel altered before publication was a New York skyline drawn before 9/11 that had originally featured the Twin Towers. Linthout's (2009) autobiographical comic about a man trying to come to terms with his son's suicide is even more radical in its use of intentionally unpolished pencil drawings, in which all the original sketch lines are still clearly visible beneath the darker outlines of the final drawings (see Chapter 5, Fig. 5.2). This suggests a grasp of reality that is terribly vulnerable and constantly threatening to dissolve completely, and yet the story feels truthful in terms of the emotional realities it conveys.[9]

Variations in style are sometimes used across one book or even within the same panel to indicate "degrees of certainty and nuances of attitude in relation to what is being recounted" (Miller 2007: 123) or to distinguish between real life and fantasy. When, for instance, Lauren Weinstein, in *Girl Stories* (2006: 191–200), discusses her adolescent obsession with her body weight, she draws a scene in which some of the ultra-thin models emerge from the pages of the magazine she is reading and tell her how unhappy and unfulfilled their lives are. In contrast to Lauren and her "real" friends, who are all drawn in full color, these imaginary interlocutors are, apart from the red of their lipstick, represented in a monochrome light beige. While Weinstein's use of stylistic variation is congruent with Kress and van Leeuwen's presumed link between visual "naturalism" and our perception of the "real," the following example is not. It is taken from Ariel Schrag's *Potential* (2008b), one of the series of four comic books chronicling the author's high school years and

FIG. 4.4 Ariel Schrag (2008b) *Potential*, p. 157 (excerpt). Copyright © 1997 Ariel Schrag.

her dawning realization that she is gay. Here, the dream sequences are always rendered in a style that, according to Kress and van Leeuwen's markers, is actually *more* naturalistic than the rest of Schrag's drawings.

The scene describes a nightmare Ariel has while sharing a bedroom with her friend (see Fig. 4.4), for whom she has developed passionate feelings but who shows little interest in her sexual advances. If we compare the first three panels with the final one, in which Ariel wakes up from her nightmare, we can see that the dream sequence is drawn in more a detailed and less abstract way, and that the style is also more highly articulated on the scales of background, depth, tone, and light and shadow. This would thus suggest that the dream is to be considered "more real" than Ariel's actual experiences.

While a dream may, of course, feel remarkably "real," I believe that Schrag's choice of drawing style for the dream sequences in *Potential* has less to do with their visual modality in relation to the other panels and more to do with practical considerations, such as the fact that realistic drawings require more investment in terms of time and effort than do the more cartoonish images that fill most of the 224 pages of the book. Schrag has developed her own narrative and stylistic conventions when it comes to indicating different states of consciousness that go beyond a simple distinction in terms of stylistic realism. In *Potential*, for instance, it is the fact that the dream sequences generally start and end with a panel showing Ariel in bed, combined with the wavy panel edges against a black background, which signal that we are dealing with a dream.[10]

Authentication through documentation

Unlike most of the more conventional comics genres, graphic memoirs frequently include photographic images and other forms of "documentary evidence" in their work, either in their "pure" form or in a graphic rendering. The ubiquity of such artifacts in graphic memoirs suggests that they must have a key role to play in persuading readers of the authenticity of a particular work. Ted Rall's (2002) *To Afghanistan and Back*, for example, uses a mixture of prose text, comic strips, and black-and-white photographs to tell the story of the author's attempts to discover the effects of America's 2001 bombing campaign upon ordinary Afghans. The book also includes his visa and press card, which were apparently scanned into the text, and several sections of maps, some of which have been redrawn in the artist's own hand. Maps perform a particularly important function in signaling the authenticity of autobiographical comics that describe someone's travels, whether this be for leisure (e.g., Neufeld 2004; Thompson 2004) or work (e.g., Delisle 2006a), probably because they seem to provide clear, unambiguous links between locations in a narrative and actual places in the real world.

However, it is undoubtedly the photograph that plays the most significant role in performing authenticity in the graphic memoir genre. When Kress and van Leeuwen say that we still define naturalistic modality on the basis of the standard 35mm color photograph, they seem to suggest that it is the photograph's high degree of iconic resemblance to its objects of representation that makes it appear so exceptionally authentic. However, it is important to remember that the myth of photographic truthfulness is based not so much on the "lifelikeness" of the images the camera produces, but rather on the photograph's apparent indexical referentiality. From its inception, it has been popularly perceived as a virtually transparent medium, with the putative capacity to transcribe reality in a completely reliable way, in the manner of "something directly stenciled off the real, like a footprint or a death mask" (Sontag 2005 [1977]: 120).

In fact, photographs have a highly complex relationship with reality. Most people are aware that photography often involves the staging of events for the camera, as well as some intervention on the part of the photographer, in terms of the choice of frame, distance, angle, exposure, and focus, for instance. Moreover, the act of taking a photograph involves the creation of a record of something that will change over time or even cease to exist. The viewer can never be certain what really happened at the time the picture was taken, while the photographer cannot know how it will be read in the future: "the very nature of photography as a medium disrupts the possibility of asserting a final and single Truth" (Kuhn and McAllister 2006: 15). Digital technology has introduced further complications, since it allows for virtually seamless modifications to be made very quickly and easily. It is now even possible to create photographically realistic images that are entirely simulated and have no basis in the material world at all, a process Frosh (2003: 177) refers to as "the miraculous perfection of the real through its fabrication."

Despite decades of discussions surrounding the problematic relationship between photographs and the "truth," an inherent belief in the photograph's direct connection to reality seems to persist.

Haverty Rugg (1997: 13) believes that photography is like autobiography, in that both "participate in a system of signs that we have learned to read—at one level—as highly indeterminate and unreliable. Below that level of doubt rests, in some persons, the desire to accept the image or the text as a readable reference to a (once-)living person." Adams (2000: 2) agrees that "apparently no amount of appealing to logic about the obvious distortions of photographs can quite sway viewers from the popular idea that there is something especially authentic or accurate about a photographic likeness." If anything, the current anxieties surrounding the development of digital photography and the increased awareness of the enhanced possibilities of manipulation appear to have led to an even greater longing for the truly authentic image (e.g., Ritchin 1990).

A good example of the use of photography to authenticate an autobiographical narrative is *The Photographer* (2009). It tells of the experiences of French photographer Lefèvre's assignment in Afghanistan, where he was documenting a "Doctors Without Borders" ("Médecins Sans Frontières," MSF) mission at the time of the war between the Soviet Union and the Mujahideen. The photographs are Lefèvre's, but his story was written and drawn by Emmanuel Guibert. One scene recounts an event Lefèvre witnessed on the long and arduous walk across several mountain ranges from Pakistan into a remote region of Northern Afghanistan, with a caravan of donkeys carrying all the supplies required to set up a basic hospital. The volunteers were accompanied by a group of Mujahideen fighters, whose leader, Najmudin, impressed everyone with his wisdom, patience, and superhuman strength— he had rescued a donkey that had slipped on a bridge simply by taking hold of its rear and lifting it up. The first panel (see Fig. 4.5) contains a drawing of a small section of the bridge with the donkey's hind legs stuck between the stones. This is followed by two photographs Lefèvre took of the scene, the first of which contains the detail depicted by Guibert and the second showing Najmudin's heroic act. As the narrator notes in the following text box: "I'm far away and there isn't enough light. I hope that the action will be visible on the photos, otherwise nobody will believe me" (p. 68).

FIG. 4.5 Guibert, Emmanuel, Didier Lefèvre and Frédéric Lemercier (2009) *The Photographer*, p. 68 (excerpt, original partially in color). Copyright © 2003, 2004, 2006 Dupuis – Guibert & Lefèvre; English translation copyright © 2009 First Second.

This page is fairly representative of the way in which photographs are used in this book to provide documentary evidence of the events Lefèvre witnessed. There is an artlessness and immediacy about the black and white pictures, which give the impression of having been taken quickly and without a lot of deliberate reflection or intervention by the photographer. Most of the photographs are taken from thumbnail contact sheets, with many events being represented through a large number of sequential moment-by-moment shots, conveying a strong sense of the actions being recorded as they unfolded over time. They thus conform to the professional norms of press photography, which typically aim to signal authenticity by making the photographer's own practices as invisible as possible (Grittmann 2003). Accordingly, press photographs appear authentic to the extent that the depicted people are presented at eye-level and from an average distance, and they are not looking at the camera. Special effects such as blurring are generally avoided, as they would draw too much attention to the mediating influence of the photographer, and black and white images tend to be perceived as more rather than less authentic, as they are still associated with serious documentary photography.

Guibert's drawings, by contrast, are generally used to fill in the gaps in the story for which no photographs were available, and as a way of conveying atmosphere and emotion. Lefèvre's return trip to Pakistan, for instance, which he foolishly decided to make without his MSF colleagues, is only sparsely documented photographically and relies heavily on Guibert's drawings. At the point at which a sick, malnourished and exhausted Lefèvre is abandoned by his Afghan guides and almost dies of exposure during a night spent on a snow-covered mountain pass, Guibert represents his friend's tribulations first in his usual style, then in silhouettes against a plain grey background and finally through twelve black panels, with nothing but a few words in grey type recounting the man's thoughts as he contemplates what seems to be certain death (*The Photographer*, pp. 210–25).

Admittedly, the vast majority of autobiographical comics use photographs much more sparingly than this. Some graphic memoirists (e.g., Barry 2002; Engelberg 2006; Small 2009) include photographs of themselves and/or family members at the beginning or the end of the book, while in others they are integrated into the text (e.g., Davison 1990; Kominsky-Crumb 2007). In many of these cases, the inclusion of photographs acts as a straightforward "sign that we are reading autobiography" (Adams 2000: 20), in the sense that it seems to "insist on something material, the *embodied* subject, the unification (to recall the autobiographical pact) of author, name, *and* body" (Haverty Rugg 1997: 13). But often photographs in graphic memoirs also fulfill a more complex role.

Miriam Katin's (2006) account of how she and her mother escaped deportation during the Nazi occupation of Hungary represents a striking illustration both of photography's unique "evidential force" (Barthes 2000 [1980]: 89) and of its potential for more ambiguous meaning. The very last page of the book shows a tattered old photograph of Miriam and her mother, which, the caption

FIG. 4.6 Miriam Katin (2006) *We Are On Our Own*, p. 21 (excerpt). Copyright © 2006 Miriam Katin.

informs us, was taken in 1946. The photo has yellowed with age, and the damaged corners and many stains give the impression that it has been removed from a photo album and handled many times. Coming as it does at the end of a harrowing tale of narrowly escaping the Nazis and living in hiding, the photo acts as material evidence of the author's survival, and as a kind of monument to her mother's bravery.

One scene shows the mother's preparations for their fake suicide and subsequent "disappearance," which includes burning all the precious family photographs (see Fig. 4.6). In the third panel parts of the mother's hand are depicted holding a photograph of Miriam's grandmother. In Mitchell's (2008: 18) terms, this is an instance of a "metapicture," a picture in which the image of another picture appears. In this case, it has been redrawn in Katin's own hand in a slightly more "naturalistic" drawing style than the other panels. As the photograph looks so authentic, we get the sense that it must have been carefully copied from an original. In fact, this is unlikely, since, according to this narrative sequence, all the family photographs in her mother's possession were destroyed. Photography is strongly associated with the act of bringing the past into the present. For victims of the persecution photographs can assume particular emotional significance, as they often come to stand for everything that was lost or destroyed. Such pictures emphasize the photograph's capacity "to hover between life and death, to capture only that which no longer exists, to suggest the desire and the necessity and, at the same time, the difficulty, the impossibility, of mourning" (Hirsch 2011: 20). The scene reflects this ambiguity, as it simultaneously conveys Katin's desire to recreate through her graphic memoir the material records of her relations and a strong sense of irretrievable loss.

Alison Bechdel's graphic memoir *Fun Home* (2006) incorporates into the story a whole range of textual artifacts, including extracts from letters, maps, the diary she kept as a child, and many photographs.[11] These are all reinterpreted through the artist's hand, while carefully preserving the visual appearance of the original documents. *Fun Home* recounts the author's memories of growing up in a small town in Pennsylvania, and her frustrated yearnings for the love of her father, whose closeted homosexuality and illicit affairs with his young students cast a deep shadow over the whole family (see Chapter 2). After her father's death, Alison discovers a photograph of the seventeen-year-old boy who for a while worked as the children's babysitter, lying semi-naked on a bed in a hotel room (pp. 100, 101).[12] She recalls a holiday by the seaside when she was eight, a trip during which her mother was absent and the youth shared a room with her father. The photograph thus seems to hint at an illicit affair, while failing to provide any real, tangible evidence. Adding to its mystery is the fact that it is included in an envelope with all the family shots from the same trip, but the date printed along one edge has been partly blotted out with a marker pen. As the autobiographical narrator notes: "It's a curiously ineffectual attempt at censorship. Why cross out the year and not the month? Why, for that matter, leave the photo in the envelope at all? In an act of prestidigitation typical of the way my father juggled his public appearance and private reality, the evidence is simultaneously hidden and revealed" (p. 101).

When photographic images are redrawn by hand, some of the aura of authenticity associated with photography is likely to be maintained, but this will be weakened by the loss of indexicality involved in the translation from one medium to another. The crucial difference between analog photography and all forms of mark-making, be they by pencil, pen, paintbrush, or using a computer-based graphic design application, is that the former lays claim to indexicality, whereas the latter involve adding to the likeness an explicit element of transformation. Unlike photography, cartooning does not generally claim to offer a direct, mimetic representation of the world but rather an interpretation of events as they are experienced by the artist, with aspects that are often deliberately exaggerated, adapted, or invented. By filtering photographs through her own unique vision, Alison Bechdel thus seems to be drawing attention to the complex relationship between photography and the "truth."[13]

Authentication through "making strange"

As several of the examples discussed above have indicated, performances of authenticity in autobiographical comics often involve a measure of self-reflexivity and irony. In contrast to the strict controls that people tend to impose on the "backstage" regions of everyday social interaction (Goffman 1969 [1959]), many autobiographical comics creators appear to relish the opportunity to lead readers behind the curtains and show them all the props, costumes, and masks—or, in other words, the formal and narrative techniques— used in the construction of a particular work. Following Bertolt Brecht's theatre theory (1978), such strategies may be regarded as contributing to the "*Verfremdungseffekt*" ("alienation effect," or "effect of making strange"). This describes the process whereby the action of a play is continuously made unfamiliar and remote in order to discourage audiences from identifying with characters and so losing the distance that is necessary in order to maintain a thoughtful and critical attitude (see also Chapter 5). An example of this is when actors break the "fourth wall," the imaginary wall at the front of the stage, by acknowledging the presence of members of the audience in some way.

When graphic memoirists employ similar tactics, the resulting increased awareness of the mediating role of the author/artist on the part of readers does not necessarily affect the perceived authenticity of a particular autobiographical work. In fact, artists who draw attention to their own interpretative practices and to the artificiality of all representation may, paradoxically, strike the reader as *more* rather than *less* authentic.[14]

One of the most straightforward strategies of "making strange" is to offer readers a frank account of the limitations of memory and the possibility of error. A good example of this can be found in *I Never Liked You* (1994), Chester Brown's account of his adolescence under the burden of his mother's increasingly fragile mental health. In a signed and dated note in the appendix the author explicitly addresses "those of you who are wondering when and where things happened." He proceeds to give a few details about dates and locations of some of the key scenes in the book, but explicitly acknowledges the possibility that he may have misremembered certain facts. In relation to his description of a car journey, during which his mother explained to her mortified sons why she wears a padded brassiere, Brown admits that he is not sure where they were going at the time, nor how close the lines he wrote for his mother are to what she actually said: "Like almost all of the dialogue in *I Never Liked You*, it's based on my memory of what was said." By being transparent about the limits of his ability to tell the absolute Truth, Brown is thus laying claim to a deeper and more sincere form of authenticity.

The reliability of memory and the impossibility of ever establishing the historical facts is also sometimes openly addressed in the text itself, as was shown in the excerpt from Baudoin's (1995) *L'éloge de la poussière* (see Fig. 4.1). An even more explicit example of this meta-narrative strategy is to be found later on in the same work, where Baudoin has reprinted a page from his previous graphic memoir, *Passe le temps* ("Time Passes") (1982, no pagination). It describes the distressing childhood experience of being followed by a stray dog, which was then shot by a deranged veteran of the war in Algeria. In *L'éloge de la poussière*, Baudoin confesses to having "twisted" the facts in the original version, since he found the actual truth too hard to bear at the time. He then recounts and draws another version of the events, according to which some of his friends from the village where he used to spend the summer holidays pushed the dog over a cliff. His final comment is that this second account of the dog's death reestablishes the "truth," "but what does that mean, the truth?" ("mais qu'est-ce que ça veut dire vérité?"). Baudoin's strategy might be described as an example of what Hatfield (2005: 124) calls "ironic authentication," "the implicit reinforcement of truth claims through their explicit rejection," which works by making "a show of honesty by denying the very possibility of being honest" (p. 126). While Baudoin is entirely frank about having diverged from the truth in a previous book, he clearly wants the reader to accept that he is sincere in his effort to expose the gaps in his memories of the past and avoid further distortion.

The making strange of a life narrative can also be achieved through the use of blatantly exaggerated and often humorous fictional elements. British comics artist Glenn Dakin's (2001) *Abe: Wrong for all the Right Reasons*, for instance, uses the character of Adam "Abe" Rat as his alter ego. This sketchily drawn cartoon character "lives in the far-flung future" and "is also the far-out superhero—Captain Oblivion" (p. 4). As the author explains in the comic-strip introduction to his book, he invented the character as a teenager, but later found that he was unable to get rid of him: "And gradually I started to use Abe to express my real feelings about real life" (p. 5). While reading about Abe's comic adventures in a strange, futuristic world, readers will always be conscious of the partly fictional nature of these stories but they are also likely to accept that they are based on Dakin's authentic thoughts and emotions.

Another way of performing authenticity is by drawing explicit attention to the visual style of representation. A comic book always offers a completely unique version of the world, since "cartooning is, inescapably, a metaphor for the subjectivity of perception" (Wolk 2007: 21; see also Gardner 2008). While the comics reader will thus always be somewhat aware of the artist as a mediating instance between a representation and the objects it depicts, *conscious* awareness of this is likely to fluctuate and to depend on the specific content and form of a story. Groensteen (2007: 61) argues that the formal features of a comic book, including, for instance, the layout of the page, and the shape and arrangement of panels and speech balloons, may be more or less "ostentatious," thus drawing attention to the presence of the artist-as-mediator to differing degrees. This form of "ostentation" depends not so much on how regular or irregular the layout is, but rather on the degree to which it is perceived to deviate from the norms associated with the medium.

The notion of ostentation suggests that the way we view any type of image is shaped by our previous experiences of how the world is typically presented to us in a particular genre. As is the case with all genres, the norms and expectations associated with graphic memoirs are constantly being challenged and redefined. Nevertheless, some generic expectations do apply. For instance, "unrealistic" proportions, speech balloons, and motion lines are such established features of cartooning that their inclusion in a particular graphic memoir is unlikely to draw our attention to the mediating role of the artist, even though they diverge fundamentally from our ordinary perceptions.

In modern comics, a "break" in the visual style has now become quite a common and acceptable way of indicating strong emotions (Groensteen 2010: 13). However, one example uses such striking and unusual breaks in style that they are likely to be rather startling for most readers. The scene is taken from Mary Fleener's (1996) account of her hedonistic life during the 1990s, *Life of the Party*. In this book, she often reverts to a highly abstract, Cubist style when describing her drug- and alcohol-fuelled hallucinations, as well as any extreme emotional states. The second and third panels on the page (see Fig. 4.7) represent Mary's contradictory feelings during

FIG. 4.7 Mary Fleener (1996) *Life of the Party*, p. 24 (excerpt). Copyright © 1996 Fantagraphics Books; all contents copyright © 1996 Mary Fleener.

a frenzied sexual encounter with a man she does not particularly like and whose bald advances she initially rejects, before finally giving in to lust. By pushing the boundaries of what readers are likely to expect in an autobiographical comic, the artist flaunts her role as mediator between the "real" world and the world created in her book. The reader is invited to accept that the abstract drawings are a sincere representation of Mary's feelings at the time, capturing not only her physical excitement but also her sense of being used by her predatory partner.[15]

Several scholars have noted the paradoxical ways in which a sense of authenticity is produced in Art Spiegelman's *Maus* (2003), which focuses obsessively on historical accuracy, while employing the deliberately artificial setting of an animal fable. Witek (1989: 100) believes that the artist's "spare and almost primitive" drawing style and his casting of all the characters in the book as animal figures enables him to challenge people's ordinary perceptions of reality and to "sidestep the 'already told' quality of the Holocaust" (p. 103). "Funny animals" are a well-established trope of traditional children's comics, and they carry with them a whole range of prior meanings and connotations. Spiegelman exposes the artificiality of this trope by "pushing it towards self-parody" (Hatfield 2005: 148): for instance, *Maus* includes a scene in which Art consults his French wife about which animal he should use to represent her, and some national stereotypes are taken to ludicrous extremes. In this way, Spiegelman reveals to us the "seams" of his narrative techniques and asks us not only to question *his* version of reality but also to reexamine some of our *own* categories and prejudices (Kannenberg 2001).

What is particularly striking about the world Spiegelman creates is the way it initially seems artificial but gradually becomes more and more "real," even natural to the reader. Cioffi (2001) suggests that the occasional photograph that Spiegelman inserts into his graphic memoir gives readers a jolt and forces them to recognize that they have been seduced into accepting a view of the world that shows people as animals and animals as people, a distortion of reality which, in effect, contributed to the propaganda which made the Holocaust possible. In this way, *Maus* awakens readers to "how images can be used to create a world both believable and fantastic, linked to actual historicity but at the same time part of another realm or dimension altogether" (p. 121).

On one of the final pages of *Maus*, the drawings of Art and his father, Vladek, are juxtaposed with a photograph of the latter in what looks like a concentration camp uniform (see Fig. 4.8). However, the medium of drawing and the medium of photography are not simply presented as diametrically opposed regarding their relationship to authenticity. As Vladek explains to his son, after his liberation from Auschwitz he had this picture taken in a studio that

offered customers the chance to pose for "souvenir photos" in a new, clean uniform. Vladek enclosed the photograph in a letter to his wife Anja, who had also survived the Holocaust and was still desperately hoping to hear from him. While its primary purpose was to reassure Anja and present her with documentary evidence that he was still alive, the picture was in fact a carefully constructed and fundamentally fraudulent portrait of Vladek as a proud and defiant hero who has survived the ordeals of the camp virtually unscathed. The portrait represents the image Vladek wanted to project of himself at the time, rather than a straightforward historical document. It is thus, in a sense, no more—but also no less—"authentic" than Spiegelman's cartoon drawings of his father in the guise of a cartoon mouse (see also Hatfield 2005).[16]

This ambivalence is emphasized by the layout of the page: the photograph looks as if it originally formed one of the panels that was subsequently cut out and placed at an angle over the other panels on the page. On the one hand, the picture forms part of the narrative world, where it is discussed and handled by Anja, Vladek, and Art. On the other, it also seems to belong to the "real" world of the readers, who are given an impression of the photograph as a concrete material object that they could, if they so wished, pick up and study. By deliberately presenting cartooning and photography as equally unreliable forms of mediation, Spiegelman thus exposes the potentially fallacious nature of *all* accounts of human history.

Indeed, of all the autobiographical comics artists discussed so far, Spiegelman can be said to have allowed his readers the most comprehensive access to the backstage regions of his life writing. In 1994, he released a CD-ROM containing not just the text of *Maus* itself, but also various "multimedia footnotes," including video clips of the author's trip to Poland, audio recordings and transcripts of the interviews he conducted with his father, early sketches, and comments about the creation and reception of the comic book (Spiegelman 1994). Anderson and Katz (2003) believe that this documentary evidence highlights the work's fundamental incompleteness and reinforces an awareness of its own constructedness and self-reflexivity. The additional materials allow readers to check the dialogue recorded in *Maus* with Vladek's original wording and to verify that Spiegelman has retained not only the most essential points his father makes, but also the unique characteristics that "make Vladek's voice recognizable—that make it, in other words, a style—and moreover imbue *Maus*'s representations of memory and of the past with authenticity" (p. 168; see also Eakin 2011).

Subverting authenticity

Some comics creators have taken the effect of making strange to such extremes that the boundaries between fact and fiction become

FIG. 4.9 Eddie Campbell (2006) *The Fate of the Artist*, p. 82 (original in color). Copyright © 2006 Eddie Campbell.

totally blurred and the very possibility of authenticity is cast into doubt. British cartoonist Eddie Campbell's (2006) *The Fate of the Artist* is a case in point. According to the text on the inside cover flap, this work offers readers "a complex meditation on the lonely demands of art amid the realities of everyday life," in which the "artist," whose part is "played by an actor," conducts "an investigation into his own disappearance." The book consists of a mind-boggling kaleidoscope of different genres, including photo-stories, longer sections of illustrated narrative text, different comics genres, and daily strips from the yellowed newspaper pages of an imaginary long ago. It also includes a vast array of different voices, some of which are clearly fictional, while others issue from the mouths of characters from Campbell's own life.

One scene is a discussion between the "artist" (who physically resembles the "real" Eddie Campbell) and a child-like crayon drawing of a stick-man. In a meta-narrative intrusion by the author/narrator into his own story (see Fig. 4.9), the crayon figure accuses the artist of wanting "everything to reflect the great cosmic joke that you imagine to be behind all existence" (p. 81), and proceeds to show him what the universe is really like: the artist has merged with the crayon scribble and both are part of a larger, rather ineptly executed artwork. "I knew it!," the artist exclaims, "all of existence is held together with paper clips and sticky tape" (p. 182).

According to Bakhtin (1981), all language is dialogic, because every utterance echoes how others have used it previously and is entangled with the points of view, value judgments, and intentions of other people. Consequently, every speech act and every written text is inevitably "heteroglot," containing within it a mix of different languages or voices. *The Fate of the Artist* makes this inherent heteroglossia explicit, by using different genres, perspectives, and voices to present the reader with an ever-shifting view of subjectivity and "reality" in general. Indeed, this book would seem to be an extreme example of the ability of comics to "parody the very notion of an original and therefore something preceding 'beyond the signs,'" and to "make fun of the recurrent notion that, in some cases, a proximity between object and sign actually exists that can be called truth" (Frahm 2000: 179, 180). In this case, the task of sifting through all the different levels of fact and fiction becomes so intractable that the issue of authenticity seems to evaporate. Instead of worrying about whether or not the author is being truthful and sincere, readers can simply sit back and enjoy the world being created for them with such extravagant virtuosity in this mock autobiographical comic.

The fake autobiography, a famous example of which is *It's a Good Life, if You Don't Weaken* (2007) by Seth (born Gregory Gallant), represents another way of subverting the notion of authenticity.[17] Using a first-person narrative throughout, this book tells the apparently plausible story of how the protagonist becomes first intrigued and then obsessed with an obscure Canadian newspaper cartoonist of the 1940s and '50s named Jack "Kalo" Kalloway, whose work appeared in the *New Yorker*. Seth is presented as a discontented and judgmental curmudgeon, who feels ill at ease in the modern world and longs for a bygone era. He embarks on a hunt for Kalo's work and eventually travels to the small town in Ontario where the cartoonist supposedly grew up. Seth goes to a lot of trouble to ensure that the story is read autobiographically, for instance by including in the book several fake Kalo cartoons that are drawn in an old-fashioned style and printed in such a manner so as to suggest that they are, indeed, more than half a century old (Beaty 2011a). In fact, Kalo is an invented character, which means that the whole search for him must also be fictional.

Nevertheless, readers with some knowledge of Gallant's real-life personality can discern a lot of interesting parallels, both between the author and his alter ego Seth, and between Seth and Kalo (Hannon 2006; Miller 2004; Tomaselli 2007). For instance, Gallant is known to be nostalgic about the popular culture, fashion, and artistic styles of the early- and mid-twentieth century, and he also looks very much like the protagonist of *It's a Good Life*, as well as dressing in the same vintage clothing. Likewise, Seth's close friend Chet is obviously closely modeled on the character of Gallant's friend and fellow cartoonist Chester Brown. And not only does Kalo's work supposedly hail from the very period Gallant/Seth so admires, he also, according to Chet, "kinda" draws in the same style (*It's a Good Life*, p. 19). Seth's fictional journey to find Kalo can thus be read if not as a "truthful" then at least as an intriguingly "authentic" story about a cartoonist trying to find meaning in his own life and work.

The European comics scene recently witnessed another case of a fake autobiography. The young French artist Judith Forest caused quite a stir when she burst onto the comics scene with her graphic memoir, *1h25*. Published in 2009 by *La Cinquième Couche*, the book derives its title from the time it takes the young woman to travel by train from Paris, where she has just graduated from the *Beaux-Arts*, to her new home in Brussels. Using the format of a drawn diary, Judith chronicles her troubled relationship with her parents, her battle against addiction, her life as an artist, and her meetings with various well-known personalities in the comics scene, including one of the publishers for *La Cinquième Couche*, Xavier Löwenthal, with whom she has an affair. *1h25* was extremely well received by readers and critics alike (e.g., Wivel 2010). Forest gave several interviews for French media outlets, including the prestigious *Arte* channel, and had a high profile on various social networking sites.

Then something astonishing happened: rumors began to surface that Judith Forest did not, in fact, exist. Several of the people mentioned in the book claimed never to have met the woman, and her artistic style was seen to be remarkably similar to that of another of her publishers, William Henne. These suspicions were apparently confirmed by Forest's (2010) second book, *Momon* ("Momon," or "Masquerade"), which recounts Judith's response to the success of *1h25* and the controversies it sparked. In addition to pencil and ink illustrations, the book contains screenshots of Judith Forest's blog, copies of newspaper reviews, and stills from the television program on which she appeared. As more and more doubts about the authenticity of the first book are raised, the autobiographical narrator starts to suspect she has been used by her three editors as a way of attracting publicity for *La Cinquième Couche*. She becomes increasingly unsure of her own identity: "Things are slipping away from me. I am no longer myself. Even my name seems too beautiful to be true. Judith, like Xavier's partner in real life. Forest, like Jean-Claude Forest, one of the inventors of the modern comic book . . . " ("Les choses m'échappent. Je ne suis plus moi-même. Mon nom même me semble trop beau pour être vrai. Judith, comme la vraie compagne de Xavier dans la vie. Forest, comme Jean-Claude Forest, l'un des inventeurs de la bande dessinée moderne . . . ") (p. 85).

Visually, Judith's disintegrating sense of self is represented through the repeated image of her gazing at herself in the mirror. On pages 49–50, she first notices a small, black stain on the mirror glass, which apparently cannot be removed; on page 96 it has grown so large that it almost entirely obscures her reflection. *What if the rumors were true?*, Judith asks herself: "And what if 'sincerity' was nothing more than a sales strategy? And what if autobiography was the whore of literary genres? And what if I had been written in just three days?" ("Et si la 'sincérité' n'était qu'un argument de vente? Et si l'autobiographie était la putain des genres littéraires? Et si j'avais été écrite en trois jours?"). Dedicated explicitly "to all those, and most especially the journalists, who have allowed me to exist" ("à tous ceux, et plus particulièrement aux journalistes, qui m'ont permis d'exister"), the book thus strongly implies what the editors finally admitted at the prestigious Angoulême comics festival in January 2011: Judith Forest is, indeed, an entirely fictional character, who was played on the radio and television by an actress (Beaty 2011b; Brethes 2011).

While *The Fate of the Artist* and *It's a Good Life* handle the issue of autobiographical authenticity with a light, playful touch, always leaving open the possibility that the original, the truthful, the sincere may yet be discovered, be it in the yarns they spin or in the wider world, the message contained in *1h25* and *Momon* is more cynical. Through the fictional character of Judith Forest, the authentic is revealed to be no more than a cunning masquerade, a way of pandering to the public's apparently insatiable appetite for revelatory autobiographical stories.

Such mock or fake graphic memoirs are still quite rare and exceptional, however. By far the majority of autobiographical comics creators are apparently still intent on signaling their fundamental honesty and integrity, typically through the use several of the authentication strategies discussed above. The strategy of making strange, whereby the mediating role of artists and the artificiality of their representations are deliberately foregrounded, is becoming a particularly popular way of performing authenticity in autobiographical comics—encouraged, perhaps, by the high critical esteem accorded to Spiegelman's *Maus*. In the following chapter, I will turn my attention to the readers of graphic memoirs, exploring the different formal and narrative means by which their interest can be stimulated and their engagement with a story and its central characters sustained.

Chapter 5

DRAWING IN THE READER

On the first page of the introductory section (pp. 1–9) to Rosalind Penfold's graphic memoir *Dragonslippers*, a young woman is shown standing on a wobbly stool and reaching for a box on the shelf above her head (see Fig. 5.1). The only light in the room emanates from a torch, which the woman offers to an unseen addressee: "Here—Would you mind holding this?" On the next page, the beam of light is directed at the pile of boxes, suggesting that the reader has entered the storyworld and is helping the woman find whatever she is looking for. As we subsequently discover, the woman represents Rosalind Penfold, and the box contains all the drawings she made in the decade she spent with a violent and manipulative older man. Now that she has finally managed to break free from this abusive relationship, she promises readers an answer to the question she assumes they must want to ask her: "*Why did I stay?* Everyone asks me that . . . // It's the *most important question*. // And the answer is *here* . . . in my *drawings!*" (pp. 6–7).

This example alerts us to the fact that all autobiographical comics have a persuasive purpose. Some works are produced initially as a form of self-expression or self-therapy, but once an author has decided to publish his or her graphic memoir, it becomes a deliberate form of communication that aims to involve readers and produce some kind of response in them, be it compassion, understanding, respect, or simply entertainment. This chapter intends to identify ways that graphic memoirs attempt to "draw in" their readers, both

FIG. 5.1 Rosalind Penfold (2006) *Dragonslippers*, no pagination.
Copyright © 2005 Rosalind B. Penfold.

in the sense of engaging their interest and emotional involvement, and in the more literal sense of including them in the story by suggesting a particular position or attitude for them to adopt.[1]

The network of more or less explicit textual structures, which invite readers to respond in a particular way and which thus anticipate "the presence of a recipient without necessarily defining him" (Iser 1978: 34), are sometimes described as the "implied reader" of a text. In *Dragonslippers*, for instance, the implied reader is a kind, helpful, and compassionate friend, who may well feel somewhat impatient with Rosalind for staying with her abusive partner for so long but who is prepared to sympathize with her reasons for acting as she did. The story thus creates the illusion of a private communication between the author and the reader, in which the former promises to reveal intimate details about her life in exchange for the latter's emotional engagement.

It is hard, however, to predict how actual readers will respond to this invitation. For several decades now, literary and media scholars have been aware of the fact that audiences are not simply passive receptacles for an already established reading or viewing position (e.g., Eco 1979; Moores 1993). German literary scholar Wolfgang Iser (1978: 22) was particularly influential in developing the concept of the "active" reader, suggesting that "the meaning of a literary text is not a definable entity but, if anything, a dynamic happening."[2] Some readers, for instance, may reject Penfold's perceptions of herself as a victim and may therefore be disinclined to "hold the torch" for her. They may even decide not to read the book—or to abandon it halfway through. In such a case, the author will have failed in her goal.

Engaging with narratives is always an imaginative activity, which prompts readers to try and understand situations, people, and values that are often alien to them. In this chapter, I consider two different mechanisms for drawing in the reader of graphic memoirs: *involvement*, and what I shall call *affiliation*. Involvement describes the general sense of connection individual readers feel either with a whole narrative or with particular scenes or characters in it. According to discourse analyst Deborah Tannen (1989), involvement is crucial to the success of both conversational interaction and literary discourse; it is often achieved by inviting readers to participate actively in a communicative act, for instance, by requiring them to supply missing information. Comics artists and scholars have argued repeatedly that the reading of comics requires a particularly active contribution on the part of the reader in the process of meaning-construction (e.g., Bearden-White 2009; Chute 2010; Eisner 1985; McCloud 1994; Scott 1999). Such claims tend to focus on the extra effort required of readers when they have to fill in the semiotic gaps between individual panels and between words and images in comics. An equally important way of encouraging reader involvement, I suggest, is through the use of multimodal rhetorical forms, which are remarkably prevalent in the graphic memoir genre.

Apart from trying to involve the readers in their stories, many graphic memoirists also wish an emotional bond with readers so that they see the world, at least momentarily, from the perspective of the autobiographical protagonist. Later in this chapter I compare and contrast what I consider to be the two most common forms of affiliation, namely *identification* and *empathy*. The concept of identification was first developed by psychoanalysts, but it was later adopted by scholars in the fields of media and cultural studies, where it refers to the patterns of attachment that are "constructed around *commonalities* imagined, felt, recognized, asserted, or imposed" (McCarthy 2009: 249). The notion of "empathy," on the other hand, describes the phenomenon of feeling *with* another person. This relies on our ability to make intuitive guesses about another's state of mind by imaginatively projecting ourselves into their situation, as well as by reading their body language, facial expressions, and behavior.

Although involvement and affiliation capture distinct processes of reader engagement, they are, in fact, inextricably intertwined in the case of graphic memoirs. As I argue in the final section of this chapter, some of the most common rhetorical devices used by autobiographical comics creators, such as metaphor, humor, and intertexuality, are dependent for their success upon the reader's ability and willingness to cooperate in the construction of meaning. They are also powerful ways of inviting engagement with characters.

Patterns of involvement

Deborah Tannen (1989: 12) defines involvement as "an internal, even emotional connection individuals feel which binds them to other people as well as to places, things, activities, ideas, memories, and words." According to her, it is not something that is simply given or absent in a particular context; rather, it constitutes a shared communicative accomplishment in conversations and in literary discourses of various kinds. She identifies two main ways in which involvement may be achieved: sound patterns, such as rhythm, repetition, and variation, and sense patterns, such as ellipsis, imagery, and tropes. The role of rhythm and repetition in graphic memoirs has already been discussed in Chapter 3 in relation to temporality, so here I will focus on sense patterns. These, Tannen (1989: 23) proposes, create involvement by inviting audience participation: "[T]he more work readers or hearers do to supply meaning, the deeper their understanding and the greater their sense of involvement with both text and author."

Ellipsis is the most general and wide-ranging of the involvement strategies Tannen (1989) describes. It refers to all the different ways in which meaning can be conveyed without its being expressed explicitly. All literature, Wolfgang Iser (1978) claims, inevitably contains "gaps," missing information that the reader fills with his or her individual projections and interpretations. In the reader's imagination, the meaning of a text may thus expand to take on a much greater significance than it would otherwise possess. This process can only be successful, however, if the reader's projections into the gaps are based on all the available evidence and if she is prepared to modify her initial hypothesis in the light of further evidence. If a text provides too much detailed information, the reading process may become tedious, but too little information runs the risk of overstretching the reader's attention span and interpretative faculties.

Many scholars place great emphasis upon the inherent "gappiness" of the comics medium, relating it both to the blank spaces in-between the panels, and to the potential disparities between verbal and visual meaning. The *Gestalt* concept of closure, which describes the universal human tendency to maintain meaning by filling in missing information, is often used to explain this process (Gordon

2004; Zakia 2002). Accordingly, incomplete familiar information, lines, or shapes are perceived as complete, as long as the distance or "interval" between elements is not too great. As closure represents an invitation to participate actively in a communicative act, it is thought to increase people's interest and sense of involvement, as well as their retrospective memory of the content of a communication.[3] *Years of the Elephant* (2004), by Flemish comics artist Willy Linthout, offers a good example of how readers of graphic novels may be invited to perceive a series of panels as a coherent narrative.

In this book the author draws heavily on his own experiences to tell the story of Charles Germonprez, a middle-aged man who is struggling to come to terms with the recent death of his son Jack, who took his own life by jumping off the roof of their apartment block. When Charles leaves the house to go to work again for the first time after this cataclysmic event, he sees that the police have drawn a chalk outline of Jack's body in the precise location where he fell, right by the entrance to the building. Charles tries to create a substitute for his son's physical presence by fixating on the outline, and in his imagination and dreams it comes alive and has spirited conversations with him. The chalk outline of the boy's fallen body thus becomes a poignant visual metaphor for Charles's terrible loss, as well as for Willy Linthout's own desperate—and finally futile—attempt to resurrect his son through his art. As the "real" Jack is never depicted in the book, not even when Charles is remembering him or dreaming about him, his physical absence is as palpable to the readers as it is to the protagonist of the story.

When a worker from the "Municipal Sanitation Department" arrives to scrub the pavement and clean away the chalk marks (see Fig. 5.2), Charles, who is out of his mind with grief and fury, chases the man away. His wife, however, is unable to understand this attitude, pointing out that, for her, "that drawing has nothing to do with our son." Like Jack, she is never portrayed in full anywhere in the book; occasionally, we see her hands or legs, but mostly she is no more than a disembodied voice originating beyond the frame of the panel. This suggests the sense of loneliness and isolation

FIG. 5.2 Willy Linthout (2009) *Years of the Elephant*, p. 81. English edition copyright © 2009 Fanfare / Ponent Mon.

extreme suffering can sometimes produce, particularly if, as in this case, two people utilize different strategies to cope with their sorrow. The book ends on a more hopeful note, when Charles finally realizes that his son has truly gone and that he desperately needs his wife (pp. 159–60). On the last two pages of the book (pp. 161–62) Charles is shown at his drawing board, for the first time looking peaceful and contented. He goes to bed, telling his son to "sleep tight" before dozing off himself. Thus the author shows that Charles is slowly beginning to accept his loss and allowing himself to share his grief with others.

In order to understand this story, readers must create a coherent narrative out of the incomplete information they are offered. The events involving Charles and the sanitation worker in panels 1/1 and 1/2, for instance, only make sense if we recognize that the man being kicked in the first image is the same person as the one Charles shouts at in the second panel, and that, in the intervening moments, he has picked himself up from the pavement and turned towards his attacker. Readers must also be able to interpret the discrepancy between Charles's words ("That's my son who's lying there!") and the drawing of the clearly inanimate chalk outline to which he is referring. Since the book does not contain any diegetic narration, readers must use all the available evidence provided by the mimetic storytelling in order to complete missing information and thereby shape their own understanding of Charles's experience of bereavement. The visual absence, in Linthout's drawings, of Charles's son and wife provides a further opportunity for readers to project their own mental images into the gaps in the narrative.

Different comics genres and individual artists tend to provide larger or smaller amounts of information, thereby demanding from their readers a more or less active participation in the construction of a story. David Hughes's *Walking the Dog* (see Fig. 5.6) uses an even more elliptic style than *Years of the Elephant*. On one level, the book centers on David's daily outings with Dexter, his wire-haired fox terrier, which he acquired, rather reluctantly, on the recommendation of his family doctor. These long and mostly uneventful walks give him the opportunity not only to mull over and vent his anger at the many things that infuriate him but also to explore some of his childhood memories and anxieties about loneliness and death. His thoughts are often presented in abstract ways, drawing on symbol, metaphor, verbo-visual humor, and often rather obscure cultural allusions. The transitions between the different elements of the story are abrupt and confusing, requiring readers to tackle the difficult task of creating meaningful links between them. On a deeper level, *Walking the Dog* can thus be interpreted as a dark and complex meditation on human suffering and the meaning—or perhaps meaninglessness—of life, but this interpretation requires a high level of commitment and involvement on the part of the reader.

As this example suggests, in graphic memoirs ellipsis is created not only by the gaps between panels and between verbal and visual information but also by specific rhetorical strategies, including metaphor, humor, and intertextuality, which require the reader to be actively engaged in the process of making meaning. The role of some of these rhetorical devices will be explored in more detail later in this chapter. First, however, I will consider the different ways in which graphic memoirs invite feelings of attachment between readers and characters in a story.

Patterns of affiliation

Whereas involvement is used to describe a sense of connection with a whole narrative or any aspects of it, the notion of *affiliation* is used in this context to refer to the act of connecting emotionally with one (or more) of the characters in a story. In the case of life writing, this character is most likely to be the autobiographical protagonist. I will focus on the two most widely discussed patterns of affiliation, namely identification and empathy.

Identification

The term *identification* is used in both everyday discourse and scholarly discussions to denote all kinds of different audience responses to characters in a story. In film and media studies, reflections on identification have traditionally referred to psychoanalytic theory, where the term describes the pathological process of denying the difference between self and other. Accordingly, the concept has been used by critics to explain the harmful influences of the popular media on groups of impressionable people, who, the argument goes, are sometimes tricked by certain texts into adopting the values of socially undesirable characters. Fredric Wertham's (1954) *Seduction of the Innocent,* in which he claimed that frequent exposure to brutal and asocial comics characters could lead children into a life of crime, is a classic example of such a view (see Chapter 1). However, the scientific community is deeply divided over whether such a total identification of audiences with media characters is a genuine and common phenomenon (e.g., Cohen 2001; Smith 1995). While children and adolescents may be susceptible to the influence of both real-life and fictional characters as they "try on" alternative ideas and values in the process of developing their own identity, it is unlikely that the majority of mature adults habitually lose themselves in the protagonists of a story, allowing their sense of self to become blurred in the process.

In this study, I use the term identification to refer to the tendency for readers to become attached to the protagonist of a graphic memoir on the basis of qualities, values, or experiences that are roughly congruent with their own.[4] Such identification typically leads readers to temporarily (or repeatedly) adopt the protagonist's perspective. According to my definition, identification thus depends, crucially, on people's ability and willingness to draw parallels between their own lives and those of the people in the stories they are reading.[5] A sense of commonality may be constructed on their perception of belonging to the same gender, social class, or generation, or else on the basis of shared values, interests, and experiences. In the case of illness narratives, for instance, strong identification with the main protagonists is probably most common among readers who have themselves experienced physical or mental disease or who have witnessed someone they love suffering in a similar way.[6]

Identification may also be encouraged through the creation of a strong sense of community among readers. Since the opportunities for individual readers to meet the author/artist or each other in person are typically limited, the occasional conference or comics festival notwithstanding, such a sense of group identity among readers can be said to constitute what Anderson (1991) has termed an "imagined community," one that is based not on kinship, physical proximity, or actual, day-to-day interaction, but rather on a deliberately created sense of belonging together and sharing important characteristics, experiences, and values. The notion of an imagined community was originally developed in relation to the birth of nationalism, which, Anderson believes, was closely linked to the emergence of mass-circulation newspapers, which gave people the illusionary feeling of a shared identity. However, I believe it can also be applied to other kinds of imagined communities that are formed on the basis of texts with a relatively wide circulation.

Rosalind Penfold makes an appeal to such a sense of belonging when, in the introduction to *Dragonslippers*, she expresses her hope that her book will help other people in unhappy relationships to "identify the warning signs of abuse" (n.p.). She ends the book by pointing out that Rosalind Penfold is a pseudonym and that there are "hundreds of thousands of 'Rosalind B. Penfolds' around the world who will recognize themselves in this story" (p. 259). This claim is reinforced through the inclusion on the final double-page spread (pp. 258–59) of nineteen "autographs," in the name of Rosalind Penfold but purporting to be in the distinctive handwriting of some of the readers that have identified with the protagonist of *Dragonslippers*. Readers are also invited to visit the website "Friends-of-Rosalind.com," where they can send in their comments and find links to support groups and charities that offer help and advice to victims of domestic violence. These strategies work together to create the impression that there is a whole community of people who have had similar experiences to Penfold or who have read *Dragonslippers* and subscribe to the values the book espouses.

As this example shows, the Internet now plays a particularly important role in creating such imagined communities of readers. Since the mid-1980s, more and more comics creators have been discovering it as a way of distributing their work. There are now said to be tens of thousands of comics from all over the world on the Web.[7] Several of the autobiographical comics I consider in this book were originally published online, thus providing authors with useful feedback channels and creating word-of-mouth publicity for their work. Brian Fies, for instance, began serializing *Mom's Cancer* (2006) on the Internet early in 2004. As the author explains in a preface to the book, he was astounded to discover how many people apparently "needed" the book and saw their own experiences reflected in it. In 2005, the Web version of *Mom's Cancer* won an Eisner Award and was subsequently republished as a book.

Even those published comics artists who do not rely solely on the Internet for the dissemination of their work still often use it to build their fan base, setting up bulletin boards, blogs, forums, and fan sections, for instance. This form of social networking is particularly common in the case of those graphic memoirs that deal with the experience of disease or abuse. Marisa Marchetto's (2006) comic about her experience of surviving breast cancer, *Cancer Vixen*, was originally published in *Glamour* magazine, before being republished as a book. Now the author has her own website, which, apart from her biography, information about her books and upcoming events, contact details, and a blog, also features a list of her personal "lifesavers," ranging from fashionable restaurants and shoe designers to the Breast Cancer Research Foundation. Thus the Internet provides readers with a forum via which they can offer feedback to comics creators, exchange views, information, and experiences with other readers, and, in some cases, establish a strong sense of mutual support.

Another example of the new potential for interaction created by the Internet is provided by German comics artist Dirk Schwieger, who spent some time living in Tokyo and used his webcomic blog to invite followers to submit specific "assignments" for him to perform and then report on in a weekly comic strip (see Chapter 3). It is likely that the readers of the original blog, in particular, were made to feel that they belonged to a community of like-minded

FIG. 5.3 Sacco, Joe (2004) *The Fixer – A Story from Sarajevo*, p. 62 (excerpt). Copyright © 2003 Joe Sacco.

individuals and that they were induced to identify strongly with the author as he performed the weekly tasks set by one of them.

The strategies for encouraging reader identification with the protagonist discussed so far are available to all autobiographers, regardless of the genre in which they work. However, graphic memoirists have some means of inviting audience engagement at their disposal that are specific to the genre (see Fig. 5.3). *The Fixer* describes Joe Sacco's complicated relationship with an army veteran, Neven, who, during the war in Bosnia, offered his services to visiting journalists—for a hefty price, of course. When Joe arrived in Bosnia in 1995, just as hostilities were ceasing, Neven took the hapless young journalist under his wing, and regaled him with tales of the gangsters and warlords who ruled the country during the war and of his own heroic exploits on the battlefield. In *The Fixer*, Joe remembers their relationship and retells Neven's stories, which seem to reflect many of the intractable ethnic, religious, and class divides of the Balkan conflict itself, but neither Joe himself nor the reader can ever be entirely sure whether Neven is telling the truth. Having just been advised by a friend that Neven is a fraud (see Fig. 5.3), Joe is utterly confused, and considers the evidence supporting Neven's stories, including the enthusiastic welcome he always receives from "salty warriors" in the street, against all the rumors he has heard about the man's boastful and unstable character.

The autobiographical narrator explicitly asks readers to put themselves in his shoes—which is an apt metaphor for the human tendency to identify with someone and to imagine the events of the narrative from his or her perspective—an invitation reiterated in panels 2 and 3 through the use of the second person pronoun ("You recall how salty warriors greeted Neven in the street . . . "). As this example demonstrates, Sacco typically draws himself with a rather expressionless face, hiding his eyes behind the shine of his owlish spectacles. In an interview with a British weekly newspaper (Cooke 2009), the artist explains that the emotional restraint that characterizes his self-portraits reflects a desire to focus on other people's thoughts and feelings rather than his own: "[S]ome people have told me that hiding my eyes makes it easier for them to put themselves in my shoes, so I've kind of stuck with it. I'm a nondescript figure; on some level, I'm a cipher. The thing is: I don't want to emote too much when I draw myself. The stories are about other people, not me. I'd rather emphasise their feelings."

Sacco's words seem to echo McCloud's (1994) theory that we tend to respond in different ways to realistic and cartoonish drawings of faces. He suggests that, while a realistic drawing of a face is seen as the face of a specific "other," simple cartoon faces remind us of the sketchy mind-pictures we use to imagine our own facial expressions as we interact with other people. Thus, cartoon drawings tend to be perceived as a reflection of ourselves, encouraging us to project our own feelings and emotions onto them: "The cartoon is a *vacuum* into which our *identity* and *awareness* are *pulled*. // [. . .] We don't just *observe* the cartoon, we *become* it" (p. 36). By acting as a *cipher* for readers' own thoughts, emotions, and values, simple cartoon figures may thus sometimes provide an ideal object of identification.

Narrative perspective, or point of view, is often believed to play a key role in encouraging or discouraging identification.

Two of the basic distinctions commonly made in this respect are between first- and third-person narration, and between internal and external "focalization," that is, the degree to which readers are allowed inside a character's head and are made aware of his or her thoughts, perceptions, and emotions (Genette 1980). It is commonly assumed that a first-person narration creates a stronger sense of closeness, naturalness and trustworthiness than a third-person narration, because in the former the reader seems to have a more direct access to the character's thoughts and emotions (Abbott 2002). Similarly, internal focalization is thought to encourage readers to understand and sympathize more with a character. Although a small number of autobiographical comic books, such as *Years of the Elephant*, have no diegetic narration at all, the overwhelming majority use first-person narration. Focalization may be through a former or current self and be more or less revelatory in terms of inner thoughts and feelings.

In comics, the concept of narrative perspective acquires a visual dimension as well. Social semioticians believe there are several ways of establishing a contact between the viewer of an image and the depicted persons (Kress and van Leeuwen 1996: 119–58). These authors claim that in pictures, as in real life, distance reflects the quality of the relationship. A close-up thus suggests an intimate relation, while a medium shot from the knees or waist upwards implies a certain distancing. A long shot may suggest either an impersonal or a completely distant relationship, depending on how far away the depicted person appears to be from the viewer. Where there is apparent "eye-contact" between a depicted character and the viewer, the former seems to be "demanding" something of the latter, whereas lack of eye contact invites detached scrutiny. The vertical angle of images is seen by these authors to encode power relationships: regarding people from above gives the viewer a symbolic power over them, an eye-level view suggests an equal relationship, and a low angle makes the depicted person appear more powerful. A horizontal angle, finally, is thought to indicate the degree of involvement a viewer is invited to feel with a person in an image, with a full frontal view indicating a maximum degree of involvement, and a profile view "from the sidelines" suggesting a sense of detachment. Characters may also be shown from behind, which, according to Messaris (1997), can either indicate complete detachment or else invite identification.

In the scene mentioned above (see Fig. 5.3), the author's cartoon alter ego, Joe, is shown at eye-level and from a slight distance in the first panel, but turned fully towards the viewer and facing directly out of the picture. According to Kress and van Leeuwen, this would indicate a relatively impersonal relationship, but one in which viewers are invited to engage with the implicit demands being made of them by the depicted person. In this case, the nature of the demand, namely for the reader to identify with Joe, is specified verbally. In the second panel we see him peering out from behind Neven's back. Neven and his warrior friends are shown from a low angle, which makes them appear powerful and imposing to the viewer, and, by implication, to Joe as well. The third panel offers us an oblique view of him, as he turns towards the disembodied voices in the dark space behind his back, a worried look on his face.

Writing about self-portraits, Cumming (2009: 26) argues that a fully frontal view of someone looking out at the viewer with a sharp, expectant gaze is the visual equivalent of direct address in written language, inviting "the purest form of reciprocity." The profile, by contrast, puts the self-portrait "straight into the third person" (p. 38), particularly when there is no eye contact between the viewer and the viewed. It is more difficult to find the equivalent of a first-person point of view in visual forms of storytelling, since readers are continually being made aware of the presence of another person. This, Hatfield (2005: 117) argues, militates against "a thoroughgoing identification of observer and observed": "While the written text in a comic may confide in the reader much like unaccompanied, first-person prose, the graphic presence of the image at once distances and inflects the autobiographer's voice. Whereas first-person prose invites complicity, cartooning invites scrutiny."

Hatfield is certainly correct in his observation that readers of comics are always aware of the embodied presence of the autobiographer, but I believe that this does not necessarily discourage readers from identifying with him or her. Identification is not ruled out by the visual presence of another person, provided that readers are able to recognize some form of commonality between that person and themselves, or to project their own qualities and values onto the cartoon character. In the example mentioned above the visual relationship between the reader and Joe is perhaps best described as one that oscillates constantly between an awareness of his "third person-ness" and a certain willingness to identify with his point of view.

An important visual means by which comics artists can suggest to their readers who is the most important character in the narrative and with whom they should identify is through what Smith (1995: 142) calls *spatial attachment*, "the way a narration may follow the spatio-temporal path of a particular character throughout the narrative, or divide its attention among many characters each tracing distinct spatio-temporal paths." If a graphic narrative follows the autobiographical protagonist around, showing all the events, people, and places as she experiences them, the reader is probably more likely to align with her perspective rather than that of the other characters.

Another way of inviting identification is by showing a character from behind or over the shoulder, which seems to offer the reader the opportunity to see the world through his eyes (Saraceni 2003). As a sequential medium, comics can also make use of what in film is called an "eyeline match," where "shot A presents someone looking at something offscreen; shot B shows us what is being looked at. In neither shot are *both* looker and object present" (Bordwell and Thompson 1993: 265). This type of point-of-view shot, according to van Leeuwen (1996: 88), "has a particularly strong 'subjective' flavor, because it allows the viewer to come face to face with both the reactor and the phenomenon." If the comics panel is regarded as the equivalent of a cinematic shot, then eyeline match occurs when a character is shown looking at something or someone outside the panel frame and the next panel reveals the object of his or her gaze.

An example of this strategy can be found in the scene from Frederik Peeters (2008) *Blue Pills*, which captures the moment in which the autobiographical protagonist is told by his new girlfriend, Cati, that she is HIV positive (see Chapter 3, Fig. 3.2). The first panel shows Frederik looking directly out of the frame, and the following panel contains an extreme close-up view of Cati's eyes, suggesting that they are gazing into each other's eyes.

When long sequences of events are shown from a point of view that coincides completely with that of the autobiographical protagonist, the sense of identification may be particularly strong. In Frédéric Boilet's (2001) *L'épinard de Yukiko*, for instance, large sections are drawn entirely from the autobiographical protagonist's perspective, so that only those of his body parts are visible that he himself would be able to see, such as his hands and feet (see Chapter 2, Fig. 2.7). However, if readers balk at the way Yukiko's body is objectified and feel no sense of commonality with Frédéric, they may well refuse to adopt the position they are being offered.

Showing the dreams, fantasies, memories, or inner experiences of autobiographical characters may also encourage reader identification. In *Cuckoo*, for instance, Madison Clell (2002) tries to make her readers understand what it feels like to suffer from Dissociative Identity Disorder by depicting herself with distinct physical identities (see Chapter 2, Fig. 2.5). The passages in Linthout's (2004) *Years of the Elephant* in which the chalk outline of Sam's body comes alive and accompanies his father to the movies and the restaurant can also be seen as an explicit invitation to the reader to enter into Charles's mind and imagine the emotional turmoil he is experiencing.

In the eighty-five graphic memoirs I consider in this book, there is one example of an autobiographical comic in which the "first-person" narration is maintained visually throughout the whole story: Danny Gregory's (2003) *Everyday Matters*, in which the author describes how he turned to drawing as a form of therapy after his wife's horrific accident, contains not a single self-portrait. Instead, it uses Danny's increasingly accomplished drawings of

FIG. 5.4 Chester Brown (1994) *I Never Liked You*, p. 53.
Copyright © 1994, 2007 Chester Brown.

his family, his dog, and hundreds of everyday objects to shows his gradual recovery from the trauma and his reengagement with the world around him (see Chapter 1, Fig. 1.3). The reader thus has no other option but to enter into Danny's mind and share his emotional and artistic journey.

While the graphic memoirs discussed so far tend to encourage reader identification, some comics creators aim at maintaining a sense of distance between the reader and the autobiographical protagonist. *I Never Liked You* (1994), by Chester Brown, offers an account of an awkward and painful adolescence. In one key scene we see Chester and his younger brother watching television in the living room (see Fig. 5.4). In the first panel they are depicted from a considerable distance and from a high, oblique angle, which creates a sense of emotional disengagement. In the second panel, we have moved in closer, and the brothers' faces are now clearly visible from an angle that is almost fully frontal and at eye-level. However, their faces are so blank and expressionless that we have no idea whether they have even heard their mother telling them to get ready for church. We then follow the obedient younger brother as he climbs the stairs to his bedroom, gets changed, and goes down to join his father, who is already waiting in the car (pp. 53–55). Meanwhile, the dialogue from the "off" between Chester and his mother indicates a vociferous argument over what is or is not appropriate for him to wear to church. The sequence ends with five panels showing, from an extreme long shot view and high angle, the car parked in front of the family house, the tiny figures of Chester and his mother emerging from the house and getting into the car, and the car finally leaving (pp. 56–57). As the narrator informs the reader in a text box stretching over three of these final panels: "Every Sunday was the same. // I'd drive my mother close to tears of exasperation . . . // . . . and would then change into my Sunday clothes" (p. 56).

As the reader gradually discovers over the course of the story, Chester's mother has severe mental health problems, which finally result in her being hospitalized and succumbing to the illness. On the few occasions that Chester visits her in the hospital, he desperately wants to tell her that he loves her, but he can never quite get himself to say so. The sense of emotional distance the artist has created in the scene above may thus be interpreted as a sign of how sad and ashamed he feels about the way he treated his mother when she was still alive. The way the events are represented indicate that Brown does not want to be too closely associated with his own former self, and that he certainly does not want his readers to identify with the young Chester. Instead, any feelings of affiliation are likely to be directed at other family members, or, perhaps, at the adult narrator, whose words implicitly convey something of the shame and regret he now feels about such episodes.[8]

Empathy

In the vernacular, identification and empathy are often used as (near-)synonyms, but, though they are related, they actually describe distinct forms of reader affiliation with characters in a story. The term "empathy" entered the English language in the early twentieth century as a translation of the German word *Einfühlung* (from *ein*, "in" or "into," and *Fühlung*, "feeling"). It is defined by Keen (2006: 208) as "a vicarious, spontaneous sharing of affect," in which "we feel what we believe to be the emotions of others."[9] The central mechanism involved in empathy can be described in the following way: Witnessing the behavior of another person—whether in real life or in a story—we imaginatively project ourselves into their situation, consider what emotions they are likely to be experiencing, and then experience similar emotions ourselves.

Since empathy is only possible if we are able to make an informed guess about what is going on in another person's head, it is closely related to mind-reading, also sometimes referred to as "theory of mind." This describes the human tendency and innate capacity to attribute to ourselves and others a particular mental state, such as thoughts, feelings, beliefs, dreams, imaginings, and desires, on the basis of observable behavior (Zunshine 2006: 6). Our mind-reading capacity and propensity to empathize are believed to have evolved gradually as humans began to live in ever-larger social groups and to face the increasingly pressing need to be able to understand, predict, and manipulate the behavior of others. These skills are seriously impaired in the case of autism (Baron-Cohen 1995), but even normally functioning individuals often make mistakes in their attributions of states of mind, both with regard to other people and themselves.[10]

In recent years, cognitive narratologists have tried to apply these findings to the reading process. They believe that literature, and the novel in particular, exercises our theory of mind mechanisms: "Just as in real life the individual constructs the minds of others from their behavior and speech, so the reader infers the workings of fictional minds and sees these minds in action from observation of characters' behavior and speech" (Palmer 2004: 11). If we believe we can understand the thoughts and feelings of the characters in a literary text, we are also more likely to empathize with them.

Although, in real-life situations, humans, like other primates, tend to empathize more with those they perceive to be members of their in-group, this association does not necessarily apply to the reading process. Indeed, for many readers, the joy of reading literature consists precisely in the opportunity it offers them to enter into another world and experience lives radically different from their own: "Readers can be strongly fascinated by characters and worlds that are unfamiliar to them, be they strange, exotic, horrible, or simply unknown" (Andringa 2004: 210). In contrast to identification, empathy thus does not depend upon the presence of a sense of commonality between the reader and the protagonist of a graphic memoir.

Empirical research suggests that the links between empathy and particular formal or narrative strategies are complex and dependent on context, as well as varying from one group of readers to another (Bourg 1996; Van Peer and Pander Maat 1996). It is not clear, for instance, whether *true*, autobiographical writing is more apt to encourage empathy than fiction, or vice versa. Keen (2006: 220) believes that a text's fictionality may unleash readers' emotional responsiveness "by releasing readers from the obligations of self-protection through skepticism and suspicion," but, at least for some readers, the supposedly more authentic nature of biography or autobiography may well be more conducive to an empathic response than "mere" fiction.

The most obvious difference between prose narratives and graphic narratives is that, in the case of the latter, the information the reader receives about a character's behavior and the situational context is presented to us mainly in a visual form. Particularly in the case of comics that contain little or no diegetic narration, readers must use all the available evidence provided by the pictures and the dialogue in order to hypothesize as to the emotions the characters are experiencing. In the case of Linthout's (2004) *Years of the Elephant*, for instance, readers must build up their own understanding of the protagonist's thoughts and emotions based on the behavior, utterances, body language, and, perhaps most importantly, the facial expressions of his cartoon alter ego.

When comics characters are frequently shown in a way that allows details of their facial expressions to be perceived, this probably encourages reader empathy. Charles Darwin (1998 [1872]) was the first to speculate that there may be a universal basis to our recognition of other people's emotions. He suggested that there is remarkable uniformity in the way particular states of mind are expressed throughout the world and that emotions and their expression are biologically innate and universal. It was not until the 1970s that Darwin's theories were tested in a series of experiments by evolutionary psychologist Paul Ekman (1971, 1987) and his associates. Using a set of photographs that were shown to people from a wide range of cultures, Ekman identified a limited number of basic human emotions—happiness, sadness, anger, disgust, fear, and surprise—which are apparently universally associated with the same distinctive physiological signals and facial expressions. "[I]t is not plausible for there to be such high agreement in so many different countries if expressions are not universal," Ekman (1999: 305) concludes. He believes that such basic emotions must be necessary for dealing with fundamental life tasks, such as recognizing whether another person is likely to be a threat to us or not.[11]

Curiosity and social necessity thus compel us to try, as best we can, to interpret other people's facial expressions, by drawing on our imagination and our knowledge of personalities and contexts. In our urge to look each other in the face, Cole (1998: 202) suggests, "is revealed our innate desire to enter into other minds, and our intense social being." By exploring the experiences of individuals who, for various reasons, cannot control their facial muscles or who are unable to recognize other people's expressions, he shows how the inability to participate fully in "facial conversations" (p. 183) can lead to difficulties not only in empathizing with others but also in experiencing and controlling one's own emotions.[12]

The fact that Ekman and others were able to demonstrate the universality of the signals and physiology of the basic emotions using photographs of human faces indicates that pictures, too, apparently appeal to the same instinctual urge to try and understand what others are like and what they may be thinking and feeling.[13] Will Eisner (1985: 100–121) is convinced that our ability and desire to read other people's emotional states from their facial expressions and body language lie at the very heart of the art of cartooning. Tan (2001) agrees; drawing on Ekman's theories, he suggests that conventional adventure comics tend to use simple and highly exaggerated facial expressions to convey the universally recognizable basic emotions, which makes them transparent to readers of all ages and levels of literacy (see also Forceville 2005). However, the faces of the characters in graphic novels, he argues, typically reflect more complex and ambiguous feelings, which require a higher level of interpretative work by the reader. In graphic memoirs, it is possible to find examples of drawings indicating basic emotions as well as some showing facial expressions that are more subtle and harder to interpret.[14]

Charles's facial expressions and body language in *Years of the Elephant* convey both types of emotion. In the drawings in panels 1/1, 1/2 and 2/1 (see Fig. 5.2), for example, it is not hard for readers to recognize his fury and, consequently, to empathize with this emotion. Charles's expressions in panels 2/2 and 3/1 are more difficult to decipher; they could be described, for instance, as vacillating somewhere between anger, grief, dismay, and confusion. The face of Chester in *I Never Liked You* (see Fig. 5.4), by contrast, is depicted throughout the book with such vacant expressions that we really have no idea what he might be thinking and feelings. As I suggested above, this has the effect of creating the feeling of an insurmountable distance between readers and the protagonist.

A similar example may be found in David Small's *Stitches: A Memoir* (2009), in which the renowned children's book illustrator describes growing up in America in the 1950s as the son of emotionally withdrawn and deeply unhappy parents who are incapable of giving their two sons the love and affection they crave. Throughout the book, David's mother and father, as well as his elder brother and maternal grandparents, are consistently represented with impassive, mask-like faces, an effect achieved in part through the fact that their eyes are almost always obscured by spectacles. This makes their emotional states difficult to fathom, both for the reader, and, by implication, for David as well. Thus the artist suggests that it was the parents who originally blocked the flow of empathy.

As a child, David is shown to be highly expressive, but in the later sections of the book he is drawn as a sullen and defensive adolescent, who hides his pain and confusion behind a constant scowl (see Chapter 2, Fig. 2.6). By this point in his life, David has clearly been conditioned by his upbringing into hiding his feelings, just as the rest of his family does. If Cole (1998) is correct in his assumption that people who are prevented from participating fully in "facial conversations" with those around them are likely to find it hard to empathize with others, then it is little wonder that David is utterly baffled by his parents' fluctuating moods. There are only one or two significant moments in the story when the masks slip a little. When David visits his dying mother in the hospital, for instance, her eyes are, for once, shown to be clearly visible behind her glasses (*Stitches*, pp. 304–7). She has a tube down her throat that prevents her from speaking, but she gives David a look that seems to express a profound sadness, or perhaps remorse, and there are tears in her eyes. For readers, who, up until this moment, have been deprived of information about her emotional state, this image is moving, almost shocking, as it suddenly demands their understanding for a hitherto remote and unsympathetic character.

Unlike identification, empathy thus does not require the reader to share any characteristics, values, or goals with the character. Writing about empathy in relation to art, Bennett (2005: 10) describes the emphatic response as being grounded "not in affinity (*feeling for* another insofar as we can imagine *being* that other) but on a *feeling for* another that entails an encounter with something irreducible and different, often inaccessible." Empathy may, therefore, play an important role in teaching us to view situations from other people's point of view and to respond with respect and understanding to the feelings of people whose experiences and outlook may be very different from our own.

However, sometimes a character in a story seems so alien to us that we are unable to fathom what he is thinking and feeling. In those cases where it was not the author's intention to create a deliberate sense of estrangement between readers and characters, a failure to empathize can be described as a failure of the imagination. Another limitation that has been identified in relation to empathy is that it may lead some people to ignore the social, cultural, and historical specificity of experience and emotion. As I will argue in the following section, the alleged "universalizing tendencies" (Keen 2007: 57) of empathy have led some critics to view all emotional responses to literary characters with deep suspicion.

Strategies for inviting both involvement and affiliation

Throughout this chapter, I have used the term "involvement" to refer to the active participation of the reader in constructing a meaningful narrative out of incomplete information, and "affiliation" to describe the act of connecting emotionally with characters in the story. Involvement and affiliation thus describe two different ways in which graphic memoirists can engage their readers. It is perfectly possible, for instance, for some autobiographical comics to involve readers without necessarily inviting empathy or identification with their protagonists (or, indeed, with any of the characters). A good example of this is Chester Brown's (1994) *I Never Liked You*, which, as I argued above, seems to create quite deliberately a sense of distance between the reader and the main protagonists, while nevertheless requiring the reader's cooperation in the process of creating a coherent narrative out of the individual panels. In the eyes of some critics, involvement and affiliation are so utterly different as to be almost mutually exclusive. They worry that a feeling response conflicts with rational aims, encouraging readers to wallow in sentiment instead of engaging critically with the contents of a text. Many human rights activists, for instance, roundly reject the "neoliberal" agenda of trying, through narrative, to evoke empathetic identification (Gilmore 2011: 157), arguing that rights activism should, instead, target "structural inequalities and formations of exploitation within and across nations" (Smith 2011: 65).

In the last century, this suspicion of sentiment and feeling was expressed strongly through the writings and plays of Bertolt Brecht, whose legacy can still be felt in Marxist-Leninist-inspired postcolonial theory. In Brecht's (1978) opinion, traditional theatrical forms encourage the audience to enter into a sort of unchallenging, hypnotic trance, an absorbed suspension of disbelief based on their complete identification with a character, to the point of giving up their own identity. Brecht railed against what he called "emotional infection," a crude form of empathy that involves "the automatic transfer of emotions to the spectator" (p. 94) and that prevents critical reasoning, that is, the recognition of the social and historical specificity of all experience. In order to counteract such tendencies, he advocated the use of various "alienation effects," which shatter the illusion of reality through experimental staging techniques (see Chapter 4).

Although Brecht's theories continue to influence literary criticism, many contemporary scholars roundly reject his central assumption that critical reasoning and affect are contradictory forms of reader engagement. As Keen (2007: 28) points out, emotional engagement with characters in a story necessarily engages both emotion and cognition: "when texts invite readers to feel . . . they also stimulate readers' thinking." Empathy, in particular, is often only possible if readers are prepared to recognize the validity of the experiences and emotions of characters who may be very different from themselves. This may actually *encourage* critical thinking. Conversely, the cognitive participation of the reader in the construction of a narrative may open the way for the emotional engagement with characters.

As was pointed out above, many of the inherent features of comics, such as the gaps between panels and the semiotic tensions between words and images, work to encourage the critical mental involvement of the audience; they can thus be described as a type of "estrangement effect" built into the very structures of the comics medium. However, these effects do not rule out the simultaneous engagement of the reader's emotions. *Years of the Elephant*, for example, uses an extremely elliptic style, while also inviting the reader's empathic identification with the autobiographical protagonist. Indeed, Whitlock (2006) believes that it is precisely the effort involved on the part of the comics reader in looking for closure that encourages a sense of affective engagement with characters who are fundamentally "other," even across deep social and cultural divides.[15]

While I agree with Whitlock's argument in principle, I believe that the inherent "gappiness" of the comics medium is not a sufficient explanation for the emotional association with the protagonists that some (but by no means all) autobiographical comics appear to invite. Instead, I argue, it is the frequent use by graphic memoirists of such rhetorical strategies as metaphor, humor, and intertexuality, which simultaneously demand the readers' active, critical co-operation and their empathic engagement, and which may thus account for the success of some autobiographical comics in evoking both involvement *and* affiliation.

Metaphor

It is striking how many different metaphors—verbal, visual, and verbo-visual—are used in graphic memoirs. Kukkonen (2008: 95) believes that comics artists use metaphor "to bring multi-layered connections and a literary complexity to narrative." In autobiographical comics, metaphors also fulfill the important function of enabling readers to draw on their own embodied experience in order to imagine the thoughts, sensations, and emotions of the characters in a story.

According to conceptual metaphor theory, metaphor is not merely "special," poetic, or rhetorical language. Rather, it is a fundamental property of human thought, which allows us to understand areas of experience that go beyond our immediate, physical experience in terms of something more concrete and embodied (Kövecses 2000; Lakoff and Johnson 1980; Lakoff and Johnson 1999). The embodied nature of metaphor suggests that many of the most basic, "primary" metaphors are understood intuitively, often at the level of unconscious or barely conscious thought processes. For example, since we all feel hot as a result of physical exertion or excitement, metaphors that express emotional intensity in terms of heat (e.g., "I'm *boiling* with anger") seem entirely natural to us (Kövecsec 2005: 18). Similarly, the conceptual metaphor TIME PASSING IS MOTION, which is realized in such common expressions as "we're *approaching* the end of the year," is likely to be founded on the universal experience of a connection between our movement through space and the passing of time (Lakoff 1993: 217).

While such primary metaphors are thought to be universal, they can be combined to form more complex connections between different areas of experience. Poets, in particular, are often able to find fresh, idiosyncratic extensions, formulations, or combinations of the entrenched metaphorical mappings that underlie our everyday language, thereby guiding us beyond their "automatic and unconscious everyday use" (Lakoff and Turner 1989: 72). When, for example, Hamlet considers his own death in terms of sleeping ("To sleep? Perchance to dream!"), William Shakespeare can be said to be using a very conventional metaphor but extending it to include the concept of death as a form of nightmare (p. 67). Lakoff and Turner have since been criticized for ignoring the existence of metaphors based on entirely novel connections between different areas of experience and for paying too little attention to linguistic and textual dimensions of metaphor creativity. Metaphorical creativity, Semino (2008: 54) argues, "needs to be considered both in terms of the novelty or otherwise of underlying conceptual mappings, and in terms of the salience and originality of individual metaphorical choices and patterns." Many literary texts, she suggests, contain "strikingly novel and arresting metaphors," which are used to express "otherwise 'ineffable' subjective experiences" (p. 38; see also Crisp 2003).

I believe that the novelty of metaphors can also relate to the semiotic modes in which they are represented. Visual metaphors, for instance, are often more specific than their verbal counterparts, capturing nuances of meaning that would be hard to convey through language and often evoking profound emotional responses (El Refaie 2003; Forceville and Urios-Aparisi 2009). Certainly many of the visual and multimodal metaphors in the eighty-five graphic memoirs I consider in this book are extremely creative. They often convey complex abstract thoughts and emotions that would be impossible to represent in any other mode or form. Such metaphors are by their very nature open to more than one interpretation, which makes their use more "risky" for authors, but also potentially more interesting for readers.

Years of the Elephant (see Fig. 5.2) uses a wide range of metaphors to describe the various stages of bereavement Charles experiences in the course of the book. His initial inability to accept the reality of his son's death and his fixation on various symbolic substitutes for his actual presence, for instance, are typical of the initial stages of mourning. In addition to the chalk outline of his son's fallen body, Charles becomes obsessed with the portable apparatus prescribed to help him breathe properly during the night, as he imagines he can hear the boy's voice through the irregular clicking noises it produces. When he puts it on, its mask and trunk-like tube make him look like an elephant, which suggests how out of place he feels in his everyday surroundings, as well as alluding to the reputed ability of elephants to remember their dead. This metaphor is entirely original, not only in terms of its underlying conceptual mappings but also in the salience and novelty of its visual form of

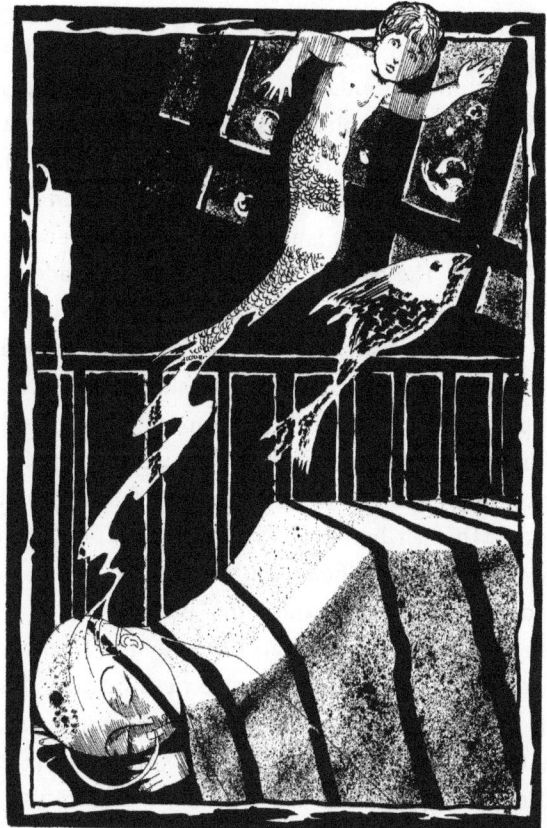

FIG. 5.5 Al Davison (1990) *The Spiral Cage*, no pagination.
Copyright © 1990 Al Davison.

expression. Toward the end of the book, Charles's sense of isolation from his wife is translated into the visual metaphor of a deep
chasm that has opened in the ground, dividing the flat into two separate spaces (pp. 143–45 and pp. 150–51). In this case, the underlying analogy between physical separation and emotional distance is
quite conventional, but its translation into a concrete, visual image
renders it novel and captivating.

My second example of the use of an original metaphor in a
graphic novel is drawn from Al Davison's (1990) *The Spiral Cage*.

Due to a serious medical condition, the young Al is bed-ridden for much of his childhood, and he creates a whole fantasy world for himself in which he embodies several heroic characters, including Superman, Batman, and a pirate, as well as more ambiguous figures such as a scarecrow and Frankenstein's monster. In one such scene, the boy is shown lying in a hospital cot, with a tube in his nose and a shaven head, indicating he is recovering from yet another operation (see Fig. 5.5). The bars of the cot cast deep shadows over his body, reinforcing the sense he is trapped in a cage. In his dreams, he becomes a boy with a fish's tail, who, on the pages following, leaps out of the water and turns joyful somersaults in the sky. However, as the sleeping child becomes dimly aware of the nurses discussing him and his strange habit of giggling and laughing all night, the mermaid boy suddenly realizes he cannot fly and falls, Icarus-like, back into the water. The half-human, half-fish creature is an apt metaphor for Al's condition, spina bifida, which renders him paralyzed from the waist down. The way in which this image is used in the story also suggests that it is not inevitable that someone with a physical impairment be a despondent and passive victim; rather, it is society's view of disability as something that utterly defines and constrains an individual that is truly "dis-abling" (see also McIlvenny 2002).

In order to access all the different levels of meaning that this one verbo-visual metaphor evokes, readers are invited to enter into the boy's mind and imagine what his thoughts and feelings might be at that moment. Each individual's interpretation of this scene is thus likely to be subtly or even quite dramatically different from the one I offered above. It is this active process of interpreting metaphorical meaning that makes some graphic memoirs so captivating for their readers, inviting both their active cooperation in constructing meaning and their emotional engagement with the protagonists.

Humor

As I pointed out in Chapter 1, the comics medium used to be closely associated with juvenile and often rather crass forms of humor.

Therefore, some readers are likely to approach any text produced in this medium with the expectation that it will be overtly humorous. Although many autobiographical comics are, indeed, at least somewhat amusing, their humor can take many different forms, with some graphic memoirists using blatant jokes and others relying on self-deprecating humor or subtle irony.

Like metaphor, a joke is a "jointly negotiated communicative accomplishment" (Holmes 2006: 33). The effort required on the part of the reader before they "get" the joke seems to create a strong sense of involvement and satisfaction. It is important to remember, however, that a joke, whether verbal or visual, is never automatically funny. It can be humorous to one person, and utterly unfunny or even offensive to another or indeed to the same person under different circumstances: "what is accepted as a joke, and so funny on that account, has first to be negotiated as a joke" (Pickering and Lockyer 2005: 9; see also El Refaie 2011). For this reason, humor is also an important tool for encouraging reader affiliation with the characters in graphic memoirs, even though it runs the risk of sometimes having the opposite effect.

Since antiquity, people have tried to understand the nature of humor and the function of human laughter (Carrell 2008). One of the earliest attempts to explain humor was the superiority or degradation theory, whose origins can be traced back to ancient Greek philosophy and whose most famous proponent was the seventeenth-century English philosopher Thomas Hobbes. According to his theory, humor is inherently aggressive. It is a hostile response to the weakness, deformity, or misfortune of others, which makes us feel a pleasant, laughter-inducing sense of "sudden glory" (Hobbes 1840 [1650]). French philosopher Henri Bergson (1911) later extended this idea to account for the beneficial effects of humor as a social corrective. His main argument was that laughter discourages the rigid or mechanical—and thus socially maladjusted—behavior of individuals and that laughter is incompatible with feelings of sympathy or pity, requiring, as he put it, "a momentary anaesthesia of the heart" (p. 5). Such aggressive forms of humor directed either at individuals or particular groups of people are often used to create a sense of *us* and *them* and sometimes even to encourage bigotry and racism (Billig 2005). Cartooning and caricature, with their "severe distortion of proportions" (Kennedy, Green and Vervaeke 1993: 253), lend themselves particularly well to derogatory humor of this kind.

There are certainly many examples of cruel mockery in graphic memoirs, most notably in the work of Robert Crumb (1998a and b) and that of Spain Rodriguez (1994). Readers who dislike this form of humor are unlikely to get very involved with the narrative or to identify with the protagonist. However, in the vast majority of graphic memoirs, much of the mockery is reserved for the autobiographical protagonist him- or herself. Joe Sacco, for instance, often presents his alter ego as a rather feeble and odd-looking "innocent abroad," who is easily taken in by the many unscrupulous characters around him (see Fig. 5.3). Peter Kuper's "unauthorized autobiography," *Stripped* (1995), employs a whole range of outrageous images to portray his own physical and sexual shortcomings as a teenager and young adult, drawing himself as a doormat, a spinning top, a worm, and a rabbit, for instance (see Chapter 2, Fig. 2.2). *Walking the Dog* (2009), by David Hughes, provides another example of the self-mockery that is so common to this genre.

In the final section of one of the book's double-page spreads, for instance, we see a typical example of one of David and Dexter's daily walks (see Fig. 5.6). The reader follows the pair as they slowly wind their way down the page, with David muttering to himself about all the people and institutions that, for whatever reason, arouse his fury. Each of the twenty-four panels shows David trudging along in a coat, hat, and thick-soled boots. His head gradually increases in size and his face becomes more and more bristly, until, in the final panel, it has acquired monstrous qualities. His swearing also increases in intensity and venom, reaching a final crescendo of profanities in the last three panels. Dexter, meanwhile, is having a wonderful time, happily engaged in those apparently pointless activities that dogs enjoy. Having ignored each other completely during the

FIG. 5.6 David Hughes (2009) *Walking the Dog*, no pagination (excerpt). Copyright © 2009 David Hughes.

whole walk, man and dog finally take account of each other in the final panel, with David praising his dog for doing his business and Dexter telling his master off for being so bad-tempered that "even breathing must annoy you."

The artist has thus portrayed himself as a laughable curmudgeon, whose only redeemable feature is his association with the lively, cheerful little dog. Seen from the point of view of superiority theorists, such self-deprecating humor could perhaps be explained as giving Hughes a way of distancing himself from an earlier self-incarnation, or else as a defensive strategy for preempting and thus undermining the effect of the mockery of others. Groensteen (1996) seems to agree with the latter theory when he points out that many autobiographical comics contain traces of the authors' efforts to deflect potential criticism or rejection by their readers, with self-mockery being one of the most common strategies. Indeed, self-deprecatory humor has become such an expected feature of the graphic memoir genre that individual artists who diverge from this convention run the risk of being perceived as pompous or self-satisfied and of losing the reader's sympathy. Self-deprecation can, of course, take various forms, not all of which are likely to strike every reader as funny. In the case of *Walking the Dog*, for instance, responses to the author's humor are likely to be influenced by the individual reader's attitudes towards swearing.

Unlike superiority theory, which is based on the assumption that we all feel a similar derision for other people's misfortunes, a psychoanalytic approach would predict different responses from individual readers, depending on their socio-cultural background and psychological predispositions. According to Sigmund Freud (1976 [1905]), jokes provide us with a release from the constant need to repress our natural aggressive and sexual desires, and are thus experienced as pleasurable. Like dreams, jokes come from the unconscious, but are then transformed into less explicit forms, thereby providing a socially acceptable way of breaking taboos. Freud's theory offers a convincing explanation of why jokes tend to be most abundant in areas where there are social inhibitions, thus providing a mirror for the norms and values operating in a particular culture or social group.

As the example above demonstrates, many areas of life that were completely taboo in Freud's lifetime are now discussed much more openly, at least in some contexts and by some groups of people. Humor relating to various bodily functions is certainly a common feature of many autobiographical comics, particularly those created by artists such as Robert Crumb, Julie Doucet, and Joe Matt, who formed part of the American comix movement or were inspired by it (see Chapter 2). A good example of deliberate irreverence towards taboos is the tongue-in-cheek declaration by Ben Snakepit (2007: 2) that his comics journal *Snake Pit 2007* "is, was, and ever shall be intended to be read on the toilet." By echoing Biblical phraseology while making reference to the toilet, Snakepit is deliberately provocative. The journal contains many references to taboo subjects; for instance, the author often refers to himself as "a lazy piece of shit" and even occasionally uses pictures of excrement to represent himself (e.g., p. 15). Readers who enjoy this form of humor are likely to derive much of their enjoyment from the idea that some sections of society will be shocked by such a flagrant disregard of taboos. They may also feel that they share the author's sense of humor and therefore be more inclined to identify with his cartoon alter ego.

Superiority and release theories are useful in helping to explain the abundance of aggressive and taboo-breaking humor in some graphic memoirs, but they are less applicable to the many instances of gentler forms of verbal and visual humor in this genre. It is this type of humor that incongruity theorists are particularly good at explaining. Like superiority theory, incongruity theory has a long and illustrious history, going back to German philosophers Kant and Schopenhauer, but being most closely associated with the English eighteenth-century philosopher John Locke. According to this theory, humor is said to emerge from the sudden and unexpected "bisociation" of two contrasting frames of reference (Koestler 1976 [1964]: 38). Linguists have applied similar ideas to the analysis of jokes, with Attardo and Raskin (1991: 308) suggesting that their humor always results from the juxtaposition of distinct semantic scripts and the abrupt shift from one to the other: "The punchline triggers the switch from the one script to the other by making the hearer backtrack and realize that a different interpretation was possible from the very beginning." The same basic principles also apply to visual forms of incongruity, which typically involve "an agile or acrobatic type of thinking—a leap, a somersault, a reversal, a sideways jump— where the outcome is unexpected" (McAlhone and Stuart 1996: 15).

In the excerpt mentioned above (see Figure. 5.6), the main joke seems to arise from our sudden perception that the mental script "man walks dog" may in fact not apply in this case, and that "dog walks man" may be the more appropriate interpretation of events. The punch line in the final panel certainly presents the dog as much more civilized than his foul-mouthed and unshaven owner. By juxtaposing his contented little dog, which lives entirely in and for the present moment, and his own bad-tempered self, which is always dwelling on the darkest moments of his past or the most anxiety-provoking thoughts about the future, the author seems to be highlighting a fatal flaw in human nature. If readers are willing and able to understand and appreciate Hughes's sense of humor, this can evoke a strong feeling of mental involvement with the story, as well as encouraging them to imaginatively project themselves into the character of David—or perhaps his little dog.

Cultural allusions and intertextual references

In some graphic memoirs, affective involvement is encouraged by alluding to the cultural knowledge specific to a particular section of society, thereby creating an imagined community of people with a common background and interests. These references are sometimes introduced as an explicit part of the story, or else they may appear in the more implicit form of intertextual references. In its broadest sense, intertextuality describes the way in which the meanings "generated by any one text are determined partly by the meanings of other texts to which it appears similar" (Fiske 1990: 166). For instance, every autobiographical comic will be read and interpreted partly through the prism of the more conventional comics, irrespective of whether there are any explicit references to these texts or not. A more restricted definition of intertextuality refers to the process by which one text *deliberately* points to or bases itself on another, which may be from the same or from a different genre (Cook 2001). As Goddard (1998: 69) argues, in such cases "the second text doesn't have to work so hard—it can take for granted that the original text has left a trace which it can use to its advantage." Readers, however, have to work particularly hard in order to recognize what is being alluded to and then use their knowledge of the original text to understand its meaning and relevance in the new context.

Joe Matt's graphic memoir about his young adulthood, *Peepshow* (1999), contains several references to his fascination with comics and comics artists. In one of the strips (p. 17), Matt imagines receiving an unexpected visit from a pompous and disdainful art critic, who accuses him of producing work that is "extremely derivative of R. Crumb," "legendary, underground cartoonist and creator of such 60's phenomenons as Mr. Natural and Fritz the

Cat!!" When Joe tries to defend himself against the accusation of copying Crumb's work, the art critic presents examples of strikingly similar panels from the comics of the two artists. Just as Joe is about to admit that he is indeed nothing more than a cheap, worthless imitation of the real thing, Robert Crumb himself appears and stabs the critic in the back. He consoles Joe and admits that he, too, was heavily influenced by other artists, including E. C. Segar and Harvey Kurtzman. The figure of Robert Crumb is drawn in a style that clearly echoes that of Crumb's self-portraits in his autobiographical work, and the comic strip ends with him abruptly exiting the comic strip in pursuit of a woman with enormous buttocks and thighs. Those readers familiar with Crumb's work are likely to be amused by this instance of intertextuality and to feel that they belong to a privileged group of people with a superior knowledge of the alternative comics scene. In his work, Joe Matt also often references his friends Chester Brown and Seth, two other Toronto-based comics artists (see also Beaty 2011a).[16]

Musical references often play an important role in graphic memoirs about an author's adolescence or young adulthood. Ariel Schrag's first two installments of her *High School Comic Chronicles* (2008a), for example, contain numerous details about the bands she worships. Similarly, *Smalltown Boy*, by Andreas Michalke (1999), is full of references to punk rock, which the teenager sees as the only means of escaping from his stultifying life in a small North German village in the mid-1980s. In a scene following the narrator's euphoric description of a summer holiday in Miami where he found a vibrant punk scene and a wide range of new bands, he has just returned to the deserted streets of his hometown (see Fig. 5.7). The sense of frustration and claustrophobia engulfing him is conveyed by the way in which the artist draws his younger self against a black background and from many different angles, thus emphasizing the bleakness and loneliness of his surroundings. Snaking its way across seven of the nine panels is a ribbon containing the lyrics of a song entitled "Young Til I Die," by the punk band 7 Seconds. This provides a visual link to the previous page, which shows Andreas at a

FIG. 5.7 Andreas Michalke (1999) *Smalltown Boy*, p. 13 (original with color tint). Copyright © 1994, 1995, 1997, 1998, 1999 Andreas Michalke.

punk concert in Miami and which is similarly overlaid with song lyrics. The words to the song also set the tone for Andreas's nihilist action of kicking the lampposts: "For me the fight has just // begun. You get in clubs, drink alcohol. It makes you feel you're ten feet tall. // I don't wanna grow up, I'm never getting old . . . " While many readers can probably identify to some extent with Andreas's adolescent rebellion, *Smalltown Boy* is likely to resonate even more for anyone who, like Michalke, grew up in a small town in the 1980s, or who is familiar with the punk music to which he refers.

Some graphic memoirs also contain references to objects of "high" culture. Alison Bechdel's *Fun Home*, for instance, is full of explicit allusions and more implicit references to feminist history, lesbian coming-out stories, and literary works, which play a central role in showing Bechdel's complicated love-hate relationship with her father (Brown Spiers 2010; Chute 2006a; Chute 2010: 175–217; Watson 2011). While it is unnecessary to be familiar with every literary work referred to in *Fun Home* in order to enjoy the narrative, the full breadth of intertextual meaning will only be available to the most well-read individuals, thus deepening their sense of involvement with the story and its protagonist. Some readers may discover commonalities between Alison's responses to particular books and their own thoughts and feelings when they read the same books. The intertextual references may thus increase their ability and willingness to identify with Alison's experiences as she grows up.

While some graphic memoirs appear to invite involvement without any emotional engagement with characters, others, particularly those that employ a lot of rhetorical devices, thus often seem to encourage both involvement and affiliation. It is impossible, however, to predict how individual readers will respond to such invitations. The exact ways in which readers of autobiographical comics get involved in the active co-construction of meaning and respond emotionally to the characters in the story could only be uncovered through empirical studies involving comics readers from many different social and cultural backgrounds, and with different levels of experience with the graphic memoir genre.

Conclusion

The goal of this book has been to identify the key formal properties and narrative techniques of a relatively new and flourishing art
form, the graphic memoir. My consideration of eighty-five autobiographical comics from North America and Western Europe
has revealed that individual works differ substantially in terms of
their subject matter, artistic style, and the degree to which they
claim to be "true" to the author's real-life experiences. While some
graphic memoirists focus on the actual, specific experiences they
have had, others use the genre to reflect upon the complex nature
of self-identity and truth, often freely mixing nuggets of fact with
blatant fiction. As comics artist Dennis P. Eichhorn points out in
an introduction to Peter Kuper's (1995: 5) graphic memoir *Stripped*,
"[we] (the autobio bunch) aren't in it for the money. We're doing
it for some hard-to-pin-down reasons that vary widely. Everyone's
motivations are different." Despite these very different motivations,
I have argued, all graphic memoirists must face the same set of fundamental challenges: they must find a way of representing themselves both verbally and visually, address the unique properties of
the human sense of time, try to convey a sense of authenticity, and,
perhaps most importantly, attract and captivate their readers.

As I suggested in the introduction, the coming together of
autobiography and the comics medium has created an opportunity
for scholars to reexamine our understanding of both the nature of
life writing and the way in which people read comics. The graphic
memoir genre has, for example, given new groups of people the

opportunity to tell their life stories to relatively large audiences. Many graphic memoirists are very "ordinary" men and women, who nevertheless have extraordinary tales to tell, for instance, about their experiences of living with a disability, surviving a serious illness, or suffering bereavement. Moreover, some of the works discussed in this book are by teenagers, whose autobiographical work would probably not have reached such a broad public if it had been created in a more conventional medium. Conversely, the comics industry, which has traditionally been dominated by professional male artists, has been opened up to new kinds of creators, including large numbers of women and those with no background in the arts or cartooning at all. The profile of the typical comics reader has also shifted, with more female and older readers showing an interest in graphic memoirs than was previously the case for conventional superhero and adventure comics.

The graphic memoir genre has provided autobiographers with new ways of understanding and representing the nature of the self, while simultaneously pushing the boundaries of the comics medium beyond the established conventions. Firstly, because of their heavy reliance on visual forms of storytelling, graphic memoirs tend to place a lot of emphasis on the importance of the body in constructing and maintaining a person's identity. Self-identity is typically represented as something that is constantly shifting and changing and which often threatens to fracture into multiple parts. Second, the comics medium, with its inherent gaps and tensions, reflects the fluid, partial, inconsistent quality of human conceptions of time. Graphic memoirists are always experimenting with new ways of conveying subjective experiences of the past and their hopes and projections for the future. Third, the use of comics to tell "true" stories from a person's life offers a new perspective on the question of what constitutes authenticity in life writing. Autobiographical comics creators commonly use both verbal and visual strategies to convey their honesty and integrity, for instance, by using either a particularly realistic or a spontaneous drawing style or by including photographic images in their books. They also frequently employ the strategy of "making strange" as a paradoxical form of authentication. Finally, graphic memoirs may open our eyes to the many different ways in which autobiographical writing can encourage the cognitive and emotional engagement of readers with a whole narrative and/or with its protagonists, through the use of multimodal metaphor and humor, for example, or by showing characters in close-up and with clearly discernible facial expressions.

Although my study has allowed me to identify some of the most common formal and stylistic properties of the graphic memoir genre, it must be remembered that comics creators are constantly discovering new ways of conveying their life stories. This is an exciting time for creators and fans of autobiographical comics. On both sides of the Atlantic, established artists are continuing to explore innovative narrative techniques and displaying increasing levels of self-reflexivity in their work. The recent cases of mock and fake graphic memoirs, for instance, suggest that growing numbers of comics creators are experimenting with ways of challenging the notion of autobiographical authenticity and of demolishing the boundaries between truth and fiction. New comics creators from many different social and cultural backgrounds enter the field every year, bringing with them their own specific attitudes and perspectives. Future years are likely to see a flowering of the graphic memoir genre in other regions of the world as well, which will doubtlessly lead to a further outpouring of artistic innovations.

Although there is some groundbreaking work on superhero comics fans by Barker (1989; 1993), Brown (2001), and Gibson (2003), for example, the readers of graphic memoirs have so far not received much attention from the academic community.[1] It is still unclear, for instance, who is attracted to autobiographical comics and what functions such stories perform for their readers. We also do not know for sure why women are apparently more interested in graphic memoirs than in traditional comics. Although I frequently referenced the reader's active role in co-constructing the meaning of autobiographical comics in this book, these claims are still largely speculative. The processes that are implicated in the construction and interpretation of meaning could only be clearly revealed through empirical studies involving a representative cross-section of comics readers. These and other fascinating questions raised by the graphic memoir genre should keep comics scholars as well as narrative, literary, media, and cultural theorists busy for many decades to come.

Notes

Introduction

1. The term was introduced in the mid-1980s by the publishing industry as part of a large PR campaign aimed at nurturing the concept of a "new breed" of adult comics. The exact origins of the term are somewhat controversial, but it seems to have been around since at least the mid-1960s, when it was used by American comics critic and magazine editor Richard Kyle (Gravett 2005: 8). Other comics scholars (e.g., Saraceni 2003; Weiner 2003) credit Will Eisner, who used it in the late 1970s as a subtitle for a collection of short stories, with the invention of the term.

2. Hillary Chute (2008; 2010) prefers the broader term "graphic narrative." The epithet "graphic" may be considered particularly apt, since many of the works it is used to describe also involve the "graphic" in the sense of explicit images of bodies involved in violent or sexual acts.

3. Two of the comics creators whose work I consider, Marjane Satrapi and Pasua Bashi, were born in Iran but now live in Western Europe. When discussing comics written originally in French, German, or Spanish, I have always used the English edition whenever available. Otherwise, all translations from the original languages are my own.

Chapter 1

1. For a perceptive analysis of reader expectations vis-à-vis the modern memoir, see Miller (2007).

2. Chute (2010: 109) discusses the same example, suggesting that the considerable amount of time that has apparently passed between the first and the second panel highlights the meaning of both fiction and autobiography "as

the material process of making." Other critical commentaries on *One! Hundred! Demons!* can be found in De Jesus (2004) and Tensuan (2006).

3. Gilmore (2001: 2) suggests that this tradition was, in fact, "never as coherent as it could be made to appear, its canonical texts formally unstable and decidedly multivoiced, and its variety as much a critique, parody, or mimicry of the Western self as evidence of it."

4. Hartmann (2002: 10) believes that the inflation of autobiographical writing in recent years may be related to the disruptive influences of increased mobility, with many people being inspired to write their life stories by the experience of displacement and Diaspora or of living among strangers: "Facing that strangeness in others, we become more aware of the other in ourselves: of what within remains ambivalent, unintegrated, in between." See Gilmore (2001: 16–19) for an alternative explanation for the current boom in life writing.

5. According to Kerby (1991: 42) there are limits to the autobiographer's freedom to (re-)interpret the facts of his or her past. Although a person's life is itself "quasi-narrative" in the sense that experience is always already caught up in story, it nevertheless serves "as a corrective or guide for the act of narration. One cannot just tell any old story without committing some form of injustice to the content of one's experience—what Sartre called 'bad faith.'" The truthfulness of an autobiographical narrative cannot, therefore, be measured against the meaning of pre-narrative experience, but it *is* possible to compare alternative interpretations of that experience and to judge their relative adequacy and aptness.

6. Although some comics have been described as "wordless," it is in fact rare to find examples of the medium where language does not play any role at all (Beronä 2001). Catherine Doherty's (2000) *Can of Worms*, for instance, does not contain any dialogue or narrative voice, but the pictures contain words that indicate sounds or actions in the storyworld (e.g., the "click" of a key unlocking the door, and the "slap" of a hand switching off the alarm clock; [see Chapter 3, Fig. 3.6]), form part of the landscape of the storyworld (e.g., names on shop fronts and street signs), or make up the carefully transcribed documents Doherty includes in her comic book.

7. Similar taxonomies of possible word-image relations have been developed in relation to children's picture books (Nikolajeva and Scott 2000; Moya Guijarro and Pinar Sanz 2009).

8. Will Eisner is famous for the spectacular splash pages he created for his *Spirit* stories, where the titles form an integral part of the pictorial landscape (Harvey 1996: 80–85).

9. Lefèvre (2000) provides an overview of the different comics formats that exist, including temporal aspects such as the frequency of publication in the case of serial publications, and the impact these can have on reader expectations and manners of consumption. Rota (2004) argues that differences in the standard

formats in France and Italy, for instance, become highly relevant when a comic book is translated.

10. While Barry's work calls attention to its hand-crafted, artisanal quality, Chute (2010: 113) argues, it is also "powerfully invested in its own populism," embracing the "low" cultural status of the mass-produced comics medium.

11. The German-speaking countries, by contrast, have had a much less tolerant attitude towards comics since World War II (Jovanomic and Koch 1999).

12. A good example of this in the UK is *Viz*, which provides deliberately crude and offensive adult humour by parodying the strait-laced British comics of the post-war period. It was first published in 1979 by a young man from Newcastle from his parents' home, and it achieved huge success from the mid-1980s to the mid-1990s, although sales have dropped off sharply since.

13. As Drucker (2008) points out, technical innovations have had a big impact on the work of comics artists, with the invention of digital front-end offset in particular offering artists a vastly increased range of creative options.

14. According to Beaty (2007), many comics creators in the European independent sector aim to make what was traditionally considered a popular medium "un-popular" in order to bring it into the realm of high culture. The current attempts by the larger publishers to bring the most successful of the small-press cartoonists under their umbrella are regarded with suspicion, as they seem to entail "the constant threat of co-optation or, worse, 'selling out'" (p. 180).

15. There are estimates that women make up only five to ten per cent of superhero comics fans in the U.S., but Healey (2009) points out that the most recent figures available appear to be from the 1990s, and she complains that female fans are often ignored by both the industry and academia. It is also difficult to obtain reliable figures regarding the readership of autobiographical comics, although, judging from personal conversations with people working in the industry, the general assumption is that more women are drawn to this genre than to conventional comic books.

16. Gardner (2008) cites the recently rediscovered work of Japanese American Henry Yoshitaka Kiyama, who depicted scenes from his life and that of three friends in San Francisco in the early twentieth century, as one of the earliest known examples of the genre. Mckinney (2011) has discovered a more troubling precursor of the graphic memoir: in the early 1960s, Coral (born Laroque Letour), who was a member of the OAS ("organisation de l'armée secrète"), a French far-right nationalist underground organization during the Algerian War, created a number of comics journals while serving time for his illegal activities. The journals consist of individual newspaper cartoon-like drawings and longer narrative sections on life in prison and events in France and Algeria. Many of the cartoons reflect Coral's extreme racist attitudes.

17. Harvey Pekar died on July 12, 2010, aged seventy.

18. As Groensteen (1996) points out, it is somewhat surprising, given the country's long history of producing serious comics for adults, that the graphic memoir genre did not really take off in France until the early 1990s. However, a number of comics artists, notably Moebius (born Jean Giraud), had in the 1970s already started to place ironic self-images into their work (Ahmed 2009). Baudoin's (1981) *Passe le temps* is another important precursor of French autobiographical comics.

19. Other graphic memoirs about a parent's experiences during the Holocaust include Martin Lemelman's (2007) *Mendel's Daughter* and Miriam Katin's (2006) *We Are On Our Own*.

20. Graphic memoirs that are centrally concerned with the author's growth of artistic consciousness might be described as belonging to the category of the *Künstlerroman*. Watson (2011: 128) suggests that this narrative form is particularly widespread among women practitioners of alternative comics.

Chapter 2

1. Watson (2011: 149) believes that *Fun Home* could not have been told as effectively in any other medium: "This act of self- and paternal creation through autographical narration is a story of relationship and legacy that depends on graphically embodying and enacting, not just telling, the family story." Other discussions of *Fun Home* can be found in Chute (2010: 175–217) and Brown Spiers (2010).

2. I will use the terms *self* and *subject* as synonyms, although the latter is more strongly associated with (post-)structuralist philosophy and the idea that the subject comes into being through language. The term *subject* also has connotations of *subjection*, for instance to a monarch, while the concept of the *self* suggests a free agent on an equal footing with other selves (Doy 2005: 7).

3. Throughout this book, I will, when necessary, follow Witek (1989) in his convention of referring to the creator of an autobiographical comic book by his or her surname, and to the narrator and protagonist by the given name. However, this is simply a heuristic device, which should not obscure the complexity of the relationships in life writing between author, narrator, and protagonist and the many overlaps between them.

4. When transcribing verbal text from comics, I use a single slash (/) to indicate a switch from one "container" of written language (e.g., balloon, text box) to another. A double slash (//) shows that the transcribed words are taken from two different panels (format adapted from Loman 2006).

5. Zunshine (2006: 67) points out that such arguments became particularly popular after Roland Barthes (1977a) had declared the "death" of the real author,

which, she argues, testifies to "the tenaciousness with which we cling to the idea that there must be some source [. . .] behind a narrative." See Palmer (2004: 16–17) for a discussion of the problems involved in trying to distinguish between the narrator and the implied author.

6. For a perceptive multimodal analysis of Joe Matt's autobiographical comics, see Jacobs (2008).

7. Some scholars (e.g., Smith 2011; Whitlock 2006) have begun to use the term "avatar" to refer to the visual incarnations of the autobiographical self in comics. In Hinduism, an avatar is the incarnate form a deity adopts to descend to the earth, but the term is now used more commonly to refer to the graphic image that represents a person in computer games, virtual worlds, and Internet forums. The act of choosing an avatar in the context of an online community is, indeed, comparable to the self-portraits produced by autobiographical comics artists in some respects. However, unlike graphic memoirists, the participants in a virtual environment are not bound to any stable physical cues such as race or gender at all, which means that they are even freer to choose multiple (ideal) versions of themselves (Soukup 2004; Turkle 1997). For this reason, I find the use of the term avatar in the context of autobiographical comics unhelpful.

8. The first published version of Davison's work, which draws heavily on the comics diary he kept for many years, was roughly chronological, while the substantially revised and extended 1990 book was organized thematically. By this time, Davison was in a fulfilled relationship, which allowed him to rewrite his life story as a positive, life-affirming tale. For a more detailed discussion of this work, see McIlvenny 2002; 2003.

9. For a more comprehensive analysis of David Small's *Stitches*, see El Refaie (2010).

10. Key scenes in *Alien* (1979), for instance, show a male character being orally "raped" by an alien being and the creature resulting from this "copulation" gnawing itself through the man's stomach. Similarly, in *The Manitou* (1978), a psychic's girlfriend finds out that a mysterious tumor growing at an astonishing rate on the base of her neck is the fetus of a four-hundred-year-old demonic witch doctor, who can control his own reincarnations (Creed 1993; Fischer 1996).

11. Russo (1997) discusses the role of the female grotesque in Bakhtin's theories.

12. Doy (2005: 52) believes that mirrors in (self-)portraits are still able to evoke a whole tradition which invites women in particular to see themselves as objects, "as sexually attractive (or not), as slender (or not), or as vain and narcissistic (always)."

13. Chute (2010: 54) comes to a similar conclusion, arguing that "Kominsky-Crumb narrates a sexual life that *includes* but is not limited to or determined by an 'objectification' and 'subordination' that she 1. finds pleasurable and 2. chooses

herself how to represent." For a discussion of the centrality of Aline's Jewishness to her visual self-representations, see Oksman (2010).

14. Some visual artists, such as Cindy Sherman and Jo Alison Feiler, use elaborately disguised photographic self-portraits as a way of commenting on social role-playing and gender stereotypes. In these cases, Cumming (2009: 258) argues, photography has the "tremendous advantage" over traditional self-portraiture of allowing artists to create a large number of different images as a way of reflecting their ever-shifting sense of self.

15. Of course, cartooning may also sometimes involve substantial exaggeration and distortion (Michelmore 2000), and some traditional comics, such as the superhero genre, have long been associated with the use of stereotypical imagery, "visually codified representations in which characters are continually reduced to their appearances" (Singer 2002: 107).

Chapter 3

1. The comics medium allows authors to place their (child) bodies in space on the page. This, Chute (2010: 114) suggests, makes the medium particularly well suited to the task of representing trauma. See also Chapter 2.

2. Cates (2011: 224) makes a similar point in relation to diary comics, suggesting that they are characterized by a temporal structure that "works to encapsulate, to parse, to describe, and ultimately to honor the present, as well as the process of the present's continuing forward development."

3. As Currie (2007) points out, the identification of prolepsis and analepsis depends on assigning priority to one section of a narrative, which, particularly in the case of narrated memory, is often not at all straightforward.

4. This method was established by Günther Müller and his associates in the 1940s. It is also used in a less rigid application by Genette (1980) and Bal (1985).

5. There is a common misconception, shared by some scholars (e.g., Dittmar 2008: 168), that comics can always be read more quickly than purely textual literature. In fact, some people may find the task of reading comics very challenging and time- consuming, particularly if they are not used to the medium.

6. There are interesting parallels between the "fuzzy temporality" characteristic of the reenactment of traumatic memories and the typical temporal structure of superhero comics. Umberto Eco (1979: 113–17) argues that superhero comics consist of stories that have already been told, in the sense that superheroes are mythic characters that belong to the ossified and indeterminate time of an epic past. But when they participate in the episodic narrative action sequences, they are subject to the ordinary dictates of time. In order to disguise this temporal paradox, superhero stories tend to develop in loops, where event strands are picked up and

repeated in slightly different forms. According to Sandifer (2008: 175), the narrative arc of the superhero comic "is best understood as a complex network of obsession and repression," stemming from the traumatic incidents that are typically part of the superhero's origin story (see also Atkinson 2009; Ndalianis 2009).

7. For more in-depth discussions of this text, see Chiu (2008), Chute (2010: 135–73), Gilmore (2011), Naghibi (2011), Tensuan (2006), and Whitlock (2006).

8. By expanding "the repertoire of trauma's representation to omission, silence, and a depiction of the void," Gilmore (2011: 161) argues, Satrapi uses her work to insist "that trauma contains within it the possibility of bearing witness, even if that means bearing witness to what was not shared or shareable."

9. A similar process seems to be at work in many single-panel cartoons, which encourage viewers to construct a mini-narrative on the basis of what is suggested by the depicted moment, and which also often presuppose a degree of cultural literacy or familiarity with current events (Edwards 1997; El Refaie 2009).

10. As I explain in El Refaie (2010b), this panel bears a striking resemblance to the sub-section of an altarpiece by the Sienese painter Sassetta, *The Meeting Of St Anthony And St Paul*, from the mid fifteenth century, which Steiner (2004) regards as a particularly good example of the continuous narrative technique. *Epileptic* is also discussed by Tabachnick (2011).

11. In movies, shots are most commonly edited together according to temporal criteria, but it is also possible to find spatial conjunctions, where we see objects that lie beside each other, and comparative conjunction, where shots are edited together according to the principle of similarity or contrast (van Leeuwen 1996). Sternberg (2004) has identified a number of non-temporal forms of sequencing in prose fiction, too.

12. Following a similar line of argumentation in relation to film, Chatman (1990: 50) defines rhythm as a correspondence between discourse-time and story-time that gradually establishes itself as the norm, "a kind of zero-degree temporal order that is understood by the spectator to correspond to the duration of events themselves."

13. There is some ambiguity over whether a larger number of images slows down or speeds up the pace of an action sequence. In apparent contradiction to Painter's account, Vernier Danehy (2008: 222) says of a particular section in a comic book that the action "picks up speed" as the page is divided into a greater number of smaller frames. This discrepancy can perhaps be explained by Dittmar's (2008: 167) observation that the more pictures are used for a sequence in the comics medium, the slower the time of narration, or discourse-time, while, paradoxically, the tempo of the narrated time, or story-time, can increase, as each picture and gutter typically stands for a shorter period of time.

14. Panels are numbered by indicating first the strip in which they appear and then their position within this strip (e.g., 2/4 refers to the fourth panel in the second strip).

15. According to *Gestalt* theory, visual elements that are similar in terms of their shape, size, or color, tend to be perceived as related. Proximity and the continuity of lines also increase the likelihood that individual elements will be grouped together (Zakia 2002).

16. Mikkonen (2010: 84) believes that the embedding of extraneous visual texts into a comic allows artists to include different temporal spaces within one panel, thereby producing "a multiple layering of time planes, without violating the conventions of plausibility." For further examples of visual echoes in *Persepolis*, see Chute (2010: 135–73) and Whitlock (2006).

17. Floating panels (or "insets") can also be used to convey temporal relationships; most commonly, they suggest a relation of tension between a stopped instant in the inclusive panel and an action in time in the inset panel(s) (Vernier Danehy 2008; Groensteen 2007).

Chapter 4

1. Gardner (2008) believes that comics autobiography typically makes fewer truth claims than either prose or image alone have done traditionally, as its formal properties—the gaps between panels and the stylized, cartoonish nature of the drawings—inevitably draw attention to the subjectivity of all memory. While this may be true for authors like Baudoin (1995), whose work constitutes an explicit investigation of the power of images and the boundaries of the imagination, those comics creators who aim to report on important geopolitical events, such as Sacco (2003, 2004) or Ted Rall (2002), are likely to place more emphasis on establishing the factuality of their accounts.

2. Several other scholars have examined the nature of authenticity in non-fiction comics (e.g., Beaty 2007, 2009; Chaney 2011; Gardner 2008; Hatfield 2005), but my own approach is unique in that it describes authenticity as a kind of performance, drawing on Goffman's theories of social interaction and Brecht's theater aesthetics. My focus on the notion of "visual authenticity" is also distinctive.

3. For a more detailed critique of the concept of "visual modality" in relation to autobiographical comics, see El Refaie (2010a).

4. In an interview about the film version of her graphic memoir *Persepolis*, Marjane Satrapi uses a striking visual metaphor to assert the authentic nature of her tale: "I'm just talking about what I've seen with my own eyes" (Bochenski 2008: 37).

5. Sadly, Engelberg died in October 2006, shortly after having completed her book.

6. An interesting parallel is discussed by Wray (2008: 173–85), who argues that *naturalness* in a scripted dialogue for public performance is intrinsically

different from *naturalness* in real conversation. The script's written format and the extra detail, directness, and contextualization required in order to render a conversation intelligible to an audience means that there will always be a gap between natural dialogue and scripted performance.

7. Tabachnick (2011: 103–5) makes a similar point when he writes that Beauchard's detailed representations of his family life in *Epileptic* appear to confirm its truthful nature: "All of the incidents and thoughts are so unusual and, at the same time, so precisely rendered in both words and drawings as to convince us of the near-impossibility of his having invented them."

8. The three other kinds of modality that Kress and van Leeuwen (1996: 168–71) identify are "technological modality," where visual truth is based on the usefulness of a visual representation as a blueprint for action, "abstract modality," where the criteria of realism are linked to the search for a deeper truth behind appearances, and "sensory modality," which is based on the ability of images to evoke pleasure or displeasure, by creating the illusion of touch, taste, or smell. For a slightly different application of Halliday's concept of "modality" to visual images, see O'Toole (1994).

9. Van Leeuwen (2001: 394) believes that the close association, in Western culture, between the spontaneous and the truthful "inner" self is due to the influence of psychoanalytic theory. Parallels can also be drawn to the much earlier notion of the "pure, ascetic" painter, who, from late Antiquity onwards, was considered able to reflect the true nature of objects by acting as a completely transparent medium (Wortmann 2003: 45–63).

10. This is, of course, only one of many ways of cueing a dream sequence. Peeters (2008), for instance, typically uses borderless panels to introduce fantasies and (day-)dreams.

11. In several interviews (Burkeman 2006; Chute 2006a and b) Bechdel talks about how she created a reference shot of herself with her digital camera by posing for every character in every panel of the book. She says that this painstaking method reflects her slightly obsessive character and a lingering sense that she cannot quite trust her own perceptions.

12. Finding the snapshot of the babysitter on the bed is what initially gave Bechdel the idea for her graphic memoir (Chute 2006b). The graphic rendition of this photograph is the only double spread in *Fun Home* and it occupies the book's exact centerfold.

13. Catherine Doherty's (2000) story of her search for her birth mother, *Can of Worms*, similarly contains a large number of excerpts from legal documents, newspaper clippings, personal letters, and her own notebooks, which have been painstakingly redrawn by Doherty in order to produce exact copies of the different handwriting styles and even of the stamp on an envelope and the barcode on the back of a greeting card, for example.

14. Another way of describing this process is to regard it as a form of "re-authentication" through ostentatious "de-authentication" (Coupland 2001).

15. As Herman (2011: 236) points out, the abrupt shifts in perspective and style also allow Flenner to mark the way the "narrating I" sometimes interprets and evaluates events very differently than the "experiencing I" did in the past.

16. For other critical work on Spiegelman's distinctive use of photographs, see Hirsch (2011), Liss (1998: 53–68), and several chapters in Geis (2003).

17. There are famous examples of fake memoirs in other genres as well, such as the teenage literary persona of JT LeRoy, who was presented to the public as a transgender vagrant, drug addict, and prostitute, but who was, in fact, the fictional creation of the American author Laura Victoria Albert. A more recent example is the American peace activist Tom MacMaster, who wrote a blog pretending to be a young gay Syrian-American woman living through repression in Damascus (Addley 2011). Each of these cases raises distinctive questions about the notion of autobiographic authenticity, which relate to the particular sociopolitical context and the specific form in which each one is told.

Chapter 5

1. German comics artist Flix draws readers into his graphic memoir *Held* (2003) in the entirely literal sense of visually depicting them: Every now and then, a group of rather earnest people of a certain age, labeled "the attentive readers," pops up to comment on the contents of the book and to ask the author's alter ego, Felix, searching questions.

2. A good example of the active role of the reader is given by the creator of *Blue Pills* (2008), Frederik Peeters, who discovered that his story was being interpreted in widely divergent ways: "A lot of people saw it as very optimistic, very joyful. Others saw it as more dramatic. Some thought the main storyline was Cati's rapport with her son, but others saw it as a love story. Everyone sees it differently" (Day 2008).

3. Saraceni (2003) and Scott (1999) have both attempted to explain the same phenomenon by drawing on discourse analysis and its related concepts of *cohesion* and *coherence*. Cohesion refers to the ways in which panels are made to hang together through formal features such as visual repetitions, overlaps, redundancies, and verbal back-referencing, while coherence describes the ability of the reader to perceive a series of images as a unified text. However, as Carrier (2000: 56) acknowledges, the exact process by which a series of comics panels are read as a sequence is still pretty much a mystery, as no one so far has been able to specify the "necessary and sufficient conditions for success in this synthesis."

4. Some scholars find it useful to distinguish between *similarity identification,* where readers recognize parallels between themselves and another, and *wish identification,* where they perceive qualities they would like to have themselves (e.g., Andringa 2004). I consider such a distinction unnecessary for my purposes.

5. Barker (1989) reveals that a large percentage of the American horror comics that caused a moral panic in the 1950s was apparently read by married women and not, as everybody assumed at the time, only by children. He explains these readership patterns by suggesting that the tales of revenge that many of these comic books contained allowed women a fantasy resolution of the many professional, economic, and sexual tensions they experienced in the years following World War II.

6. As Couser (1997: 3) points out, *identity politics,* the "idea that one's identity and politics are, or ought to be, based in some shared attribute—such as race, ethnicity, or gender," has gradually been extended to include the shared experience of illness and disability as well. For people who have no immediate experience of a particular disease, he suggests, illness narratives may instead "serve to expose and dramatize what we would prefer to ignore most of the time, to arouse and (ideally) assuage our anxiety about our somatic selves" (p. 9).

7. In August 2011, the Webcomics List (http://www.thewebcomiclist.com/) listed over 18,400 separate webcomics. See McCloud (2000) for a discussion of the specific narrative properties of webcomics.

8. The title of the book, *I Never Liked You,* which ostensibly quotes the words a young girlfriend says to Chester when he treats her in a particularly ruthless manner (p. 155), can also be interpreted as a comment on his own former self.

9. Empathy can be distinguished from sympathy, in which a supportive feeling (such as pity) about another person's emotions occurs (Keen 2007: 5; see also Neill 1996).

10. Contemporary neuroscience has developed several ways of investigating empathy, for instance, by measuring changes in a person's heart rate and skin conductance, or through Functional Magnetic Resonance Imaging (fMRI). Evolutionary psychologist Baron-Cohen (2002) believes that the typical female brain is hard-wired for empathy to a greater extent than the male brain. For a critical response to this claim, see Keen (2007: 6–12).

11. For a critical discussion of Ekman's theories and, in particular, his neglect of the important role of language and culture in our perception of emotions, see Shweder (1991: 245), who remarks that "[i]t is ludicrous to imagine that the emotional functioning of people in different cultures is basically the same. It is just as ludicrous to imagine that each culture's emotional life is unique."

12. In a fascinating series of experiments, Neal and Chartrand (2011) discovered that emotion perception was significantly impaired in people who had

received Botox treatment, a cosmetic procedure that reduces muscular feedback from the face. These findings appear to support the claim by embodied cognition theorists that emotion perception is based partly on the facial feedback signals generated when we automatically mimic the expressions displayed on other people's faces.

13. In a study by Simon Baron-Cohen and colleagues (reported in O'Connell 1997: 64–65), British, Spanish, and Japanese adults were shown portraits by Velazquez and by the contemporary British artist David Hockney, which displayed a range of complex emotions, such as contempt, regret, and distrust. In all three cultures, there was a high level of agreement among the respondents in their description of the emotion the artists had depicted. The sparse line-drawings of Hockney's portraits actually seemed to be easier to understand than the more information-rich oil paintings by the Spanish artist.

14. Studies of how readers interpret political cartoons (El Refaie 2009; El Refaie and Hörschelmann 2010) have revealed that the same facial expression is often perceived and described in astonishingly divergent ways by the different respondents.

15. Gardner's (2008) claim that the graphic memoir simultaneously demands both distance and identification from the reader seems to be following a similar line of thought.

16. Some French comics artists make a regular appearance in each other's work, too. Trondheim, for example, features in *Journal d'un album* ("Journal of an Album") by Dupuy and Berberian (1994: part 4, page 9) and in *Livret de Phamille* ("F[ph]amily Record Booklet") by Menu (1995: "Cerisy," p. 6). Judith Forest's fake graphic memoirs, *1h25* (2009) and *Momon* (2010), contain multiple references to well-known personalities in the Franco-Belgian comics scene (see Chapter 4).

Conclusion

1. There is also a growing body of critical work that focuses on the reader of comics and graphic narratives from an educational or visual literacy perspective (e.g., Frey and Fisher 2008).

Autobiographical Comics

B., David. 2005. *Epileptic*. London: Jonathan Cape.

Barry, Lynda. 2002. *One! Hundred! Demons!* Seattle, WA: Sasquatch.

———. 2009. *What It Is*. London: Jonathan Cape.

Bashi, Pasua (2009) *Nylon Road: A Graphic Memoir of Coming of Age in Iran*. New York: St. Martin's Griffin.

Baudoin, Edmond. 1981. *Passe le temps*. Paris: Futuropolis.

———. 1995. *L'éloge de la poussière*. Paris: L'Association.

Bechdel, Alison. 2006. *Fun Home: A Family Tragicomic*. London: Jonathan Cape.

Boilet, Frédéric. 2001. *L'épinard de Yukiko*. Angoulême: ego comme x.

Brabner Joyce, and Harvey Pekar. 1994. *Our Cancer Year*. Illustrations by Frank Stack. New York: Running Press Book Publishers.

Brick. 2010. *Depresso, Or: How I Learned to Stop Worrying And Embrace Being Bonkers!* London: Knockabout.

Brown, Chester. 1992. *The Playboy*. Montreal: Drawn & Quarterly.

———. 1994. *I Never Liked You*. Montreal: Drawn & Quarterly.

Brown, Jeffrey. 2005. *Every Girl is the End of the World for Me*. Marietta, GA: Top Shelf.

———. 2009. *Funny Misshapen Body: A Memoir*. New York: Touchstone.

Cabanes, Max. 1991. *Heart Throbs*. London: Xpresso Books.

Campbell, Eddie. 2000. *Alec: The King Canute Crowd*. Marietta, GA: Top Shelf.

———. 2001. *Alec: How to Be an Artist*. Marietta, GA: Top Shelf.

———. 2006. *The Fate of the Artist*. New York and London: First Second.

Clell, Madison. 2002. *Cuckoo*. Portland, OR: Green Door Studios.

Crumb, Robert. 1992. *My Troubles With Women*. San Francisco: Last Gasp.

———. 1998. *The Death of Fritz the Cat: The Complete Crumb Vol. 8*. Seattle, WA: Fantagraphics.

Cunningham, Darryl. 2010. *Psychiatric Tales*. London: Blank Slate.

Dakin, Glenn. 2001. *Abe: Wrong for all the Right Reasons*. Marietta, GA: Top Shelf.

Davison, Al. 1990. *The Spiral Cage: An Autobiography*. London: Titan Books.

Delisle, Guy. 2006a. *Pyongyang: A Journey in North Korea*. London: Jonathan Cape.

———. 2006b. *Shenzhen: A Travelogue From China*. London: Jonathan Cape.

Doherty, Catherine. 2000. *Can of Worms*. Seattle, WA: Fantagraphics Books.

Doucet, Julie. 2004. *My New York Diary*, 2nd edn. Montreal: Drawn & Quarterly.

Dupuy, Philippe, and Charles Berberian. 1994. *Journal d'un album*. Paris: L'Association.

Eisner, Will. 2007. *Life, in Pictures: Autobiographical Stories*. New York: Norton.

Engelberg, Miriam. 2006. *Cancer Made Me a Shallower Person: A Memoir in Comics*. New York: Harper Collins.

Fies, Brian. 2006. *Mom's Cancer*. New York: Harry N. Abrams.

Fleener, Mary. 1996. *Life of the Party*. Seattle, WA: Fantagraphics.

Flix. 2003. *Held*. Hamburg: Carlsen.

———. 2004. *Sag was*. Hamburg: Carlsen.

Forest, Judith. 2009. *1h25*. Brussels: La Cinquième Couche.

———. 2010. *Momon*. Brussels: La Cinquième Couche.

Gallardo, María, and Miguel Gallardo. 2010. *María y yo*. Bilbao: Astiberri.

Gloeckner, Phoebe. 1998. *A Child's Life and Other Stories*. Berkeley, CA: Frog.

Green, Justin. 1995. *Binky Brown Sampler*. San Francisco: Last Gasp.

Gregory, Danny. 2003. *Everyday Matters: A Memoir*. New York: Hyperion.

Guibert, Emmanuel. 2008. *Alan's War: The Memories of G. I. Alan Cope*. New York and London: First Second.

———, Didier Lefèvre, and Frédéric Lemercier. 2009. *The Photographer*. New York and London: First Second.

Hughes, David. 2009. *Walking the Dog*. London: Jonathan Cape.

Jensen, Thor. 2007. *Red Eye, Black Eye*. Gainesville, FL: Alternative Comics.

Katin, Miriam. 2006. *We Are On Our Own*. Montreal: Drawn & Quarterly.

Kominsky-Crumb, Aline. 2007. *Need More Love: A Graphic Memoir*. London: MQ Publications.

Kuper, Peter. 1995. *Stripped*. Seattle, WA: Fantagraphics Books.

Lasko-Gross, Miss. 2006. *Escape from "Special."* Seattle, WA: Fantagraphics Books.

Lay, Carol. 2008. *The Big Skinny: How I Changed my Fattitude*. New York: Villard.

Lemelman, Martin. 2007. *Mendel's Daughter*. London: Jonathan Cape.

Linthout, Willy. 2009. *Years of the Elephant*. Wisbech: Fanfare/Ponent Mon.

Mahler, Nicolas. 2007. *Kunsttheorie versus Frau Goldgruber*. Berlin: Reprodukt.

Marchetto, Marisa Acocella. 2006. *Cancer Vixen: A True Story*. London: HarperCollins.

Matt, Joe. 1999. *Peepshow*. Montreal: Drawn & Quarterly.

———. 2003. *Fair Weather*. Montreal: Drawn & Quarterly.

Mawil, Markus. 2008. *We Can Still Be Friends*. London: Blank Slate Books.

Menu, Jean-Christophe. 1995. *Livret de Phamille*. Paris: L'Association.

Michalke, Andreas. 1999. *Smalltown Boy*. Berlin: Reprodukt.

Neaud, Fabrice. 1996. *Journal (1): Février 1992–septembre 1993*. Angoulême: ego comme x.

Neufeld, Josh. 2004. *A Few Perfect Hours and Other Stories From Southeast Asia & Central Europe*. Self-published, distributed through: Gainesville, FL: Alternative Comics.

Peeters, Frederik. 2008. *Blue Pills: A Positive Love Story*. London: Jonathan Cape.

Pekar, Harvey. 2005. *The Quitter*. New York: Vertigo.

———. 2007. *Another Day*. New York: Vertigo.

Penfold, Rosalind B. 2006. *Dragonslippers: This is What an Abusive Relationship Looks Like*. London: Harper Press.

Rall, Ted. 2002. *To Afghanistan and Back*. New York: NBM.

Sacco, Joe. 2003. *Palestine*. London: Jonathan Cape.

———. 2004. *The Fixer—A Story from Sarajevo*. London: Jonathan Cape.

Satrapi, Marjane. 2006. *Persepolis. The Story of a Childhood* and *The Story of a Return*. London: Jonathan Cape.

Seth. 2007. *It's a Good Life, If You Don't Weaken*. London: Jonathan Cape.

Schrag, Ariel. 2008a. *Awkward and Definition. The High School Comic Chronicles of Ariel Schrag*. New York: Touchstone.

———. 2008b. *Potential. The High School Comic Chronicles of Ariel Schrag*. New York: Touchstone.

———. 2009. *Likewise. The High School Comic Chronicles of Ariel Schrag*. New York: Touchstone.

Schwieger, Dirk. 2008. *Moresukine*. New York: ComicsLit.

Small, David. 2009. *Stitches: A Memoir*. New York and London: Norton.

Snakepit, Ben. 2007. *Snake Pit 2007*. Bloomington, IN: Microcosm Publishing.

Sophie. 2004. *Belly Button Comix #2*. Seattle, WA: Fantagraphics.

Spain, Rodriguez. 1994. *My True Story*. Seattle, WA: Fantagraphics.

Spiegelman, Art. 2003. *The Complete Maus*. London: Penguin.

Streeten, Nicola. 2011. *Billy, Me & You*. Brighton: Myriad Editions.

Thompson, Craig. 2003. *Blankets*. Marietta, GA: Top Shelf.

———. 2004. *Carnet de Voyage*. Marietta, GA: Top Shelf.

Trondheim, Lewis. 2007. *Little Nothings Vol.1: The Curse of the Umbrella*. New York: ComicsLit.

Valentino, Jim. 1995. *Vignettes: The Autobiographical Comix of Valentino*. San Juan Capistrano, CA: Image Comics.

Weinstein, Lauren R. 2006. *Girl Stories*. New York: Henry Holt.

References

Abbott, H. Porter. *The Cambridge Introduction to Narrative*. Cambridge: Cambridge University Press. 2002.

Abel, Jessica and Matt Madden. *Drawing Words & Writing Pictures: Making Comics: Manga, Graphic Novels, and Beyond*. New York: First Second. 2008.

Adams, Timothy Dow. *Light Writing and Life Writing: Photography in Autobiography*. Chapter Hill and London: University of North Carolina Press, 2000.

Addley, Esther. "Syrian Lesbian Blogger Is Revealed Conclusively to be a Married Man." *The Guardian* 13 June 2011. Available at: http://www.guardian.co.uk/world/2011/jun/13/syrian-lesbian-blogger-tom-macmaster (accessed 4 August 2011).

Ahmed, Maaheen. "Moebius, Gir, Giraud, Gérard: Self-visualizations." *International Journal of Comic Art* 11(2): 421–31. 2009.

Anderson, Benedict. *Imagined Communities: Reflections on the Origin and Spread of Nationalism*. 2nd ed. London and New York: Verso. 1991.

Anderson, John C., and Bradley Katz. "Read Only Memory: *Maus* and Its Marginalia on CD-ROM." Deborah R. Geis, ed. In *Considering Maus: Approaches to Art Spiegelman's "Survivor's Tale" of the Holocaust*. Tucaloosa and London: University of Alabama Press: 159–74. 2003.

Anderson, Linda. *Autobiography*. London and New York: Routledge. 2001.

Andringa, Els. "The Interface Between Fiction and Life: Patterns of Identification in Reading Autobiographies." *Poetics Today* 25(2): 205–40. 2004.

Atkinson, Paul. "The Time of Heroes: Narrative, Progress, and Eternity in *Miracleman*." Angela, Ndalianis, ed. In *The Contemporary Comic Book Superhero*. London and New York: Routledge: 44–63. 2009.

Attardo, Salvatore and Victor Raskin. "Script Theory Revis(it)ed: Joke Similarity and Joke Representation Model." *Humor: International Journal of Humor Research* 3(4): 293–347. 1991.

Baetens, Jan. "Graphic Novels: Literature Without Text?" *English Language Notes, Special Issue* (Graphia: The Graphic Novel and Literary Criticism) 46(2): 77–88. 2008.

——. "Revealing Traces: A New Theory of Graphic Enunciation." Robin Varnum and Christina T. Gibbons, eds. In *The Language of Comics: Word and Image.* Jackson: University Press of Mississippi: 145–55. 2001.

Bakhtin, Mikhail M. *The Dialogic Imagination: Four Essays.* Holquist, Michael, ed. Translated by Caryl Emerson and Michael Holquist. Austin: University of Texas Press. 1981.

——. "Rabelais and his World." Translated by Hélène Iswolsky. 1984. Pam Morris, ed. In *The Bakhtin Reader: Selected Writings of Bakthin, Medvedev and Voloshinov.* London: Edward Arnold: 194–244. 1994.

Bal, Mieke. *Narratology: Introduction to the Theory of Narrative.* Toronto, Buffalo, London: University of Toronto Press. 1985.

Barker, Martin. *Comics: Ideology, Power and the Critics.* Manchester and New York: University of Manchester Press. 1989.

——. "Getting a Conviction: Or, How the British Horror Comics Campaign Only Just Succeeded." John A. Lent, ed. In *Pulp Demons: International Dimensions of the Postwar Anti-Comics Campaign.* Cranbury, NJ, London, Mississauga, Ontario: Associated University Presses: 69–92. 1999.

——. "On Seeing How Far You Can See: On Being a 'Fan' of *2000 AD.*" In Buckingham, David, ed. *Reading Audiences: Young People and the Media,* Manchester: Manchester University Press: 159–83. 1993.

Baron-Cohen, Simon. *The Essential Difference: Men, Women and the Extreme Male Brain.* London: Allen Lane. 2002.

——. *Mindblindness: An Essay on Autism and Theory of Mind.* Cambridge, MA and London: Massachusetts Institute of Technology Press. 1995.

Barrington, Judith. *Writing the Memoir: From Truth to Art.* 2nd ed. Portland, Oregon: The Eighth Mountain Press. 2002.

Barthes, Roland. *Camera Lucida: Reflections on Photography.* New York: Farrar, Straus and Giroux. 2000 (1980).

——. *Image, Music, Text.* London: Fontana. 1977a.

——. *Roland Barthes by Roland Barthes.* Translated by Richard Howard. London: Macmillan. 1977b.

Bartual, Roberto. "William Hogarth's *A Harlot's Progress*: The Beginnings of a Purely Pictographic Sequential Language." *Studies in Comics* 1(1): 83–05. 2010.

Bateman, John A. *Multimodality and Genre: A Foundation for the Systematic Analysis of Multimodal Documents.* Houndmills and New York: Palgrave Macmillan. 2008.

Bearden-White, Roy. "Closing the Gap: Examining the Invisible Sign in Graphic Narratives." *International Journal of Comic Art* 11(1): 347–62. 2009.

Beaty, Bart. "Autobiography as Authenticity." Jeet Heer and Kent Worcester, eds. In *A Comics Studies Reader*. Jackson: University Press of Mississippi: 226–35. 2009.

———. "Hillary Chute and the Dynamics of Autobiography." *Comics Journal* 29 April. 2011a. Available at: http://www.tcj.com/hillarychuteautobiography/ (accessed 16 June 2011).

———. "Selective Mutual Reinforcement in the Comics of Chester Brown, Joe Matt, and Seth." Michael A. Chaney, ed. In *Graphic Subjects: Critical Essays on Autobiography and Graphic Novels*. Wisconsin, MA and London: Wisconsin University Press: 247–59. 2011b.

———. *Unpopular Culture: Transforming the European Comic Book in the 1990s.* Toronto, Buffalo, London: University of Toronto Press. 2007.

Bell, Roanne and Mark Sinclair. *Pictures & Words: New Comic Art and Narrative Illustration*. London: Laurence King. 2005.

Bennett, Jill. *Empathic Vision: Affect, Trauma, and Contemporary Art*. Stanford, CA: Stanford University Press. 2005.

Berger, Arthur Asa. *Narratives in Popular Culture, Media, and Everyday Life.* Thousand Oaks, London, New Delhi: Sage. 1997.

Berger, John. *Ways of Seeing*. London: Penguin. 1972.

Bergson, Henri. "The Idea of Duration." Keith Pearson, Keith Ansell, and John Mullarkey, eds. 2002. In *Henri Bergson. Key Writings*. New York and London: Continuum: 49–77. 1889.

———. *Laughter: An Essay on the Meaning of the Comic*. London: Macmillan. 1911.

Beronä, David A. "Pictures Speak in Comics Without Words: Pictorial Principles in the Work of Milt Gross, Hendrik Dorgathen, Eric Drooker, and Peter Kuper." Robin Varnum and Christina T. Gibbons, eds. In *The Language of Comics: Word and Image*. Jackson: University Press of Mississippi: 19–39. 2001.

Bersani, Leo. *The Freudian Body: Psychoanalysis and Art*. New York: Columbia University Press. 1986.

Billig, Michael. *Laughter and Ridicule: Towards a Social Critique of Humour.* London: Sage. 2005.

Bochenski, Matt. "Citizen Marji." *Little White Lies: Truth & Movies* 16(2): 34–37. 2008.

Booth, Wayne C. *The Rhetoric of Fiction*. Chicago and London: University of Chicago Press. 1961.

Bordwell, David and Kristin Thompson. *Film Art: An Introduction*. 4th ed. New York: McGraw-Hill. 1993.

Bourg, Tammy. "The Role of Emotion, Empathy, and Text Structure in Children's and Adults' Narrative Text Comprehension." Roger J. Kreuz and Mary S. MacNealy, eds. In *Empirical Approaches to Literature and Aesthetics*. Norwood, NJ: Ablex: 241–60. 1996.

Brecht, Bertolt. *Brecht On Theatre: The Development of an Aesthetic*. Translated by John Willett. New York and London: Hill and Wang/Eyre Methuen. 1978.

Brethes, Romain. "Canular Belge à Angoulême." *Le Point.fr* 29 January 2011. Available at: http://www.lepoint.fr/culture/canular-belge-a-angouleme-29-01-2011-1289191_3.php (accessed 4 August 2011).

Brown, Jeffrey A. *Black Superheroes, Milestone Comics, and their Fans*. Jackson: University Press of Mississippi. 2001.

Brown Spiers, Miriam. "Daddy's Little Girl: Multigenerational Queer Relationships in Bechdel's Fun Home." *Studies in Comics* 1(2): 315–35. 2010.

Bruner, Jerome. "The Autobiographical Process." Robert Folkenflik, ed. In *The Culture of Autobiography: Constructions of Self-Representation*. Stanford, CA: Stanford University Press: 38–56. 1993.

Bucholtz, Mary and Kira Hall. (2004) "Theorizing Identity in Language and Sexuality Research." *Language in Society*, 33(4): 469–515. 2004.

Burkeman, Oliver. "A Life Stripped Bare." *The Guardian*, 16 October 2006. Available at: http://www.guardian.co.uk/books/2006/oct/16/biography .oliverburkeman (accessed 13 February 2011).

Butler, Judith. *Bodies that Matter: On the Discursive Limits of "Sex."* New York and London: Routledge. 1993.

——. "Performative Acts and Gender Constitution: An Essay in Phenomenology and Feminist Theory." Katie Conboy, Nadia Medina, and Sarah Stanbury, eds. In *Writing on the Body: Female Embodiment and Feminist Theory*. New York and Chichester, West Sussex: Columbia University Press: 401–17. 1997.

Caputi, Jane. "The Pornography of Everyday Life." Marian Meyers, ed. In *Mediated Women: Representations in Popular Culture*. Cresskill, N.J: Hampton Press: 57–79. 1999.

Carney, Sean. "The Ear of the Eye, or, Do Drawings Make Sounds?" *English Language Notes, Special Issue* (Graphia: The Graphic Novel and Literary Criticism) 46(2): 193–209. 2008.

Carrell, Amy. "Historical Views of Humor." Victor Raskin, ed. In *The Primer of Humor Research*. Berlin and New York: Mouton de Gruyter: 303–32. 2008.

Carrier, David. *The Aesthetics of Comics*. University Park, PA: The Pennsylvania State University. 2000.

Carrier, Mélanie. "*Persepolis* et les Révolutions de Marjane Satrapi." *Belphégor* 4(1). 2004. Available at: http://etc.dal.ca/belphegor/vol4_no1/articles/04_01_Carrie_ satrap_fr.html (accessed 24 February 2011).

Caruth, Cathy. "Introduction." Cathy Caruth, ed. In *Trauma: Explorations in Memory*. Baltimore and London: John Hopkins University Press: 151–57. 1995.

Cates, Isaac. "The Diary Comic." Michael A. Chaney, ed. In *Graphic Subjects: Critical Essays on Autobiography and Graphic Novels*. Wisconsin, MA and London: Wisconsin University Press: 209–26. 2011.

Chaney, Michael A. "Introduction." Michael A. Chaney, ed. In *Graphic Subjects: Critical Essays on Autobiography and Graphic Novels*. Wisconsin, MA and London: Wisconsin University Press: 3–9. 2011.

Chatman, Seymour. *Coming to Terms: The Rhetoric of Narrative in Fiction and Film*. Ithaca and London: Cornell University Press. 1990.

Chiu, Monica. "Sequencing and Contingent Individualism in the Graphic, Postcolonial Spaces of Satrapi's *Persepolis* and Okubo's *Citizen 13660.*" *English Language Notes, Special Issue* (Graphia: The Graphic Novel and Literary Criticism) 46(2): 99–114. 2008.

Chute, Hillary. "Comics as Literature? Reading Graphic Narrative." *PMLA* 123(2): 452–65. 2008.

———. "Gothic Revival. Old Father, Old Artificer: Tracing the Roots of Alison Bechdel's Exhilarating New 'Tragicomic,' *Fun Home.*" *Village Voice*. 2006a. Available at: http://www.villagevoice.com/2006-07-04/books/gothic-revival (accessed 24 February 2011).

———. *Graphic Women: Life Narrative and Contemporary Comics*. New York and Chichester, West Sussex: Columbia University Press. 2010.

———. "An Interview with Alison Bechdel." *Modern Fiction Studies* 52(4): 1004–13. 2006b.

Cioffi, Frank L. "Disturbing Comics: The Disjunction of Word and Image in the Comics of Andrzej Mlecyko, Ben Katchor, R. Crumb, and Art Spiegelman." Robin Varnum and Christina T. Gibbons, eds. In *The Language of Comics: Word and Image*. Jackson: University Press of Mississippi: 97–122. 2001.

Cohen, Jonathan. "Defining Identification: A Theoretical Look at the Identification of Audiences with Media Characters." *Mass Communication & Society*. 4(3): 245–64. 2001.

Cohen, Robin. *Frontiers of Identity: The British and the Others*. London and New York: Longman. 1994.

Cohn, Neil. "A Visual Lexicon." *The Public Journal of Semiotics* 1(1): 35–56. 2007. Available at: http://semioticsonline.org/issues/pjos-1-1.pdf (accessed 24 February 2011).

Cohn, Neil. "Navigating Comics: Reading Strategies of Page Layouts." 2008. Available at: http://www.emaki.net/essays/pagelayouts.pdf (accessed 24 February 2011).

Cole, Jonathan. *About Face*. Cambridge, MA and London: Massachusetts Institute of Technology Press. 1998.

Cook, Guy. *The Discourse of Advertising*. 2nd ed. London: Routledge. 2001.

Cooke, Rachel. "Eyeless in Gaza." *Observer*, 22 November 2009. Available at: http://www.guardian.co.uk/books/2009/nov/22/joe-sacco-interview-rachel-cooke (accessed 24 February 2011).

Coupland, Nikolas. "Dialect Stylization in Radio Talk." *Language in Society* 30(3): 345–75. 2001.

Coupland, Nikolas. "Sociolinguistic Authenticities." *Journal of Sociolinguistics* 7(3): 417–31. 2003.

Couser, G. Thomas. *Recovering Bodies: Illness, Disability, and Life Writing.* Madison: University of Wisconsin Press. 1997.

Creed, Barbara. *The Monstrous-Feminine: Film, Feminism, Psychoanalysis.* London and New York: Routledge. 1993.

Crisp, Peter. "Conceptual Metaphor and Its Expression." Joanna Gavins and Gerard Steen, eds. In *Cognitive Poetics in Practice.* London and New York: Routledge: 99–113. 2003.

Culler, Jonathan. "Story and Discourse in the Analysis of Narrative." Mieke Bal, ed. In *Narrative Theory: Critical Concepts in Literary and Cultural Studies*, vol. 1 (Major Issues in Narrative Theory). London and New York: Routledge: 117–37. 2004.

Cumming, Laura. *A Face to the World: On Self-Portraits.* London: Harper Press. 2009.

Currie, Mark. *About Time: Narrative, Fiction and the Philosophy of Time.* Edinburgh: Edinburgh University Press. 2007.

Damasio, Antonio R. *Descartes' Error: Emotion, Reason, and the Human Brain.* New York: Putnam. 1994.

Darwin, Charles. *The Expression of the Emotions in Man and Animals.* 3rd ed. New York, Oxford: Oxford University Press. 1998 (1872).

Day, Elizabeth. "Frame by Frame: How to Make a Cartoon Drama Out of a Crisis." *Observer*, 23 March 2003. Available at: http://www.guardian.co.uk/books/2008/mar/23/culture.features (accessed 24 February 2011).

De Jesus, Melinda L. "Liminality and Mestiza Consciousness in Lynda Barry's *One Hundred Demons.*" *MELUS* 29(1): 219–52. 2004.

De Man, Paul. "Autobiography as De-facement." *Modern Language Notes* 94: 919–30. 1979.

Descartes, René. *Meditations and Other Metaphysical Writings.* Translated by Desmond M. Clarke. London: Penguin. 2000 (1641).

Dittmar, Jakob F. *Comic-Analyse.* Konstanz: UVK. 2008.

Doy, Gen. *Picturing the Self: Changing Views of the Subject in Visual Culture.* London and New York: I.B. Tauris. 2005.

Drucker, Johanna. "What Is Graphic About Graphic Novels?" *English Language Notes, Special Issue* (Graphia: The Graphic Novel and Literary Criticism) 46(2): 39–55. 2008.

Eakin, Paul John. *How Our Lives Become Stories: Making Selves.* Ithaca, NY and London: Cornell University Press. 1999.

———. "Reading Comics: Art Spiegelman on CD-ROM." Michael A. Chaney, ed. In *Graphic Subjects: Critical Essays on Autobiography and Graphic Novels.* Wisconsin, MA and London: Wisconsin University Press: 13–16. 2011.

Eco, Umberto. *The Role of the Reader: Explorations in the Semiotics of Texts.* Bloomington: Indiana University Press. 1979.

Edwards, Janis L. *Political Cartoons in the 1988 Presidential Campaign: Image, Metaphor, and Narrative.* New York and London: Garland. 1997.

Egan, Susanna. *Mirror Talk: Genres of Crisis in Contemporary Autobiography.* Chapel Hill and London: University of North Carolina Press. 1999.

Eisner, Will. *Comics and Sequential Art: Principles and Practice of the World's Most Popular Art Form.* Paramus, NJ: Poorhouse. 1985.

Ekman, Paul. "Basic Emotions." Tim Dalgleish and Mick J. Power, eds. In *Handbook of Cognition and Emotion.* New York: Wiley & Sons: 45–60. 1999.

———. "Constants Across Cultures in the Face and Emotion." *Journal of Personality and Social Psychology* 17(2): 124–29. 1971.

———. "Universals and Cultural Differences in the Judgments of Facial Expressions of Emotion." *Journal of Personality and Social Psychology* 53(4): 712–17. 1987.

El Refaie, Elisabeth. "Multiliteracies: How Readers Interpret Political Cartoons." *Visual Communication* 8(1): 181–205. 2009.

———. "Of Men, Mice, and Monsters: Embodiment and Body Image in David Small's Graphic Memoir *Stitches*." *The Journal of Graphic Novels and Comics* 3(1). 2012.

———. "The Pragmatics of Humor Reception: Young People's Responses to a Newspaper Cartoon." *HUMOR: International Journal of Humor Research* 24(1): 87–108. 2011.

———. "Subjective Time in David B's Graphic Memoir *Epileptic*." *Studies in Comics* 1(2): 281–99. 2010a.

———. "Understanding Visual Metaphor: The Example of Newspaper Cartoons." *Visual Communication* 2(1): 75–96. 2003.

———. "Visual Modality Versus Authenticity: The Example of Autobiographical Comics." *Visual Studies* 25(2): 162–74. 2010b.

———, and Kathrin Hörschelmann. "Young People's Readings of a Political Cartoon and the Concept of Multimodal Literacy." *Discourse: Studies in the Cultural Politics of Education* 31(2): 195–207. 2010.

Etcoff, Nancy. *Survival of the Prettiest: The Science of Beauty.* New York: Doubleday. 1999.

Ewert, Jeanne. "Art Spiegelman's *Maus* and the Graphic Narrative." Marie-Laure Ryan, ed. In *Narrative Across Media: The Languages of Storytelling.* Lincoln and London: University of Nebraska Press: 178–93. 2004.

Featherstone, Mike. "The Body in Consumer Culture." Mike Featherstone, Mike Hepworth, and Bryan S. Turner, eds. In *The Body: Social Process and Cultural Theory*. London, Newbury Park and New Delhi: Sage: 170–96. 1991.

Ferrara, Alessandro. "Authenticity Without a True Self. Phillip Vannini and Patrick J. Williams, eds. In *Authenticity in Culture, Self, and Society*. Farnham, Surrey and Burlington, VT: Ashgate: 21–35. 2009.

Fingeroth, Danny. *Disguised as Clark Kent: Jews, Comics, and the Creation of the Superhero*. New York and London: Continuum. 2007.

Fischer, Lucy. "Birth Traumas: Parturition and Horror in *Rosemary's Baby*." Barry Keith Grant, ed. In *The Dread of Difference: Gender and the Horror Film*. Austin: University of Texas Press: 412–31. 1996.

Fiske, John. *Introduction to Communication Studies*. 2nd ed. London and New York: Routledge. 1990.

Forceville, Charles. "Visual Representations of the Idealized Cognitive Model of Anger in the Asterix Album 'La Zizanie.'" *Journal of Pragmatics* 37(1): 69–88. 2005.

Forceville, Charles, and Eduardo Urios-Aparisi, eds. *Multimodal Metaphor*. Berlin, New York: Mouton-de Gruyter. 2009.

——, Kurt Veale, and Kurt Feyaerts "Balloonics: The Visuals of Balloons in Comics." Joyce Goggin and Dan Hassler-Forest, eds. In *The Rise and Reason of Comics and Graphic Literature: Critical Essays on the Form*. Jefferson, NC: McFarland: 56–73. 2010.

Frahm, Ole. "Weird Signs. Comics as Means of Parody." Anne Magnussen and Hans-Christian Christiansen, eds. In *Comics and Culture: Analytical and Theoretical Approaches to Comics*. Copenhagen: Museum Tusculanum Press: 177–91. 2000.

Freud, Sigmund. *Jokes and Their Relation to the Unconscious*. Translation James Strachey. Harmondsworth: Penguin. 1976 (1905).

Frey, Nancy, and Douglas Fisher, eds. *Teaching Visual Literacy: Using Comic Books, Graphic Novels, Anime, Cartoons, and More to Develop Comprehension and Thinking Skills*. Thousand Oaks, CA: Corwin Press. 2008.

Frosh, Paul. *The Image Factory: Consumer Culture, Photography and the Visual Content Industry*. Oxford, New York: Berg. 2003.

Gardner, Jared. "Autobiography's Biography, 1972–2007." *Biography* 31(1): 1–26. 2008.

Geis, Deborah R., ed. *Considering Maus: Approaches to Art Spiegelman's "Survivor's Tale" of the Holocaust*. Tuscaloosa and London: University of Alabama Press. 2003.

Genette, Gérard. *Narrative Discourse*. Translated by Jane E. Lewin. Oxford: Blackwell. 1980.

———. *Paratexts: Thresholds of Interpretation*. Translated by Jane E. Lewin. Cambridge: Cambridge University Press. 1997.

Gibson, Mel. "'You can't read them, they're for boys!' British Girls, American Superhero Comics and Identity." *International Journal of Comic Art* 5(1): 305–24. 2003.

Gilmore, Leigh. *The Limits of Autobiography: Trauma and Testimony*. Ithaca, NY and London: Cornell University Press. 2001.

———. "Witnessing *Persepolis*: Comics, Trauma, and Childhood Testimony." Michael A. Chaney, ed. In *Graphic Subjects: Critical Essays on Autobiography and Graphic Novels*. Wisconsin, MA and London: Wisconsin University Press: 157–63. 2011.

Gloeckner, Phoebe. "Autobiography: The Process Negates the Term." Michael A. Chaney, ed. In *Graphic Subjects: Critical Essays on Autobiography and Graphic Novels*. Wisconsin, MA and London: Wisconsin University Press: 178–79. 2011.

Goddard, Angela. *The Language of Advertising*. London and New York: Routledge. 1998.

Goffman, Erving. *The Presentation of Self in Everyday Life*. Harmondsworth, Middlesex: Penguin. 1969 (1959).

Gombrich, E. H. *Art and Illusion: A Study in the Psychology of Pictorial Representation*. 5th ed. London: Phaidon. 1977.

Gordon, Ian E. *Theories of Visual Perception*. 3rd ed. Hove and New York: Psychology Press. 2004.

Gravett, Paul. *Graphic Novels: Stories to Change Your Life*. London: Aurum Press. 2005.

Grittmann, Elke. "Die Konstruktion von Authentizität. Was ist echt an den Pressefotos im Informationsjournalismus?" Thomas Knieper and Marion Müller, eds. In *Authentizität und Inszenierung von Bilderwelten*. Cologne: Herbert von Harlem Verlag: 123–49. 2003.

Groensteen, Thierry. "Les petites cases du Moi: L'autobiographie en band dessinée." *Neuvième Art* January: 58–69. 1996.

———. "Why Are Comics Still in Search of Cultural Legitimization?" Anne Magnussen and Hans-Christian Christiansen, eds. In *Comics and Culture: Analytical and Theoretical Approaches to Comics*. Copenhagen: Museum Tusculanum Press: 29–41. 2000.

Groensteen, Thierry. "Le réseau et le lieu: pour une analyse des procédures de tressage iconique." Mireille Ribière and Jan Baetens, eds. In *Time, Narrative & the Fixed Image* (*Temps, Narration & Image Fixe*). Amsterdam and Atlanta, GA: Rodopi: 117–29. 2001.

———. "The Monstrator, the Recitant, and the Shadow of the Narrator." *European Comic Art* 3(1): 1–21. 2010.

———. *The System of Comics*. Translated by Bart Beaty and Nich Nguyen. Jackson: University of Mississippi. 2007.

Gubrium, Jaber F., and James A. Holstein "The Everyday Work and Auspices of Authenticity." Phillip Vannini and Patrick J. Williams, eds. In *Authenticity in Culture, Self, and Society*. Farnham, Surrey and Burlington, VT: Ashgate: 122–38. 2009.

Hajdu, David. *The Ten-Cent Plague: The Great Comic-Book Scare and How It Changed America*. New York: Picador. 2008.

Hall, Edward T. *The Silent Language*. 2nd ed. New York: Anchor Press. 1973.

Hall, Stuart. "Encoding, Decoding." S. During, ed. In *The Cultural Studies Reader*. New York, London: Routledge: 90–103. 1993.

Halliday, M.A.K. *An Introduction to Functional Grammar*. 2nd ed. London and Melbourne, Auckland: Edward Arnold. 1994.

Hannon, Gerald. "Retro Man." *Toronto Life* January. 2006. Available at: http://www.torontolife.com/features/retro-man/ (accessed 24 February 2011).

Hartman, Geoffrey. *Scars of the Spirit: The Struggle Against Inauthenticity*. New York: Palgrave MacMillan. 2002.

Harvey, Robert C. *The Art of the Comic Book: An Aesthetic History*. Jackson: University of Mississippi. 1996.

———. "Comedy at the Juncture of Word and Image: The Emergence of the Modern Gag Cartoon Reveals the Vital Blend." Robin Varnum and Christina T. Gibbons, eds. In *The Language of Comics: Word and Image*. Jackson: University Press of Mississippi: 75–96. 2001.

Hatfield, Charles. *Alternative Comics: An Emerging Literature*. Jackson: University Press of Mississippi. 2005.

———. "An Art of Tensions." Jeet Heer and Kent Worcester, eds. In *A Comics Studies Reader*. Jackson: University Press of Mississippi: 132–48. 2009.

———. "How to Read a . . ." *English Language Notes, Special Issue* (Graphia: The Graphic Novel and Literary Criticism) 46(2): 129–49. 2008.

Hausken, Liv. "Coda: Textual Theory and Blind Spots in Media Studies." Marie-Laure Ryan, ed. In *Narrative Across Media: The Languages of Storytelling*. Lincoln and London: University of Nebraska Press: 391–203. 2004.

Haverty Rugg, Linda. *Picturing Ourselves: Photography and Autobiography*. Chicago and London: University of Chicago Press. 1997.

Healey, Karen. "When Fangirls Perform: The Gendered Fan Identity in Superhero Comics Fandom." Angela Ndalianis, ed. In *The Contemporary Comic Book Superhero*. London and New York: Routledge: 144–63. 2009.

Herman, David. "Narrative Worldmaking in Graphic Life Writing." Michael A. Chaney, ed. In *Graphic Subjects: Critical Essays on Autobiography and Graphic Novels*. Wisconsin, MA and London: Wisconsin University Press: 231–43. 2011.

———. *Story Logic: Problems and Possibilities of Narrative*. Lincoln and London: University of Nebraska Press. 2002.

Herrnstein Smith, Barbara. "Narrative Versions, Narrative Theories." Mieke Bal, ed. In *Narrative Theory: Critical Concepts in Literary and Cultural Studies*, vol. 1 (Major Issues in Narrative Theory). London and New York: Routledge: 95–216. 2004.

Hirsch, Marianne. "Mourning and Postmemory." Michael A. Chaney, ed. In *Graphic Subjects: Critical Essays on Autobiography and Graphic Novels*. Wisconsin, MA and London: Wisconsin University Press: 17–44. 2011.

Hobbes, Thomas. *Human Nature*. Volume 4. London: John Bohn. 1840 (1650).

Hodge, Robert, and Gunther Kress. *Social Semiotics*. Ithaca: Cornell University Press. 1988.

Holmes, Janet. "Sharing a Laugh: Pragmatic Aspects of Humor and Gender in the Workplace." *Journal of Pragmatics* 38(1): 26–50. 2006.

Horn, Robert E. *Visual Language: Global Communication for the 21st Century*. Bainbridge Island, WA: MacroVU. 1998.

Huxford, John. "Beyond the Referential: Uses of Visual Symbolism in the Press." *Journalism* 2(1): 45–71. 2002.

Hyland, Ken. *Metadiscourse*. London and New York: Continuum. 2005.

Iser, Wolfgang. *The Act of Reading: A Theory of Aesthetic Response*. London and Henley: Routledge and Kegan Paul. 1978.

Jacobs, Dale. "Multimodal Constructions of Self: Autobiographical Comics and the Case of Joe Matt's *Peepshow*." *Biography* 31(1): 59–84. 2008.

Jewitt, Carey, and Gunther Kress, eds. *Multimodal Literacy*. New York and Oxford: Peter Lang. 2003.

Jovanomic, Goran, and Ulrich Koch. "The Comics Debate in Germany Against Dirt and Rubbish, Pictorial Idiotism, and Cultural Analphabetism." John A. Lent, ed. In *Pulp Demons: International Dimensions of the Postwar Anti-Comics Campaign*. Cranbury, NJ, London, Mississauga, Ontario: Associated University Presses: 93–128. 1999.

Kannenberg, Gene. "'I Looked Just Like Rudolph Valentino': Identity and Representation in *Maus*." Jan Baetens, ed. In *The Graphic Novel*. Leuven: Leuven University Press: 79–89. 2001.

Keen, Suzanne. *Empathy and the Novel*. Oxford and New York: Oxford University Press. 2007

———. "A Theory of Narrative Empathy." *Narrative* 14(3): 207–236. 2006.

Kennedy, John M., Christopher D. Green, and John Vervaeke. "Metaphoric Thought and Devices in Pictures." *Metaphor and Symbolic Activity* 8(3): 243–55. 1993.

Kerby, Anthony Paul. *Narrative and the Self*. Bloomington and Indianapolis: Indiana University Press. 1991.

Khordoc, Catherine. "The Comic Book's Soundtrack: Visual Sound Effects in *Asterix*." Robin Varnum and Christina T. Gibbons, eds. In *The Language of Comics: Word and Image*. Jackson: University Press of Mississippi: 156–73. 2001.

King, Nicola. *Memory, Narrative, Identity: Remembering the Self*. Edinburgh: Edinburgh University Press. 2000.

Koestler, Arthur. *The Act of Creation*. London: Hutchinson & Co. 1976 (1964).

Kolakowski, Leszek. *Bergson*. Oxford and New York: Oxford University Press. 1985.

Kövecses, Zoltán. *Metaphor and Emotion: Language, Culture, and Body in Human Feeling*. Cambridge: Cambridge University Press. 2000.

———. *Metaphor in Culture: Universality and Variation*. Cambridge: Cambridge University Press. 2005.

Kress, Gunther. "Text as the Punctuation of Semiosis: Pulling at Some of the Threads." Ulrike Hanna Meinhof and Jonathan Smith, eds. In *Intertextuality and the Media: From Genre to Everyday Life*. Manchester: Manchester University Press: 132–154. 2000.

———. "What Is Mode?" Carey Jewitt, ed. In *The Routledge Handbook of Multimodal Analysis*. London and New York: Routledge: 54–67. 2009.

Kress, Gunther, and Theo van Leeuwen. *Reading Images: The Grammar of Visual Design*. London: Routledge. 1996.

Kristeva, Julia. *Powers of Horror: An Essay on Abjection*. Translated by Leon S. Roudiez. New York: Columbia University Press. 1982.

Kuhn, Annette, and Kirsten Emiko McAllister. "Locating Memory: Photographic Acts." An Introduction." Annette Kuhn and Kirsten Emiko McAllister, eds. In *Locating Memory: Photographic Acts*. New York, Oxford: Berghahn Books: 1–17. 2006.

Kukkonen, Karin. "Beyond Language: Metaphor and Metonymy in Comics Storytelling." *English Language Notes, Special Issue* (Graphia: The Graphic Novel and Literary Criticism) 46(2): 89–98. 2008.

Kunzle, David. "Rodolphe Töpffer's Aesthetic Revolution." Jeet Heer and Kent Worcester, eds. In *A Comics Studies Reader*. Jackson: University Press of Mississippi: 17–24. 2009.

Lacan, Jacques. *Écrits: A Selection*. Translation Alan Sheridan. London: Tavistock Publications. 1977.

Lakoff, George. "The Contemporary Theory of Metaphor." Andrew Ortony, ed. In *Metaphor and Thought*. 2nd ed. Cambridge: Cambridge University Press: 202–25. 1993.

Lakoff, George, and Mark Johnson. *Metaphors We Live By*. Chicago and London: The University of Chicago Press. 1980.

———. *Philosophy in the Flesh: The Embodied Mind and Its Challenge to Western Thought*. New York: Basic Books. 1999.

Lakoff, George, and Mark Johnson. *More Than Cool Reason: A Field Guide to Poetic Metaphor.* Chicago and London: University of Chicago Press. 1989.

Laneyrie-Dagen, Nadeije. *How to Read Paintings.* London: Chambers. 2004.

Le Poidevin, Robin. *The Images of Time: An Essay on Temporal Representation.* Oxford: Oxford University Press. 2007.

Leder, Drew. *The Absent Body.* Chicago and London: University of Chicago Press. 1990.

Lefèvre, Pascal. "The Importance of Being 'Published': A Comparative Study of Different Comics Formats." Anne Magnussen and Hans-Christian Christiansen, eds. In *Comics and Culture: Analytical and Theoretical Approaches to Comics.* Copenhagen: Museum Tusculanum Press: 91–105. 2000.

Lejeune, Philippe. *On Autobiography.* Minneapolis: University of Minnesota Press. 1989.

Lemke, Jay L. "Travels in Hypermodality." *Visual Communication* 1(3): 299–325. 2002.

Lent, John A. "Introduction: The Comics Debates Internationally: Their Genesis, Issues, and Commonalities." John A. Lent, ed. In *Pulp Demons: International Dimensions of the Postwar Anti-Comics Campaign.* Cranbury, NJ and London, Mississauga, Ontario: Associated University Presses: 9–41. 1999.

Liss, Andrea. *Trespassing Through Shadows: Memory, Photography, and the Holocaust.* Minneapolis: University of Minnesota Press. 1998.

Loman, Andrew. "'Well-intended Liberal Slop': Allegories of Race in Spiegelman's *Maus*." *Journal of American Studies* 40(3): 551–71. 2006.

MacKinnon, Kenneth. *Representing Men: Maleness and Masculinity in the Media.* London: Arnold. 2003.

Magnussen, Anne. "The Semiotics of C. S. Peirce as a Theoretical Framework for the Understanding of Comics." Anne Magnussen and Hans-Christian Christiansen, eds. In *Comics and Culture: Analytical and Theoretical Approaches to Comics.* Copenhagen: Museum Tusculanum Press: 193–207. 2000.

Mainardi, Patricia. "The Invention of Comics." *Nineteenth-Century Art Worldwide: A Journal of Nineteenth Century Culture* 6(1). 2007. Available at: http://www.19thc-artworldwide.org/index.php/component/content/article/46-spring07article/145-the-invention-of-comics (accessed 24 February 2011).

Manguel, Alberto. *Reading Pictures: What We Think About When We Look at Art.* New York: Random House. 2002.

Masschelein, Anneleen. "Foreword." *Image & Narrative: Online Magazine of the Visual Narrative* (Autofiction and/in Image—Autofiction visuelle II) 22. 2008. Available at: http://www.imageandnarrative.be/inarchive/autofiction2/masschelein.html (accessed 12 February 2011).

Maynard, Patrick. "The Time It Takes." Jan Baetens, ed. In *The Graphic Novel.* Leuven: Leuven University Press: 191–210. 2001.

McAlhone, Beryl, and David Stuart. *A Smile in the Mind: Witty Thinking in Graphic Design.* London: Phaidon. 1996.

McCarthy, E. Doyle. "Emotional Performances as Dramas of Authenticity." Phillip Vannini and Patrick J. Williams, eds. In *Authenticity in Culture, Self, and Society.* Farnham, Surrey and Burlington, VT: Ashgate: 241–55. 2009.

McCloud, Scott. *Making Comics: Storytelling Secrets of Comics, Manga and Graphic Novels.* New York: Harper. 2006.

———. *Reinventing Comics.* New York: Paradox Press. 2000.

———. *Understanding Comics: The Invisible Art.* New York: Harper Perennial. 1994.

McIlvenny, Paul. "The Disabled Male Body 'Writes/Draws' Back: The Graphic Fictions of Masculinity and the Body in the Autobiographical Comic *The Spiral Cage.*" Nancy Tuana, William Cowling, Maurice Hamington, Greg Johnson, and Terrance MacMullan, eds. In *Revealing Male Bodies.* Bloomington, IN: Indiana University Press: 100–124. 2002.

———. "Disabling Men: Masculinity and Disability in Al Davison's Graphic Autobiography, *The Spiral Cage.*" Søren Ervø and Thomas Johansson, eds. In *Bending Bodies: Moulding Masculinities.* Volume 2. Aldershot, Hants: Ashgate Press: 238–58. 2003.

Mckinney, Mark. "The Other Origins of Bande Dessinée Autobiography." Conference Paper Given at the *Joint International Conference of Graphic Novels, Bande Dessinées and Comics,* Manchester, UK, 5–8 July 2011.

Merleau-Ponty, Maurice. *Phenomenology of Perception.* Translated by Colin Smith. London and Henley-on-Thames: Routledge and Kegan Paul. 1962.

Messaris, Paul. *Visual Persuasion: The Role of Images in Advertising.* Thousand Oaks, California: Sage. 1997.

Michelmore, Christina. "Old Pictures in New Frames: Images of Islam and Muslims in Post World War II American Political Cartoons." *The Journal of American Culture* 23(4): 37–50. 2000.

Mikkonen, Kai. "Remediation and the Sense of Time in Graphic Narratives." Joyce Goggin and Dan Hassler-Forest, eds. In *The Rise and Reason of Comics and Graphic Literature: Critical Essays on the Form.* Jefferson, NC: McFarland: 74–86. 2010.

Miller, Ann. *Reading Bande Dessinée: Critical Approaches to French-Language Comic Strip.* Bristol and Chicago: Intellect. 2007.

Miller, Bryan. "An Interview with Seth." *Bookslut* June 2004. Available at: http://www.bookslut.com/features/2004_06_002650.php (accessed 24 February 2011).

Miller, Nancy K. "Cartoons of the Self: Portrait of the Artist as a Young Murderer—Art Spiegelman's *Maus.*" Deborah R. Geis, ed. In *Considering* Maus: *Approaches to Art Spiegelman's "Survivor's Tale" of the Holocaust.* Tuscaloosa and London: University of Alabama Press: 44–59. 2003.

Miller, Nancy K. "The Entangled Self: Genre Bondage in the Age of the Memoir." *PMLA* 122(2): 537–48. 2007.

Mitchell, Adrielle Anna. "Distributed Identity: Networking Image Fragments in Graphic Memoirs." *Studies in Comics* 1(2): 257–79. 2010.

Mitchell, W. J. T. "Beyond Comparison." Jeet Heer and Kent Worcester, eds. In *A Comics Studies Reader*. Jackson: University Press of Mississippi: 116–23. 2009.

———. *Picture Theory*. Chicago and London: University of Chicago Press. 1994.

———. "Visual Literacy or Literary Visualcy?" James Elkins, ed. In *Visual Literacy*. New York and London: Routledge: 11–29. 2008.

Mitter, Partha. "The Hottentot Venus and Western Man: Reflections on the Construction of Beauty in the West." Elizabeth Hallam and Brian V. Street, eds. In *Cultural Encounters: Representing "Otherness."* Routledge: London and New York: 35–50. 2000.

Montgomery, Martin. "Defining 'Authentic Talk.'" *Discourse Studies* 3(4): 397–405. 2001.

Moores, Shaun. *Interpreting Audiences: The Ethnography of Media Consumption*. London, Thousand Oaks, and New Delhi: Sage. 1993.

Morgan, David. "You Too Can Have a Body Like Mine: Reflections on the Male Body and Masculinities." Sue Scott and David Morgan, eds. In *Body Matters: Essays on the Sociology of the Body*. London and Washington, DC: Falmer Press: 69–88. 1993.

Moya Guijarro, A. Jesús, and Maria-Jesús Pinar Sanz. "On Interaction of Image and Verbal Text in a Picture Book: A Multimodal and Systemic Functional Study." Eija Ventola and A. Jesús Moya Guijarro, eds. In *The World Told and the World Shown: Multisemiotic Issues*. New York: Palgrave Macmillan: 107–23. 2009.

Mulvey, Laura. "Visual Pleasure and Narrative Cinema." Jessica Evans and Stuart Hall, eds., 1999. In *Visual Culture: The Reader*. London: Sage: 381-89. 1973.

Naghibi, Nima. "A Story Told in Flashback: Remediating Marjane Satrapi's *Persepolis*." Michael A. Chaney, ed. In *Graphic Subjects: Critical Essays on Autobiography and Graphic Novels*. Wisconsin, MA and London: Wisconsin University Press: 164–77. 2011.

Ndalianis, Angela. "Enter the Aleph: Superhero Worlds and Hypertime Realities." Angela Ndalianis, ed. In *The Contemporary Comic Book Superhero*. London and New York: Routledge: 270–90. 2009.

Neal, David T., and Tanya L. Chartrand. "Embodied Emotion Perception: Amplifying and Dampening Facial Feedback Modulates Emotion Perception Accuracy." *Social Psychological and Personality Science* 21 April 2011. Available at: http://spp.sagepub.com/content/early/2011/04/21/1948550611406138 (accessed 14 June 2011).

Neill, Alex. "Empathy and (Film) Fiction." Noël Carroll and David Bordwell, eds. In *Post-Theory: Reconstructing Film Studies*. Madison: University of Wisconsin Press: 175–94. 1996.

Nikolajeva, Maria, and Carole Scott, Carole. "The Dynamics of Picturebook Communication." *Children's Literature in Education* 31(4): 225–39. 2000.

Nixon, Sean. "Exhibiting Masculinity." Stuart Hall, ed. In *Representation: Cultural Representations and Signifying Practices*. London: Sage: 293–330. 1997.

Nochlin, Linda. "Women, Art, and Power." Norman Byrson, Michael Ann Holly, and Keith Moxey, eds. In *Visual Theory: Painting and Interpretation*. Cambridge: Polity: 13–46. 1991.

O'Connell, Sanjida. *Mindreading: An Investigation Into How We Learn to Love and Lie*. London: Heinemann. 1997.

Oksman, Tahneer. "Visualizing the Jewish Body in Aline Kominsky-Crumb's *Need More Love*." *Studies in Comics* 1(2): 213–32. 2010.

Olney, James. *Memory and Narrative: The Weave of Life-Writing*. Chicago and London: University of Chicago Press. 1998.

O'Sullivan, Kerry. *Understanding Ways: Communicating Between Cultures*. Alexandria, NSW: Hale & Iremonger. 1994.

O'Toole, Michael. *The Language of Displayed Art*. London: Leicester University Press. 1994.

Painter, Clare. "Children's Picture Book Narratives: Reading Sequences of Images." Anne McCabe, Mick O'Donnell, and Rachel Whittaker, eds. In *Advances in Language and Education*. London and New York: Continuum: 40–59. 2007.

Palmer, Alan. *Fictional Minds*. Lincoln and London: University of Nebraska Press. 2004.

Peirce, Charles Sanders. *Collected Papers of Charles Sanders Peirce*. Volume 2, *Elements of Logic*. Charles Hartshorne and Paul Weiss, eds. Cambridge, MA: Harvard University Press. 1960.

Pickering, Michael, and Sharon Lockyer. "Introduction: The Ethics and Aesthetics of Humour and Comedy." Sharon Lockyer, and Michael Pickering, eds. In *Beyond A Joke: The Limits of Humour*. Houndsmill and New York: Palgrave: 1–24. 2005.

Preston, John. "Crumb's Comforts." *Daily Telegraph* 15 March 2005. Available at: http://www.telegraph.co.uk/culture/art/3638764/Crumbs-comforts.html (accessed 24 February 2011).

Ricoeur, Paul. "Narrative Time." Mieke Bal, ed. In *Narrative Theory: Critical Concepts in Literary and Cultural Studies*. Volume 3 (Political Narratology). London and New York: Routledge: 327–47. 2004.

Ritchin, Fred. "Photojournalism in the Age of Computers." Carol Squiers ed. In *The Critical Image*. Seattle: Bay Press: 28–37. 1990.

Robins, Kevin. *Into the Image: Culture and Politics in the Field of Vision*. London and New York: Routledge. 1996.

Rota, Valerio. "The Translation's Visibility: David B.'s *L'Ascension du Haut Mal* in Italy." *Belphégor* 4(1). 2004. Available at: http://etc.dal.ca/belphegor/vol4_no1/articles/04_01_Rota_davidb_fr.html (accessed 24 February 2011).

Russo, Mary. "Female Grotesques: Carnival and Theory." Katie Conboy, Nadia Medina, and Sarah Stanbury, eds. In *Writing on the Body: Female Embodiment and Feminist Theory*. New York and Chichester, West Sussex: Columbia University Press: 318–36. 1997.

Ryan, Marie-Laure. "Introduction." Marie-Laure Ryan, ed. In *Narrative Across Media: The Languages of Storytellling*. Lincoln and London: University of Nebraska Press: 1–40. 2004.

Sabin, Roger. *Adult Comics: An Introduction*. London and New York: Routledge. 1993.

———. *Comics, Comix & Graphic Novels*. London: Phaidon. 1996.

Said, Edward. *Orientalism*. New York: Vintage. 1979.

Sandifer, Philip. "Amazing Fantasies: Trauma, Affect, and Superheroes." *English Language Notes, Special Issue* (Graphia: The Graphic Novel and Literary Criticism) 46(2): 175–92. 2008.

Saraceni, Mario. *The Language of Comics*. London and New York: Routledge. 2003.

Scannell, Paddy. "Authenticity and Experience." *Discourse Studies* 3(4): 405–11. 2001.

Schierl, Thomas. "Der Schein der Authentizität: Journalistische Bildproduktion als nachfrageorientierte Produktion scheinbarer Authentizität." Thomas Knieper and Marion Müller, eds. In *Authentizität und Inszenierung von Bilderwelten*. Cologne: Herbert von Harlem Verlag: 150–67. 2003.

Schirato, Tony, and Jen Webb. *Understanding the Visual*. London: Sage. 2004.

Schneider, Greice. "Comics and the Everyday Life: From *Ennui* to Contemplation." *European Comic Art* 3(1): 37–63. 2010.

Schwalbe, Michael. "We Wear the Mask: Subordinated Masculinity and the Persona Trap." Phillip Vannini and Patrick J. Williams, eds. In *Authenticity in Culture, Self, and Society*. Farnham, Surrey and Burlington, VT: Ashgate: 139–52. 2009.

Scott, Clive. *The Spoken Image: Photography & Language*. London: Reaktion Books. 1999.

Semino, Elena. *Metaphor in Discourse*. Cambridge: Cambridge University Press. 2008.

Shalom, Albert. *The Body/Mind Conceptual Framework and the Problem of Personal Identity: Some Theories in Philosophy, Psychoanalysis and Neurology*. Atlantic Highlands, NJ: Humanities Press International. 1985.

Shildrick, Margrit. *Embodying the Monster: Encounters with the Vulnerable Self*. London, Thousand Oaks, New Delhi: Sage. 2002.

Shweder, Richard A. *Thinking Through Cultures: Expeditions in Cultural Psychology.* Cambridge, MA: Harvard University Press. 1991.

Singer, Marc. "'Black Skins' and White Masks: Comic Books and the Secret of Race." *African American Review* 36(1): 107–19. 2002.

Skinn, Dez. *Comix: The Underground Revolution.* London: Collins & Brown. 2004.

Smith, Murray. *Engaging Characters: Fiction, Emotion, and the Cinema.* Oxford: Oxford University Press. 1995.

Smith, Sidonie. "Human Rights and Comics: Autobiographical Avatars, Crisis Witnessing, and Transnational Rescue Networks." Michael A. Chaney, ed. In *Graphic Subjects: Critical Essays on Autobiography and Graphic Novels.* Wisconsin, MA and London: Wisconsin University Press: 61–72. 2011.

——. *Subjectivity, Identity and the Body: Women's Autobiographical Practices in the Twentieth Century.* Bloomington: Indiana University Press. 1993.

Sontag, Susan. *Illness as Metaphor and AIDS and Its Metaphors.* London: Penguin. 1991.

——. *On Photography.* New York: RosettaBooks, electronic edition. 2005 (1977).

Soukup, Charles. "Multimedia Performance in a Computer-mediated Community: Communication as a Virtual Drama." *Journal of Computer Mediated Communication* 9(4). 2004. Available at: http://jcmc.indiana.edu/vol9/issue4/soukup.html (accessed 24 February 2011).

Spiegelman, Art. *The Complete Maus.* CD-ROM. New York: The Voyager Company. 1994.

Spurgeon, Tom. "Interview with Lynda Barry." *Comics Reporter.* 2008. Available at: http://www.comicsreporter.com/index.php/cr_sunday_interview_lynda_barry/ (accessed 24 February 2011).

Stacey, Jackie. *Teratologies: A Cultural Study of Cancer.* London and New York: Routledge. 1997.

Staniszewski, Mary Anne. *Believing is Seeing: Creating the Culture of Art.* New York and London: Penguin. 1995.

Steiner, Wendy. "Pictorial Narrativity." Marie-Laure Ryan, ed. In *Narrative Across Media: The Languages of Storytellling.* Lincoln and London: University of Nebraska Press: 145–77. 2004.

Sternberg, Meir. "Telling in Time (I): Chronology and Narrative Theory." Mieke Bal, ed. In *Narrative Theory: Critical Concepts in Literary and Cultural Studies.* Volume 2 (Special Topics). London and New York: Routledge: 93–137. 2004.

Stöckl, Hartmut. "In Between Modes: Language and Image in Printed Media." Eija Ventola, Charles Cassily, and Martin Kaltenbacher, eds. In *Perspectives on Multimodality.* Amsterdam: Benjamins: 9–30. 2004.

——. "Typography: Body and Tress of a Text—A Signing Mode Between Language and Image." *Visual Communication* 4(2): 205–14. 2005.

Sturken, Marita, and Lisa Cartwright. *Practices of Looking: An Introduction to Visual Culture.* Oxford and New York: Oxford University Press. 2001.

Tabachnick, Stephen E. "Autobiography as Discovery in *Epileptic*." Michael A. Chaney, ed. In *Graphic Subjects: Critical Essays on Autobiography and Graphic Novels*. Wisconsin, MA and London: Wisconsin University Press: 101–16. 2011.

Talon, Durwin S. *Comics Above Ground: How Sequential Art Affects Mainstream Media*. Raleigh, NC: TwoMorrows Publishing. 2004.

Tan, Ed S. "The Telling Face in Comic Strip and Graphic Novel." Jan Baetens, ed. In *The Graphic Novel*. Leuven: Leuven University Press: 31–46. 2001.

Tannen, Deborah. *Talking Voices: Repetition, Dialogue, and Imagery in Conversational Discourse*. Cambridge: Cambridge University Press. 1989.

Taylor, Charles. (1989) *Sources of the Self: The Making of the Modern Identity*. Cambridge: Cambridge University Press.

Tensuan, Theresa. "Comic Visions and Revisions in the Work of Lynda Barry and Marjane Satrapi." *Modern Fiction Studies* 52(4): 947–64. 2006.

——. "Up from Surgery: The Politics of Self-representation in Women's Graphic Memoirs of Illness." Michael A. Chaney, ed. In *Graphic Subjects: Critical Essays on Autobiography and Graphic Novels*. Wisconsin, MA and London: Wisconsin University Press: 180–94. 2011.

Tomaselli, Susan. "It's a Good Life, If You Don't Weaken (review)." *3:AM Magazine*. 2007. Available at: http://www.3ammagazine.com/3am/its-a-good-life-if-you-dont-weaken/ (accessed 24 February 2011).

Turkle, Sherry. "Multiple Subjectivity and Virtual Community at the End of the Freudian Century." *Sociological Inquiry* 67(1): 72–84. 1997.

Turner, Mark. *The Literary Mind: The Origins of Thought and Language*. New York and Oxford: Oxford University Press. 1996.

Tyner, Kathleen R. *Literacy in a Digital Age: Teaching and Learning in the Age of Information*. Mahwah, NJ and London: Lawrence Erlbaum. 1998.

Van der Kolk, Bessel A., and Onno van der Hart. "The Intrusive Past: The Flexibility of Memory and the Engraving of Trauma." Cathy Caruth, ed. In *Trauma: Explorations in Memory*. Baltimore and London: John Hopkins University Press: 158–82. 1995.

Van Leeuwen, Theo. *Introducing Social Semiotics*. London: Routledge. 2005.

——. "Moving English: The Visual Language of Film." Sharon Goodman and David Graddol, eds. In *Redesigning English: New Texts, New Identities*. London and New York: Routledge: 81–105. 1996.

——. "Rhythmic Structures of the Film Text." Teun A. van Dijk, ed. In *Discourse and Communication: New Approaches to the Analysis of Mass Media Discourse and Communication*. Berlin and New York: Gruyter: 217–32. 1985.

——. (2006) "Towards a Semiotics of Typography." *Information Design Journal* 14(2): 139–55. 2006.

——. "What Is Authenticity?" *Discourse Studies* 3(4): 392–97. 2001.

Van Peer, Willie, and Henk Pander Maat. "Perspectivation and Sympathy: Effects of Narrative Point of View." Roger J. Kreuz and Mary Sue MacNealy, eds.

In *Empirical Approaches to Literature and Aesthetics*. Norwood, NJ: Ablex: 143–54. 1996.

Vannini, Phillip, and Patrick J. Williams. "Authenticity in Culture, Self, and Society." Phillip Vannini and Patrick J. Williams, eds. In *Authenticity in Culture, Self, and Society*. Farnham, Surrey and Burlington, VT: Ashgate: 1–18. 2009.

Varnum, Robin, and Christina T. Gibbons. "Introduction." Robin Varnum and Christina T. Gibbons, eds. In *The Language of Comics: Word and Image*. Jackson: University Press of Mississippi: ix-xix. 2001.

Vernier Danehy, Cécile. "Textual Absence, Textual Color: A Journey Through Memory—Cosey's *Saigon-Hanoi*." Mark McKinney, ed. In *History and Politics in French-Language Comics and Graphic Novels*. Jackson: University Press of Mississippi: 212–36. 2008.

Versaci, Rocco. *This Book Contains Graphic Language: Comics as Literature*. New York and London: Continuum. 2007.

Vice, Sue. "It's About Time": The Chronotope of the Holocaust in Art Spiegelman's *Maus*." Jan Baetens, ed. In *The Graphic Novel*. Leuven: Leuven University Press: 47–60. 2001.

Wägenbaur, Thomas. "Memory and Recollection: The Cognitive and Literary Model." Thomas Wägenbaur, ed. In *The Poetics of Memory*. Tübingen: Stauffenburg-Verlag: 3–22. 1998.

Walsh, Richard. "The Narrative Imagination Across Media." *Modern Fiction Studies* 52(4): 855–68. 2006.

Waskul, Dennis D., and Phillip Vannini. "Introduction: The Body in Symbolic Interaction." Dennis D. Waskul and Phillip Vannini, eds. In *Body/Embodiment: Symbolic Interaction and the Sociology of the Body*. Aldershot: Ashgate: 1–18. 2006.

Watson, Julia. "Autographic Disclosures and Genealogies of Desire in Alison Bechdel's *Fun Home*." Michael A. Chaney, ed. In *Graphic Subjects: Critical Essays on Autobiography and Graphic Novels*. Wisconsin, MA and London: Wisconsin University Press: 123–56. 2011.

Weiner, Stephen. *Faster Than a Speeding Bullet: The Rise of the Graphic Novel*. New York: Nantier, Beall, Minoustchine. 2003.

Weiss, Gail. *Body Images: Embodiment as Intercorporeality*. New York and London: Routledge. 1999.

Wells, Liz, ed. *Photography: A Critical Introduction*. 2nd ed. London: Routledge. 2000.

Wertham, Fredric. *Seduction of the Innocent*. New York: Rinehart. 1954.

White, Glyn. *Reading the Graphic Surface: The Presence of the Book in Prose Fiction*. Manchester and New York: Manchester University Press. 2005.

Whitlock, Gillian. "Autographics: The Seeing "I" of the Comics." *Modern Fiction Studies* 52(4): 965–79. 2006.

——, and Anna Poletti. "Self-regarding Art." *Biography* 31(1): v-xxiii. 2008.

Witek, Joseph. *Comic Books as History: The Narrative Art of Jack Jackson, Art Spiegelman, and Harvey Pekar*. Jackson: University Press of Mississippi. 1989.

——. "Justin Green: Autobiography Meets the Comics." Michael A. Chaney, ed. In *Graphic Subjects: Critical Essays on Autobiography and Graphic Novels*. Wisconsin, MA and London: Wisconsin University Press: 227–30. 2011.

Wivel, Matthias. "Establishing Shots—Judith Forest's *1h25*." *Comics Journal* 25 July 2010. Available at: http://classic.tcj.com/international/establishing-shots-judith-forests-1h25/ (accessed 4 August 2011).

Wolf, Naomi. *The Beauty Myth*. London: Vintage. 1991.

Wolk, Douglas. *Reading Comics: How Graphic Novels Work and What They Mean*. Cambridge, MA: Da Capo Press. 2007.

Wortmann, Volker. *Authentisches Bild und authentisierende Form*. Cologne: Herbert von Halem Verlag. 2003.

Wray, Alison. *Formulaic Language: Pushing the Boundaries*. Oxford: Oxford University Press. 2008.

Zakia, Richard D. *Perception and Imaging*. Boston and Oxford: Focal Press. 2002.

Zunshine, Lisa. *Why We Read Fiction: Theory of Mind and the Novel*. Columbus: Ohio State University Press. 2006.

Index

www.ingramcontent.com/pod-product-compliance
Lightning Source LLC
Chambersburg PA
CBHW031131250226
40156CB00004B/65